# Differentiating Instruction *with* Technology
## in K–5 Classrooms

GRACE E. SMITH

STEPHANIE THRONE

**International Society for Technology in Education**
EUGENE, OREGON · WASHINGTON, DC

# Differentiating Instruction *with* Technology *in K–5 Classrooms*

**Grace E. Smith**
**Stephanie Throne**

**Acquisitions Editor:** Scott Harter
**Development Editor:** Mike Van Mantgem
**Production Editor:** Lynda Gansel
**Production Coordinator:** Maddelyn High
**Graphic Designer:** Signe Landin
**Rights and Permissions Administrator:** Diane Durrett

**Copy Editor:** Nancy Olson
**Cover Design:** Signe Landin
**Book Design and Production:** Kaelin Chappell Broaddus

**Library of Congress Cataloging-in-Publication Data**

Smith, Grace E.
  Differentiating instruction with technology in K-5 classrooms / Grace E.
Smith, Stephanie Throne. — 1st ed.
    p. cm.
    Includes bibliographical references.
    ISBN-13: 978-1-56484-233-6 (pbk.)
    1. Individualized instruction. 2. Educational technology. 3. Teaching—Aids and devices.
4. Elementary school teaching. I. Throne, Stephanie. II. International Society for Technology in Education.
III. Title.
    LB1031.S62 2007
    371.39′4—dc22

                                                          2007020503

First Edition
ISBN: 978-1-56484-223-6

Printed in the United States of America

**International Society for Technology in Education (ISTE)**

Washington, DC, Headquarters:
        1710 Rhode Island Ave. NW, Suite 900, Washington, DC 20036-3132
Eugene, Oregon, Office:
        175 West Broadway, Suite 300, Eugene, OR 97401-3003
Order Desk: 1.800.336.5191
Order Fax: 1.541.302.3778
Customer Service: orders@iste.org
Book Publishing: books@iste.org
Rights and Permissions: permissions@iste.org
Web: www.iste.org

# ABOUT ISTE

The International Society for Technology in Education (ISTE) is the trusted source for professional development, knowledge generation, advocacy, and leadership for innovation. A nonprofit membership association, ISTE provides leadership and service to improve teaching, learning, and school leadership by advancing the effective use of technology in PK–12 and teacher education.

Home of the National Educational Technology Standards (NETS), the Center for Applied Research in Educational Technology (CARET), and the National Educational Computing Conference (NECC), ISTE represents more than 85,000 professionals worldwide. We support our members with information, networking opportunities, and guidance as they face the challenge of transforming education. To find out more about these and other ISTE initiatives, visit our Web site at **www.iste.org**.

As part of our mission, ISTE Book Publishing works with experienced educators to develop and produce practical resources for classroom teachers, teacher educators, and technology leaders. Every manuscript we select for publication is carefully peer-reviewed and professionally edited. We look for content that emphasizes the effective use of technology where it can make a difference—increasing the productivity of teachers and administrators; helping students with unique learning styles, abilities, or backgrounds; collecting and using data for decision making at the school and district levels; and creating dynamic, project-based learning environments that engage 21st-century learners. We value your feedback on this book and other ISTE products. E-mail us at **books@iste.org**.

# ABOUT THE AUTHORS

 **Grace E. Smith** received a PhD in instructional (educational) technology from Wayne State University. Her experience includes 10 years as a teacher and reading specialist in public and private schools and 8 years as a technology curriculum coordinator for a school district of 10,000 students. She has also worked as the director of continuing professional education at a business college, as an educational consultant, and as an adjunct professor at two universities, where she taught writing and technology courses.

 **Stephanie Throne** received a PhD in Spanish literature from the University of Michigan at Ann Arbor. She has extensive experience in developing online educational materials and at one point was the first instructor at her institution to offer online foreign language classes. Assignments necessitating the use of technology have always played an important role in all of her classes. She currently works as an independent contractor for adult, high school, elementary, and preschool Spanish classes and as a private tutor for students of college level Spanish, elementary reading, and math.

# CONTENTS

# INTRODUCTION

The purpose of *Differentiating Instruction with Technology in K–5 Classrooms* is to help you strengthen your teaching skills by adding technology tools to differentiated instructional strategies. As with most other endeavors, you'll probably find that the key to using technology with differentiated instruction is to move slowly.

You can try out as many or as few strategies in this book as you wish. Some strategies or activities require more preparation time than others, and some will be a more natural fit with your style of teaching. All chapters contain a resource section of links based on the topic at hand. These resources are to provide examples and ideas for trying out the activities in your own classroom.

Here's a caveat from your authors. Although all Web sites in this book were tested prior to publication, sites change addresses frequently. If you find that a link doesn't work, try using the title provided with each link (the title is placed before the URL listing) as your search term. In other words, if the link for the Center for Applied Research in Educational Technology (CARET) doesn't work, search using the phrase "Center for Applied Research in Educational Technology" or CARET. You should be able to find the site without too much trouble.

The content and resources in this book are designed to supply you with some concrete plans to test ways you might combine technology with differentiated instruction. More important, we hope it will serve as a stepping-stone to inspire you to create your own plans for your own students.

We've always liked books that feature overviews and contents-at-a-glance. What follows is a snapshot of this book's chapters in an easy-to-read table.

# Strategies-At-a-Glance

| Chapter | Differentiated Instruction Strategy or Practice | Conventional Classroom Focus | Differentiated Instruction Classroom Focus | Technology Features |
|---|---|---|---|---|
| 1 | Overview and Principles | Use of paper and pencil or low-tech tools to learn or extend learning | Use of computer and Internet technology to learn or extend learning | Personalization, privacy, collaboration, organization, authentic learning |
| 2 | Interest | Not often assessed, sometimes ignored | Built on student interests and passions, interest centers and groups, new forms of expression; link interests with curriculum; share interests | I-Search, WebQuests, Jigsaw groups, group investigations, Internet |
| 3 | Readiness | Sometimes used with reading and math groups (high, middle, low) | Flexible groups based on readiness, Equalizer tool, scaffolding, tiered assignments | Flexible groups, tiered assignments created with technology tools |
| 4 | Learning Profile | Not often assessed, sometimes ignored | Learning style preferences assessed and honored; learning environment considered; multiple intelligences, cultural-influenced, and gender-based preferences considered and sometimes the structure for learning activities | Assessment tools created in technology applications, teacher anecdotal records stored in handhelds or Word documents |
| 5 | Content | Teacher + textbooks | Flexible group learning; non-text resources; variety of resources based on readiness, interest, and learning profile; curriculum compacting; learning contracts | Content software, Internet sites, multimedia, video streaming |
| 6 | Process | Teacher-driven | Student choices, multiple intelligences, interest groups and centers | Student choices, choice board, interactive sites and software |

*continued*

| Chapter | Differentiated Instruction Strategy or Practice | Conventional Classroom Focus | Differentiated Instruction Classroom Focus | Technology Features |
|---|---|---|---|---|
| 7 | Product | Non-digital tools such as crayons and paper, dioramas, handwritten reports by individuals | Group reports, projects, and authentic artifacts using non-digital tools | Digital tools for authentic product creation and sharing of information (Publisher, PowerPoint, Word, Paint, Internet) |
| 8 | Encore Subjects | Often whole-class, teacher-driven activities, with exception of pairing or grouping; use of other DI strategies and technology dependent upon teacher knowledge and availability of funds for tech resources | Flexible grouping, learning centers or stations, interest centers or stations, group reports or projects, tiered instruction, authentic documents, varied printed texts and traditional audiovisual resources, skills-based differentiation | Tech-driven flexible grouping, learning centers or stations, interest centers or stations, and tiering; interactive/virtual sites and software; digital tools for authentic documents and product creation; WebQuests and R.A.F.T.s; podcasts, labs, student handhelds and multimedia; student choice and choice boards |
| 9 | Assessment | Student assessment after completing a unit or chapter | Use of a wide range of pre-, ongoing, and post-assessment tools | Software, online, and teacher-made assessments |
| 10 | Management | Teacher-driven whole group | Flexible groups, frequent feedback, both oral and written | Voice/e-mail, talking text, student-managed projects, discussion groups, electronic feedback |

## CHAPTER 1

# Overview *and* **Principles** *of* Differentiated Instruction

NCLB, IEP, GLCE, MI, 6 + 1 Traits—are any of these acronyms a part of your everyday language? As teachers, we have our own jargon, which is often based on current educational trends and philosophies.

Sometimes it can seem overwhelming to keep abreast of all the latest developments and buzzwords in our profession. While many of the changes and advances become an important part of our curricula and repertoire, others fall by the wayside because we learn they aren't as effective as advertised.

The waning popularity of particular approaches or tactics doesn't necessarily mean that their methodologies are inherently flawed but that our teaching practices are keenly shaped by such external factors as cultural shifts, changes in the family dynamic, and technology improvements. So as the "business" of education undergoes changes, we, too, must make modifications to reach students of different backgrounds and levels of ability.

Yet another acronym you're undoubtedly familiar with is DI, or differentiated instruction. Perhaps unlike some of the acronyms listed above that represent various educational theories or practices, DI has the potential to play a vital and sustained role in the classrooms of the future. While older movements and strategies may fade and new ones develop, the essential premise of DI gives promise to its being long-lasting. It offers a unique flexibility to withstand change over a significant period of time. Why is this?

The core of DI is a broad framework that offers multiple approaches to meeting learners' needs. Our classrooms today are more diverse than ever, with a wide range of interests, levels of readiness, and learning styles. In addition to this breadth of academic diversity, we encounter a challenging array of cultural and familial differences that strongly influence our students' social and learning personalities. As teachers, we're faced with meeting the unique needs of each and every student. We're also charged with ensuring high levels of student achievement across the board.

As opposed to some educational theories and methods of the past, DI actually embraces the recognition of cultural, familial, and academic differences among students. Teachers who practice DI modify their instruction to address that diversity and to meet curricular objectives. At the same time, in the DI classroom, educators don't bear *all* the responsibility for student learning and achievement. Students have responsibilities, too.

How can DI possibly help educators rise to the doubly difficult challenge of meeting the demands placed on them to produce high achievement results while concurrently addressing the variety of academic, cultural, and familial diversity in our classrooms? Let's examine some key components of differentiated instruction to understand its fundamental value.

- DI encourages the modification of instruction to address student diversity and to meet curricular objectives.

- DI emphasizes student accountability for learning and high levels of participation through flexible grouping and simultaneous activities, such as learning centers and WebQuests.

- DI features group-driven tasks, but it also relies on whole-class and individualized instruction to complement group work. It focuses on the quality of activities versus the quantity of work assigned.

- DI promotes a comfortable yet challenging learning environment. Teachers realize that their organization and presentation of content profoundly affects students' motivation to learn and their perceived ability to comprehend. Inspired students feel safe in their learning communities and are intrigued by the subject matter at hand.

- DI depends on pre-, ongoing, and post-assessment that utilizes both traditional and nontraditional evaluation methods, such as teacher observation, self-assessment, and project work.

- Teachers who apply DI concepts show a willingness not only to learn more about their students but also to modify instruction to support student needs. As a result, student surveys and other tools used to learn about students are important.

- DI is guided by the constructivist, or student-centered, approach to teaching and learning. Constructivism, one of the big ideas in education that arose during the early 1990s, is the belief that students create or construct their own knowledge and understanding by building on previous learning. Constructivist learning is active rather than passive. Constructivist teachers relinquish their traditional role of "sage on the stage" (the omnipotent keeper of knowledge) to become the "guide on the side" (the facilitator of experiences and opportunities for children to learn).

- In student-centered classrooms, planning, teaching, and assessment are focused on the needs and abilities of students. Why? Because constructivists believe learning is most meaningful when topics are connected to students' needs and interests and when the students themselves are actively engaged in creating, understanding, and connecting to knowledge. Students are motivated to learn when they feel they have a real share in their own learning. In a student-centered classroom, students are given options and are included in decision-making processes. The focus in these classrooms is on choices, rather than on one size fits all. Students are regarded as individuals with thoughts and issues that merit consideration and thoughtfulness.

- DI practitioners make instructional decisions based on student readiness, interests, and learning profile as well as on content, process, and product. Even more recently, teachers who practice DI have begun to focus on student affect and the learning environment.

That said, what about technology? How does it impact learning? What does research about technology in the classroom tell us thus far?

# Research on the Impact of Technology on Learning

According to the Center for Applied Research in Educational Technology (CARET), a project of the International Society for Technology in Education in partnership with Education Support Systems and the Sacramento County Office of Education, technology can help improve student performance in six key ways:

1. **"Technology improves student performance when the application directly supports the curriculum objectives being assessed."** In other words, technology is most effective when integrated with curriculum content.

2. **"Technology improves performance when the application provides opportunities for student collaboration."** Studies show that paired and collaborative learning in conjunction with technology enhances student performance.

3. **"Technology improves performance when the application adjusts for student ability and prior experience, and provides feedback to the student and teacher about student performance or progress with the application."** This finding supports the differentiated instruction practices of coaching and mentoring as well as sharing responsibility for learning.

4. **"Technology improves performance when the application is integrated into the typical instructional day."** This finding supports classroom and content learning with technology as opposed to lab learning with technology.

5. **"Technology improves performance when the application provides opportunities for students to design and implement projects that extend the curriculum content being assessed by a particular standardized test."** Student-created products, multimedia, and video streaming are examples of how technology can extend curriculum content.

6. **"Technology improves performance when used in environmentswhere teachers, the school community, and school and district administrators support the use of technology."** In addition to performance improvements tied to administrative support for technology, findings show that integration of technology with instruction, professional development for teachers, and computer use at home and school with differentiated products and student entry points combine to improve performance.

Differentiated instruction focuses on teaching strategies that give diverse students multiple options for taking in and processing information, making sense of ideas, and expressing learning. Technology tools can support good instruction and offer personalized learning environments in which students interact with software, conduct research, create products, and communicate with others outside their school. Both differentiated instruction and technology tools are important for 21st-century education, aka digital age learning.

According to a study by the North Central Regional Educational Laboratory (NCREL) titled "enGauge 21st Century Skills: Literacy in the Digital Age," "[T]echnology has catapulted us into a knowledge-based global society." As a result of technology, what students learn and how and when they learn are changing.

NCREL advises that technology influences learning in these three ways:

1. Technology drives change. As a result, success in society will require skill sets in the 21st century significantly different from those of the past.

2. Technology serves as a bridge to more engaging, relevant, meaningful, and personalized learning, all of which can lead to higher academic achievement.

3. Technology provides a platform for using timely and relevant data to shape personalized learning.

The enGauge 21st Century Skills shown in Table 1.1 are well matched with the principles and practices of differentiated instruction. Combining differentiated instruction strategies with technology will help students attain the 21st -century skills sets.

TABLE **1.1** ■ The enGauge 21st Century Skills

| Digital-Age Literacy | ■ Basic, scientific, economic, and technological literacies<br>■ Visual and information literacies<br>■ Multicultural literacy and global awareness |
| --- | --- |
| Inventive Thinking | ■ Adaptability and managing complexity and self-direction<br>■ Curiosity, creativity, and risk taking<br>■ Higher-order thinking and sound reasoning |
| Effective Communication | ■ Teaming, collaboration, and interpersonal skills<br>■ Personal, social, and civic responsibility<br>■ Interactive communication |
| High Productivity | ■ Prioritizing, planning, and managing for results<br>■ Effective use of real-world tools<br>■ Ability to produce relevant, high-quality products |

The enGauge skills sets offer a quick look at what students will need for the future. What, though, is that state of technology in today's schools? Is there ample and strategic technology integration to help prepare and propel students to actualize 21st-century skills? The following section provides a quick review.

# Status of Technology Use in Schools

The use of technology in classrooms appears to range from none, or minimal, to frequent. Although various agencies and groups across the United States have collected data, there's little uniformity on what should be collected and how. As a result, it's difficult, if not impossible, to determine from a global perspective how much technology is used in elementary schools today.

"Technology Counts" is a report (in print and digital formats) produced annually by *Education Week*. *Education Week* surveys the states to measure the status of K–12 education technology and then creates individual state technology reports based on several criteria: state overview, access to technology, use of technology, the capacity to use technology, state data systems, and data access/analysis tools. *Education Week* analyzes each of the six major categories and makes comparisons among states. A grade is given for each category, and each state receives an overall grade as well. Readers who use the *Education Week* Web site (www.edweek.org) can make online comparisons between their own states and others. If you don't have a personal subscription, your school district or regional school district may subscribe.

The "Technology Counts 2006" report is the ninth report *Education Week* has completed in as many years. Although many states have made great strides toward improving technology in the schools, it's disheartening to read this year's survey results. Why? Because of the 50 states and the District of Columbia, only two states received an A grade for overall technology: West Virginia (94) and Virginia (92). The six states ranking lowest received D+ to D- grades: Hawaii (69), Massachusetts (69), Oregon (66), Rhode Island (65), Minnesota (65), and Nevada (62). The remaining states range from North Dakota, with a B grade (86), through Oklahoma, with a C- grade (70). The overall technology grade average is C+, with a score of 77.

Other recent studies can give you a taste of the status of technology across the country and prompt you to check out your own state's score in the "Technology Counts 2006" report. Or you might contact your state department of education to see what's planned for technology in the near future.

In the 2003 "Use, Support and Effect of Instructional Technology" (UseIT) study of several schools in Massachusetts, some interesting findings were noted at the Grade 5 level:

- Students use computers in school but less than at home.
- Fifth-graders use computers in school more than 8th- and 11th-graders do; but 24.5% of 5th-graders don't use computers, 39.6% use computers for 15 minutes or less per day, and 33.4% use computers ranging from 15 to 60 minutes every day to once per month.
- Teachers use computers during instruction less than students do.

- Key factors affecting elementary classroom use include
  - home use, skills, and beliefs about technology;
  - teachers' pedagogical beliefs and practices;
  - student technology skill level;
  - principals' beliefs about technology;
  - principals' emphasis on technology and pressure to use technology.

Another study, the 2005 "National Teacher Survey," shows that a gap exists between technology for teachers and technology for teaching because the need for data management has begun to supersede the need for instructional use. Why is data management so important? According to *eSchoolNews*, "New technologies, combined with the strict accountability demands of the No Child Left Behind Act (NCLB), have combined to create a climate in which 'Data-informed Instruction' is flourishing. The NCLB has introduced a number of new buzzwords into the lexicon of K–12 educators—and the most significant of them all just might be 'data-driven decision making.'

"Simply put, this concept involves the collection and analysis of test results, demographic information, and other student data to make more informed decisions about instruction—and, given the stringent requirements of NCLB, it's a practice that is no longer an option for today's school leaders, but a necessity."

Other key findings from the survey show:

- Teachers cite computers as effective tools, but only about 54% integrate them into daily instruction.
- Seasoned teachers indicate no resistance to classroom technology.
- Classroom instructional use of computers ranks 4th in the role of technology use by teachers (1st is administrative functions, 2nd is communication, and 3rd is research and planning).

A fourth study, "Effect of the *unitedstreaming* Application on Educational Performance," reports that those students who received instruction that incorporated *unitedstreaming* videos showed dramatic improvement in achievement. *Unitedstreaming* is a browser-based Internet content delivery system developed by Discovery Education. It consists of a collection of more than 4,000 videos and 40,000 chaptered clips of standards-based educational videos, teacher guides, black line masters, student activities, clip art, quizzes, and teacher resources. Conclusions drawn from the study reveal three primary reasons that multimedia and technology are effective in the classroom:

1. Multimedia and technology use engages students, which in turn leads to students who are more attentive, knowledgeable, and higher achieving.

2. Multimedia and technology use leads to teachers who are better prepared and more effective.

3. Multimedia and technology use in the classroom changes the nature of interaction in ways that help students learn.

In its report on the NetDay 2005 Speak Up Event, NetDay, a national nonprofit organization, summarized national data on technology use in education collected from 185,000 student surveys and 15,000 teacher surveys.

The surveys focused on technology products and Internet tools used by teachers and students and how they're using them. Surveys also focused on trends, obstacles and issues, and student achievement through technology.

Survey results determined that:

- Students are innovative users of technology and adopt new technologies to support learning and lifestyles.

- Communication is a key motivator for students, driving their use of technology for learning and for personal use.

- Younger students continue to adopt sophisticated technologies, especially those favored by older siblings.

- Students and teachers want access to current technology tools when they need it. Restrictions to technology use for learning frustrate them.

- Teachers' technology use does not keep up with advances in how students use technology.

- Students believe that technology enriches their learning experiences and prepares them for a competitive job market.

- Students use technology tools for communication, research, completing school projects, and checking on their grades.

- Teachers use technology tools for preparing lessons, keeping records, communication, and research.

As other studies are reported, we'll have a better picture of how technology is used in education. The Irving, Texas, "Laptop Surveys for Teachers" report, for example, offers insight into how laptops are changing instruction in the school district. It would be helpful to see similar studies conducted in each subject area to assess the learning issues specific to that content. However, what remains constant is that knowing how to use technology is increasingly necessary on many levels to function in our society. Teachers need to integrate technology into their classrooms to personalize and facilitate learning, to nourish learners' engagement with curriculum content, and to prepare students for the world of work.

While many teachers still struggle with how to use technology and integrate it into classroom content, those who are more sophisticated in their use of technology may not have thought much about how to use it in a differentiated classroom. In other words, you might be a master at differentiated instruction but not know how to add technology as a differentiation tool. Or you might be a techno whiz but not know much about differentiated instruction.

The power of two—differentiated instruction + technology—will soon be apparent to teachers who successfully use technology in a differentiated environment. Technology is a highly motivating, interactive tool that can be used to personalize students' instruction according to their learning styles, interests, and readiness. Web resources and multimedia software greatly expand learning options and provide information access way beyond the school textbook and media center. Technology can help teachers shape and deliver instruction to meet the needs of all students, assist in the improvement of student thinking, provide for research and presentation products, and improve communication. This book is about combining technology with differentiated instruction in ways that empower student learning.

# Technology Features That Support Differentiated Instruction in Elementary Classrooms

Over the last 30 years, studies have shown that the teacher is the most important factor in student learning. Research from Marzano, Pickering, and Pollock (2001) reveals the nine essential instructional strategies most likely to improve student achievement in all grades and any content area. As states and districts become increasingly accountable for academic performance (No Child Left Behind legislation), teachers must become more aware of the instructional strategies that work, and they must employ them.

The nine categories of instructional strategies are listed in order of effectiveness in the first column of Table 1.2 on the following page. Column two lists their corresponding elements in differentiated instruction. Column three lists tech tools such as software and Web sites that support differentiated instruction.

TABLE **1.2** ■ **Nine categories of instructional strategies most likely to help students learn**

| | | |
|---|---|---|
| 1. Recognizing similarities and differences | Graphic organizers such as the Venn diagram and Comparison matrix<br><br>Represent similarities and differences in graphic or symbolic form<br><br>Sorting, classifying, using metaphors and analogies | Inspiration and Kidspiration software<br><br>Web-based/downloadable graphic organizers<br><br>Word processing tables (Word software) |
| 2. Summarizing information and taking notes | Beginning, middle, end<br><br>Clarifying information<br><br>Teacher-prepared and student-prepared comments<br><br>Webbing | Cornell Note-taking Forms<br><br>Inspiration and Kidspiration software<br><br>NoteStar<br><br>Read•Write•Think Notetaker<br><br>Word processing notes (Word software) |
| 3. Reinforcing effort and providing recognition | Effective praise and rewards<br><br>Effort and achievement rubrics and charts<br><br>Personalizing recognition<br><br>Success stories of people who persisted during difficult times | Kids Are Authors (Scholastic)<br><br>Microsoft Publisher certificates<br><br>Online certificates<br><br>Personal achievement logs<br><br>Word processing feedback notes (Word software) |
| 4. Homework and practice | Planners and organizers<br><br>Vary student and teacher feedback | Content-related software<br><br>Homework help sites to extend learning beyond the classroom<br><br>Word processing planners and organizers (Word software)<br><br>Word processing feedback notes (Word software) |
| 5. Nonlinguistic representations:<br>■ Creating graphic representations<br>■ Drawing pictures and pictographs<br>■ Engaging in kinesthetic activity<br>■ Generating mental pictures<br>■ Making physical models | Cause and effect organizers<br><br>Concept organizers<br><br>Drawing pictures, illustrations, and pictographs<br><br>Graphic organizers<br><br>Physical models and movement<br><br>Time-sequence organizers | Digital cameras<br><br>Graph Club software<br><br>Inspiration and Kidspiration software<br><br>Kid Pix software<br><br>Micro Worlds software<br><br>Excel spreadsheet software<br><br>Paint software (Microsoft Windows accessory)<br><br>PowerPoint software<br><br>TimeLiner software<br><br>Virtual manipulative software or Web sites |

*continued*

TABLE **1.2** ■ Nine categories of instructional strategies most likely to help students learn *(continued)*

| Effective Instructional Strategies | Application to Differentiated Classrooms | Related Tech Tools |
|---|---|---|
| 6. Cooperative and collaborative learning groups by ability, interest, and other criteria | Flexible groups by interest, learning style, and readiness<br>Individual and group accountability<br>Vary groups by size and objectives<br>Think–Pair–Share strategy | Group investigations<br>Individual and group assessments<br>Jigsaw groups<br>Multimedia software<br>Scavenger hunts<br>ThinkQuests<br>WebQuests |
| 7. Setting objectives and providing feedback | Learning contracts for achieving specific goals<br>Ongoing assessment<br>Praise<br>Rubrics<br>Self-assessment<br>Student-led feedback<br>Teacher feedback that's timely, specific, and constructive | Electronic journaling (Word software)<br>Learning logs (Word software)<br>Project-based learning checklists (Web-based)<br>RubiStar and other rubric generators<br>Word processing checklists (Word software)<br>Word processing contracts (Word software) |
| 8. Generating and testing hypotheses | Decision making<br>Historical investigation<br>Invention<br>Making predictions<br>Problem solving | Graph Club<br>Kids' mysteries<br>Kidspiration and Inspiration hypothesis Webs<br>Internet research<br>Online graphing generator<br>PowerPoint slideshows<br>Science Court software<br>Word or Publisher reports, mini-books, and advertisements |
| 9. Questions, cues, and advance organizers | Advance organizers<br>Anticipation guides<br>Cubing and ThinkDots activities<br>KWL charts<br>Pause after asking questions | Cubing and ThinkDots templates<br>Inspiration/Kidspiration advanced organizers<br>Online or Word-created KWL charts<br>Word Personal Agendas<br>Word narrative advance organizers |

## Resources for Chapter 1

| | |
|---|---|
| **Center for Applied Research in Educational Technology (CARET)** | http://caret.iste.org |
| **Education Commission of the States Policy Brief: Student Performance and Teacher Accountability** | www.ecs.org/clearinghouse/12/28/1228.doc |
| **Education Week's Technology Counts 2006** | www2.edweek.org/rc/articles/2004/10/15/tc-archive.html |
| **Effect of the *unitedstreaming* Application on Educational Performance** | http://caret.iste.org/index.cfm?StudyID=852&fuseaction=studySummary |
| **eSchoolNews** | www.eschoolnews.com/resources/reports/datadrivendecisionmaking/ |
| **Integrating Technology into the Classroom Using Instructional Strategies** | www.tltguide.ccsd.k12.co.us/instructional_tools/Strategies/Strategies.html |
| **Irving, Texas, Laptop Surveys for Teachers report** | www.iittl.unt.edu/irving/IrvingTeacherReport2005.pdf |
| **Kids Are Authors** | http://teacher.sckholastic.com/activities/kaa/ |
| **MysteryNet's Kids Mysteries** | http://kids.mysterynet.com |
| **2005 National Teacher Survey** (Teachers Talk Tech 2005) | http://newsroom.cdwg.com/features/2005NatlTeacherSurvey.pdf<br>http://newsroom.cdwg.com/features//TTTCompleteResults.pdf |
| **NetDay 2005 Speak Up Event** | www.netday.org/SPEAKUP/pdfs/SpeakUpReport_05.pdf |
| **No Child Left Behind** | www.ed.gov/nclb/ |
| **North Central Regional Educational Laboratory (NCREL) report: enGauge 21st Century Skills: Literacy in the Digital Age** | www.ncrel.org/engauge/skills/engauge21st.pdf |
| **NoteStar** | http://notestar.4teachers.org |
| **Use, Support and Effect of Instructional Technology** | www.bc.edu/research/intasc/PPT/USEIT_NECC070203.ppt |
| **Who Is Accountable for Children's Education?** | www.pbs.org/newshour/btp/pdfs/stlouis_accountability_2005.pdf |

## CHAPTER 2

# Using Technology *to* Differentiate *by* Interest

Multiple intelligences expert Thomas Armstrong affirms, "Giving students choices is as much a fundamental principle of good teaching as it is a specific intrapersonal teaching strategy" (1994, p. 83). We couldn't agree more.

If you look around your building or district, you'll find colleagues who have set up interest centers in their classrooms. Maybe you have some, too. The point is that an interest-driven learning environment engages children. Teachers know that when learners are interested in a topic, they put in more effort, retain more information, and connect what they're learning to prior knowledge. In other words, interest-based activities help motivate children to learn.

In this chapter, we offer strategies and tools for using technology to differentiate by interest. We focus primarily on the inquiry-based learning strategies of I-Searches, Jigsaw groups, R.A.F.T.s, and WebQuests. We also offer some technology resources to support investigations in the classroom.

Before we dig into the specifics of these strategies, let's review the basics of differentiation by interest.

## Differentiating by Interest

Differentiating by interest means crafting activities that permit students to explore their own interests and develop new ones. When tasks promote curiosity, learning becomes more appealing to all students, even those who struggle most or are the most reluctant to learn.

Although some educators (parents, too!) might not view it as such, student choice is a powerful ally for teachers and a great incentive for students. Researching topics of personal interest encourages students to become more actively involved in the learning process, which in turn boosts their levels of accountability.

A user-friendly characteristic of differentiating by interest is that its core concepts aren't overly complex. If you need some guidelines as to what your students' interests are, ask them, or use a convenient tool such as an online interest survey or questionnaire.

## Technology-enhanced Instructional Strategies Focusing on Student Interest

You may already differentiate by interest in your classroom by using learning centers or groups, literature circles, and independent or exploratory study. Such activities are fairly common in elementary classrooms.

We're going to take differentiating by interest a step further by adding technology to the mix. Adding such technology as draw and paint software, presentation and publishing software, brainstorming tools, and Web resource tools allows teachers to personalize learning, vary the process by which learning is achieved, and produce products (artifacts) based on what students have discovered and learned.

Table 2.1 lists four instructional strategies that focus on student interests. Note that the strategies we've chosen are inquiry based or inquiry oriented. Inquiry-based learning strategies have much in common with those of differentiated instruction because they're founded on a constructivist perspective that promotes a high degree of accountability for one's own learning, concept-based problem solving, and collaborative learning. In Table 2.1, we've provided a definition of each interest-based strategy, along with how it works in the classroom.

Now that you've seen a brief overview of the interest-based strategies that represent the core pedagogy of the sample lesson plans of this chapter, we'd like to give you more specifics about each one.

TABLE **2.1** ■ Instructional strategies that focus on student interests

| Strategy | Definition | How It Works in the Classroom |
|---|---|---|
| **I-Searches** | Student-driven investigative research paper or other product based on a "genuine itch" (interest, passion) as defined by creator Ken Macrorie. | 1. Students individually use the Web, electronic research tools, and other resources to investigate a topic of interest.<br>2. Students individually use technology such as Web research tools, word processing templates, draw and paint software, and brainstorming tools for creating, writing, publishing, and presenting information to their peers. |
| **Jigsaw Groups** | A peer teaching strategy in which students focus on a specific interest or topic with the assistance of a jigsaw group. In the jigsaw group, students discuss definitive aspects of their shared interest or topic and brainstorm how they'll present key information to their home groups. | 1. Working in cooperative home teams students use electronic tools such as Web resources, online self-assessments, notes and planning templates, and other resources to investigate a portion of a task that's assigned by the teacher.<br>2. After reassignment to their jigsaw group, students use technology such as software-based and Web-based research tools, as well as presentation and publishing software for creating, writing, publishing, and presenting information to their peers. |
| **R.A.F.T** | R.A.F.T. stands for role, audience, format, and topic. It was created originally to combine reading and writing in unconventional ways.<br>Students design a new product that demonstrates their conceptual understanding of teacher-identified skills and ideas. | 1. Teacher determines the content students are to learn and then identifies the specifics of four components: role, audience, format, and topic.<br>2. Students confer with teacher about which role they'll assume.<br>3. Students individually use Web or electronic research tools, hyperlinks, and hints in the R.A.F.T. table to locate information.<br>4. Students individually use technology such as paint and draw software, graphic organizer software, and word processing software for creating, writing, publishing, and presenting their final product. |
| **WebQuests** | Team (or sometimes individualized) activities using the Internet to help students grapple with complex, open-ended questions. Tasks are research- or interest-based, or both, and require problem-solving skills such as evaluation, analysis, and synthesis of resources. | 1. Working in a cooperative team, students use Web research tools to investigate a teacher-designed topic of interest.<br>2. Working in a cooperative team, students use technology such as Web research tools, Web page creation tools, and puzzle creation tools for creating, writing, publishing, and presenting information to their peers. |

Preceding each sample lesson plan, you'll find a profile section that describes the function, advantages, and components of each strategy, plus the steps you need to follow to create activities that use the strategy. You'll find information about the related technologies used in the lesson plan. We'll provide a brief description of how the technologies will be used in the lesson plan, as well as any implementation challenges. Lastly, we'll supply a description of the technologies, where to find them, and where to get help when implementing them. While we realize you may have tried all or some of these strategies in your own classroom, it's also possible you may not have had any experience with them at all. If you're lacking experience or feel like you need a quick review of any of the strategies, turn first to the information sheet before looking at the sample lesson plan.

# I-Search Strategy

We begin with the I-Search, an attractive alternative to the conventional research paper.

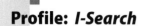

## Profile: *I-Search*

### Function

To enable a greater understanding of the research process as well as the production of a quality artifact by means of self-selection of an intriguing topic.

### Advantages

- Increases student commitment through freedom to choose individualized topic and product format and style.
- Enhances understanding of the research process, thereby improving writing, organizational, and presentation skills.
- Permits use of multiple technologies such as word processing, publishing software, brainstorming tools, Web research tools, and draw and paint software and inquiry-based learning.

### Components

**A.** Selecting a topic/Posing questions based on immersion activities/What do I want to know?

**B.** Finding answers/Developing a search plan

**C.** Searching for and using information/Gathering, analyzing, and synthesizing information

**D.** Developing the final product/Showing what I've learned/Representing knowledge

### Steps to Create an I-Search

The I-Search comprises four steps that have many different names or titles, so we've listed more than one for each step.

**1.** For component A:
- Develop a broad or general theme and determine the core concepts students must comprehend.
- Figure out a hook that will encourage students' interest in the topic along with their willingness to discuss any previous knowledge of, or experience with, the theme.

- Prepare possible questions to use as you brainstorm with students about what questions they want to answer or subtopics they might want to investigate.

- Put together a brief overview of the four phases of the I-Search process for the students so that they know what's ahead.

- Consider how you might help students select their own topics, possibly using a KWL (What I **K**now—What I **W**ant to Know—What I **L**earned) chart, interest maps or inventories, or journaling (about "what if" questions, their likes, things they wonder about, etc.).

2. For component B:

- Demonstrate strategies students might use to collect information.

- Direct students toward electronic sources, possible interviews, printed sources, and other resources that will assist them in the research process.

- Disseminate rubrics, guidelines, timelines, and information about your expectations for the final product, as well as the research process.

3. For component C:

- Assist students as they endeavor to make sense of the information they're gathering.

- Teach them to use graphic organizers as a classification tool.

4. For component D:

- Reexamine the rubrics and other evaluation criteria to make sure students are on track.

- Continue to guide them toward helpful resources as needed.

- Support them in the creation of their final products as needed.

## Related Technologies: *I-Search Lesson Plan*

### *Word Processing Templates*

**How word processing templates will be used in the activity**: In the accompanying lesson plan, students type biographical information into a word processing template (Word) or a publishing template (Publisher). To complete this activity, students must know how to input information into the pre-designed templates, and you must be able to create one ahead of time.

As an additional option, you may elect to have students use a word processing template as a part of the brainstorming phase. You could prepare a template that students fill in during class discussion (such as a KWL chart) or provide a template with a journal question or an interest inventory that prompts them to think about the topic at hand and identify their primary interests.

**Implementation challenges**: In most cases, word processing templates are very user friendly. Sometimes misalignment problems might occur, or students will forget to save their documents or changes to them.

| *Resources for Word Processing Templates* | |
|---|---|
| **Description** | Templates are pre-created forms or files accessible in word processing programs that you customize by filling in personalized information. A word processing program, such as Word, enables you to create and format a document on the computer and edit it without retyping the document. You save your document as a file on your computer or on a disk, CD, or flash drive. |
| **Where to find the templates** | In most cases, a word processing program such as Word will come with your computer or be supplied and installed by someone in the technology department at your school. You may purchase it almost anywhere online or at traditional stores, such as office supply stores, bookstores, department store chains, and electronics stores. |
| **Where to get help** | Word has a built-in help feature with searchable contents. If you can't find the answer to your question, it will ask you if you wish to search for the answer via Microsoft's Answer Wizard on the Web. In addition, the additional resources below may be helpful to you. |
| | **Word Home Page—Microsoft Office Online** |
| | http://office.microsoft.com/en-us/word/ |
| | *Microsoft's home page provides templates, blogs, a product guide, help, and FAQs.* |
| | **Online Technology Practice Modules—Word** |
| | www.Internet4classrooms.com/online_word.htm |
| | **Essential Microsoft Office XP: Tutorials for Teachers** |
| | www.pitt.edu/~edindex/OfficeindexXP2.html |
| | *This is an online book that supplies a set of tutorials to help teachers learn not only Word, but also Excel, PowerPoint, and Access, as well as the drawing tools.* |
| | **Online Technology Tutorials** |
| | www.kent.k12.wa.us/KSD/IT/TSC/prof_dev/tutorials.html |
| | *This is a thorough site from Kent School District that provides multiple tutorials for Word, PowerPoint, Excel, FrontPage, Publisher, Outlook, Access, Inspiration, Kid Pix, and many others. It offers additional resources on technology integration, PC basics, and other software and hardware tools.* |

## *Web Research Tools*

**How Web research tools will be used in the activity**: In the lesson plan below, students will use Web resource tools to find facts that they need to generate a biographical summary for their final products. Minimally, students must be able to use kid-safe search engines to hunt by keywords to track down historical information. You can assist your students by guiding them to some useful Web sites and by modeling how to collect and organize information.

**Implementation challenges**: When using the Web, there's always a possibility that a Web site might be down, under repair, or nonexistent. Computer servers and other equipment may impact Internet connection speed and performance. If your school has filtering software, sites that you or your students may wish to access could be blocked, depending on content. More challenged readers might move more slowly as they scan the sites to search for useful information.

| Resources for Web Research Tools | |
|---|---|
| **Description** | Search engines, dictionaries, encyclopedias, online databases, library catalogs, Web sites, and other online resources that enable you to locate information based on keywords, dates, or topics. |
| **Where to find software** | There are countless resources on the Web. |
| **Where to get help** | Paint has a built-in help feature with searchable contents. If you can't find the answer to your question, check the resources below. |
| | **Kids' Tools for Searching the Internet**<br>www.rcls.org/ksearch.htm |
| | **Ask for Kids**<br>www.askforkids.com |
| | **CyberSleuth Kids**<br>www.cybersleuth-kids.com |
| | **KidsClick!**<br>www.kidsclick.org |
| | **NoodleQuest**<br>www.noodletools.com/noodlequest/ |
| | **Kids Online Resources**<br>www.kidsolr.com/reference/ |
| | **Thinkfinity Search**<br>www.marcopolosearch.org |

## *Draw and Paint Software*

**How draw and paint software will be used in the activity**: In the lesson plan below, students must know how to create a picture with draw and paint software (Paint or Kid Pix) and be able to insert it into the word processing or publishing software template.

**Implementation challenges**: Even children with little experience seem to warm up very quickly to draw and paint software. It takes some practice to become familiar and adept with the drawing tools, and it doesn't allow for much fine detail.

| Resources for Draw and Paint Software | |
|---|---|
| **Description** | Programs that allow you to simulate the action of drawing and painting via computer. Drawing and painting tools are housed in a toolbox. |
| **Where to find the software** | Programs such as Paint normally come with your computer. |
| **Where to get help** | Paint has a built-in help feature with searchable contents. If you can't find the answer to your question, check the resources below. |
| | **Lakewood Public Library's Microsoft Paint Tutorial** |
| | www.lkwdpl.org/classes/MSPaint/paint.html |
| | **How to Use Microsoft Paint** |
| | www.teachers.ash.org.au/geparker/how_to_use_microsoft_paint.htm |
| | **Microsoft Paint Tutorial** |
| | www.lesley.edu/faculty/ahunt/MSPttutr.htm |

## *Kidspiration, Inspiration, Brainstorming Tools, and Graphic Organizers*

**How brainstorming tools and graphic organizers will be used in this activity**: In the accompanying lesson plan, you may choose to use electronic learning tools such as Kidspiration or Inspiration to assist in the brainstorming phase of the activity. Students might create idea maps or Webs as a means to select a topic that intrigues them.

**Implementation challenges**: Although it's not difficult to learn, you'll need to show your students how to use various graphics and other tools first, and you'll need to allow for some practice sessions.

| Resources for Kidspiration and Inspiration | |
|---|---|
| **Description** | Kidspiration and Inspiration are learning tools that foster brainstorming, categorizing, and organizational skills. These software programs help students to construct, classify, and sequence information, as well as to understand different perspectives through the creation of visual images such as idea maps, concept maps, Webs, and storyboards. |
| **Where to find the software** | Inspiration Software Inc. is the manufacturer. You may download a free trial from the company's site, www.inspiration.com. You may order the product directly from the manufacturer, but you can also find it at many online and traditional department stores, electronics stores, educational stores, and bookstores. In many cases, departments within schools make their own decisions as to whether they wish to purchase it for use by their staff. |
| **Where to get help** | **Inspiration Software Inc.'s technical support page (for both Kidspiration and Inspiration)**<br><br>www.inspiration.com/techsupport/index.cfm?fuseaction=inspiration<br><br>*This site includes a tutorial, quick tour, FAQs, upgrade information, and tips.*<br><br>**Grosse Pointe Public Schools' sites on Inspiration and Kidspiration**<br><br>www.gpschools.org/ci/ce/computer/inspire/inspiration.htm<br><br>www.gpschools.org/ci/ce/computer/inspire/kidspiration.htm<br><br>*These sites offer tutorials and sample uses for classroom activities, using both products.*<br><br>**Lee's Summit R-7 School District Technology Integration pages on Inspiration and Kidspiration**<br><br>http://its.leesummit.k12.mo.us/kidspiration.htm<br><br>http://its.leesummit.k12.mo.us/inspiration.htm<br><br>**Teacher2Teacher.com's Kidspiration 2.1 Training Guide**<br><br>www.teacher2teacher.com/samples/Kids_2.1_TG_SampleCh3.pdf |

# Lesson Plan

## I-Search—Explorers

| | |
|---|---|
| **Grade** | 5 |
| **Subject Area** | Social Studies |
| **Curriculum Standards** | **National Council for the Social Studies Standards addressed:**<br><br>All students will sequence, chronologically, the following eras of American history and key events within these eras to examine relationships and explain cause and effect:<br><br>NSS-USH.5–12.1 Era 1: The Meeting of Three Worlds (beginnings to 1620)<br><br>NSS-USH.5–12.2 Era 2: Colonization and Settlement (1585–1763)<br><br>**National Educational Technology Standards for Students (NETS·S) addressed:** (see appendix for full list)<br><br>1. Creativity and Innovation: 1.a., 1.b.<br>2. Communication and Collaboration: 2.b.<br>3. Research and Information Fluency: 3.a., 3.b., 3.c., 3.d.<br>4. Critical Thinking, Problem Solving, and Decision Making: 4.b. |
| **Lesson Summary** | Students choose an explorer to investigate. They write a summary of the explorer's life, accomplishments, the country he sailed for, and dates of birth and death. Then they type the information into a bookmark template. Students also create an original portrait of the explorer (and optional ship) to insert into the template. After proofreading, bookmarks are printed, glued on tag board, and laminated (optional). |
| **Materials** | ■ Bookmark template (Publisher or Word)<br>■ Color printer (preferred). If color printer isn't available, print in black and white, then hand color with pencils or crayons.<br>■ Laminating machine (optional)<br>■ Yarn or ribbon for tassel or trim |
| **Web Resources** | **Make it Happen!: The I-Search Unit**   www2.edc.org/FSC/MIH/i-search.html<br><br>**Information Inquiry for Teachers**   http://eduscapes.com/info/isearch.html<br><br>**Literacy Matters: I-Search**   www.literacymatters.org/lessons/isearch.htm<br><br>**Explorer Links**   http://edtech.kennesaw.edu/Web/explorer.html<br><br>**eMINTS: Explorers of North America**   www.emints.org/ethemes/resources/S00001141.shtml |
| **Lesson Activities** | 1. Students select an early explorer they wish to investigate by using tools such as brainstorming, a KWL chart, interest inventories and maps, and journaling or discussion questions, or both.<br><br>2. Using print and Internet resources, students research facts about their explorers, such as date of birth and death, country they sailed for, what they discovered, problems and successes, contribution to exploration, and so forth. Prior to beginning their research, assist students by modeling how to collect and organize the information they find. See the "Modeling How to Collect and Organize Information Students Encounter During Research" section for help in this process. In addition, share rubrics and other tools that will be used to evaluate students' final products.<br><br>3. Students create a bookmark-sized summary of the key points in their explorer's life. |

*continued*

## *I-Search—Explorers*

| | |
|---|---|
| **Technology Activity Options** | 1. Create graphic of explorer in Paint, Kid Pix, or other graphic program.<br>2. Type summary or highlights into bookmark template.<br>3. Insert graphic into template. Print and assemble. Laminate if desired.<br>4. See examples at www.gpschools.org/monteith/Staff/fifth/Kellogg/ss.htm. |
| **Differentiation/ Extension** | ■ More capable students can create longer and more detailed artifacts or products.<br>■ Less capable students may create shorter and less detailed artifacts, and may need scaffolding. |
| **Evaluation** | ■ Use rubrics to evaluate students on research, writing, and technology components. See sample rubric below.<br>■ Use a journal or other product for student self-reflection. |

TABLE **2.2** ■ Rubric for Explorers lesson bookmark

| Category | 4 | 3 | 2 | 1 |
|---|---|---|---|---|
| **Research Effort** | Stays on task 90%–100% of the time to complete research. Very self-directed. | Stays on task 80%–89% of the time. Focuses on what needs to be done most of the time. | Stays on task 70%–79% of the time. Needs prodding from teacher. | Stays on task only 60%–69% of the time. Doesn't complete all necessary research. |
| **Layout and Design** | The bookmark includes the two necessary graphics and completely follows the required formatting (on both sides of the bookmark). It's appealing, colorful and reader friendly. | The bookmark includes the two necessary graphics, but doesn't fulfill all of the formatting requirements. | The bookmark is missing one graphic or doesn't follow the required formatting. | The bookmark is missing both graphics and doesn't follow the required formatting. |
| **Biographical Content** | Shows a 90%–100% understanding of the topic. The bookmark includes all required elements. | Shows 80%–89% understanding of the topic. The bookmark is missing one required element. | Shows 70%–79% understanding of parts of the topic. The bookmark is missing two required elements. | Shows only 60%–69% understanding of the topic. The bookmark is missing three or more required elements. |
| **Spelling and Grammar** | There are no grammatical or spelling mistakes on the bookmark. | There are one to two grammatical or spelling mistakes on the bookmark. | There are three grammatical or spelling mistakes on the bookmark. | There are four or more grammatical or spelling mistakes on the bookmark. |

FIGURE **2.1** ■ Explorer bookmark researched and illustrated by fifth grade student

Created by Kamala K.

## Modeling How to Collect and Organize Information Students Encounter During Research

First, check your curriculum resources to see if any resources (in print or online) are suggested. Look over those that are available to you. Next, go to the Web to search for additional resources.

In most cases, you'll seek out two types of sites: 1) note-taking forms that will assist your students in the collection and organization of information, and 2) safe sites containing biographical information about the selected explorers.

We suggest you pick a sample explorer, which means you'll not allow the children to choose one for their own bookmarks. We recommend you visit a handful of sites with your students to show them how to find the required information and how to place it into an appropriate note-taking form. If you haven't tried any Web-based booking and tagging programs to help lighten your load, you might want to test them out. Furl (www.furl.net) and del.icio.us (http://del.icio.us/) are social bookmarking Web services that you may use to search for, store, categorize, and share links. Tags are words that you create to describe the bookmarked links.

If you wish to allow students to search for their own biographical sites, consider using some kid-friendly search tools such as KidsClick! or Ask for Kids. We found a neat Web site for kids created by the Kentucky Virtual Library (The KYVL for Kids Research Portal—Step 3: Take Notes: www.kyvl.org/html/kids/p3_notes/notes.html). It examines eight different types of note-taking strategies. You might want to share and review some or all of these strategies with your students and allow them to use the strategy they feel most comfortable with. We offer a useful list of resources for other helpful forms (for note-taking and other tasks) at the end of this chapter.

# Jigsaw Group Strategy

Now that you've learned about I-Search and reviewed a lesson plan for an I-Search explorers project, take a look at another strategy. Jigsaw groups provide an unusual opportunity for students to use both collaborative and individual skills as they assume responsibility for teaching others about a specific interest.

## Profile: *Jigsaw Group*

### Function

To develop peer teaching and presentation skills via a cooperative learning activity that centers on a particular area of interest.

### Advantages

- Boosts abilities in team building, collaboration, and leadership. Enhances community atmosphere in the classroom.
- Improves skills in researching, questioning, listening, and presentation.
- Encourages familiarity with multimedia, such as presentation or publishing software. Encourages familiarity with such research software as an online encyclopedia or database.

### Components

- **A.** Identification of sections of text or subtopics of current theme to study
- **B.** Division of students into *home* groups
- **C.** Additional regrouping of students into *expert* groups according to common subtopics or sections of text, followed by group research
- **D.** Preparation of instructional materials and techniques by *expert* group members
- **E.** Instruction by *expert* members upon return to *home* groups
- **F.** Assessment

### Steps to Create a Jigsaw Group

1. For component A, choose the chapter(s) of the text you wish to use.
   - Option A: divide the chapter(s) into the appropriate number of sections (to match the number of home groups).
   - Option B: select the appropriate number of subtopics needed (to match the number of members in a home group).

- You might give students the option of voicing their preferences via an interest survey (as to which subtopics or text sections they might like to research).

- Describe the jigsaw technique to the students so that they know what to anticipate.

2. For component B, form four to six diverse home groups and select a captain for each group. Each member of every home group will become an expert on a topic.

3. For component C, rearrange home group members with the same topic into their appropriate expert group. Each expert group uses a variety of materials to research its topic.

    - Model strategies students might use to research information.

    - Point students toward electronic sources, printed sources, and other resources that will assist them in the research process.

    - Share rubrics, guidelines, timelines, and information about your expectations for the final product, as well as the research process.

4. For component D, expert group members determine how they'll teach what they've learned to members of their home group.

    - Assist students as they attempt to identify the most important information to share.

    - Support them in the creation of their final products and coach them as they polish their presentations. Provide opportunities to practice their presentations.

5. For component E, expert group members jigsaw back to their home group to teach what they've learned.

    - Home group members take notes and listen as each member teaches.

    - If you allow each group to present information simultaneously in various parts of the classroom, float from group to group to monitor progress and evaluate students.

    - If you ask groups to present individually at the front of the class-room, guide a discussion at the end of each presentation that involves clarification of unclear points and resolution of any student questions. Evaluate students as they present their information.

6. For component F, everyone is assessed on the topics taught by student experts.

    - Consider having your students fill out both self-assessment and peer-assessment forms that they'll turn in to you.

    - Complete final assessment for each individual student.

# Related Technologies: *Jigsaw Group Lesson Plan*

## *Rubric-Creation Tools*

**How rubric-creation tools will be used in the activity**: The majority of sample activities and lesson plans in this book require the use of one or more rubrics as a part of the evaluation process. You may decide to use an online rubric generator or another rubric-creation tool to produce a rubric.

**Implementation challenges**: Rubistar is extremely user friendly. If you wish to access your rubric online, make sure you save your work. You might save a copy of your rubric offline so that it will be available to you even if the Web site is down.

| *Resources for Rubric-Creation Tools* | |
| --- | --- |
| **Description** | Rubric generators such as Rubistar reduce your preparation time because they quickly build simple or very detailed rubrics based on the specifications you input. |
| **Where to find the tools** | http://rubistar.4teachers.org |
| **Where to get help** | On the Rubistar site, there's a tutorial along with sample rubrics. If you wish to register, you may do so for free. |

## *Presentation Software*

**How presentation software will be used in the activity**: In the jigsaw group lesson plan, students must know how to create a slideshow to present key information about a topic or to create a quiz-like game.

**Implementation challenges**: Presentation software usually provides a structured layout, which helps students. But at the same time students might choose many options to enhance their slideshow. It takes a little time to become familiar with all of the options and how to place objects (such as imported pictures or clip art) on the slides.

| Resources for Presentation Software | |
|---|---|
| **Description** | Presentation software, such as PowerPoint, supplies templates for slides, charts, and other diagrams that you design to communicate information in a clear and attractive format. Presentation software offers an extensive list of options that you may choose to enhance the layout of your material, such as text, graphics, sounds, video, backgrounds, fonts, color schemes, lettering styles, clip art, and so forth. |
| **Where to find the software** | In most cases, presentation software such as PowerPoint will come with your computer or be supplied and installed by someone in the technology department at your school. You may purchase it almost anywhere online or at traditional stores, such as office supply stores, bookstores, department store chains, and electronics stores. |
| **Where to get help** | PowerPoint has a built-in help feature with searchable contents. If you can't find the answer to your question, it will ask you if you wish to search for the answer via Microsoft's Answer Wizard on the Web. Following are some additional Web-based resources:<br><br>**Internet4Classrooms: Online Technology Practice Modules—PowerPoint**<br>www.Internet4classrooms.com/on-line_powerpoint.htm<br>*This site has wonderful resources for templates, sample PowerPoint presentations, tutorials, and integration ideas.*<br><br>**PowerPoint Home Page—Microsoft Office Online**<br>http://office.microsoft.com/en-us/powerpoint/<br>*This is Microsoft's home page for their product, and it has links for help, a product guide, and templates.*<br><br>**The PowerPoint FAQ List**<br>www.pptfaq.com<br>*This site offers help, tips, templates, how-tos, add-ins, bugs, tutorials, and other tech-related issues, such as versions, compatibility, exporting, importing, and on and on!*<br><br>**PowerPoint in the Classroom**<br>www.pptfaq.com<br>*This is a tutorial site that you may use with your students.* |

### Publishing Software

**How publishing software will be used in this activity**: In this lesson, students have the option of creating a board game in Publisher if they don't wish to create a game or presentation in PowerPoint. They must be familiar with the graphics tools they may use to fashion a product that looks like a game board.

**Implementation challenges**: Publishing software presents some of the same challenges as presentation software, such as familiarity with enhancements, alignment, and placement.

## Resources for Publishing Software

| | |
|---|---|
| **Description** | Desktop publishing software, such as Publisher, enables you to use templates or to create free-form communicative materials such as newsletters, brochures, invitations, banners, and so forth. This software offers a plethora of tools to customize the layout and design of your document to create a professional-looking final product. |
| **Where to find the software** | In most cases, publishing software such as Publisher will come with your computer or be supplied and installed by someone in the technology department at your school. You may purchase it almost anywhere online or at traditional stores, such as office supply stores, bookstores, department store chains, and electronics stores. |
| **Where to get help** | Publisher has a built-in help feature with searchable contents. If you can't find the answer to your question, it will ask you if you wish to search for the answer via Microsoft's Answer Wizard on the Web. Following are some other helpful resources:<br><br>**Northside Independent School District's Publisher Training (10 videos)**<br>www.nisd.net/scobee/online_training/publisher/pub_training.htm<br><br>**Microsoft's How-to Articles for Teachers (on Publisher, Word, Excel, and PowerPoint)**<br>www.microsoft.com/education/classtipsarchive.mspx<br><br>**Microsoft's Templates Home Page**<br>http://office.microsoft.com/en-us/templates/default.aspx |

# Lesson Plan

## Jigsaw Group—Volcanoes

| | |
|---|---|
| **Grade** | 4 |
| **Subject Area** | Science |
| **Curriculum Standards** | **National Science Standard addressed:**<br><br>NS.K–4.3 Life Science: As a result of activities in grades K–4, all students should develop understanding of:<br>■ Properties of earth materials<br>■ Objects in the sky<br>■ Changes in earth and sky<br><br>**National Educational Technology Standards for Students (NETS•S) addressed:** (see appendix for full list)<br>1. Creativity and Innovation: 1.a., 1.b.<br>2. Communication and Collaboration: 2.a., 2.b.<br>3. Research and Information Fluency: 3.a., 3.b., 3.c., 3.d.<br>4. Critical Thinking, Problem Solving, and Decision Making: 4.b. |

*continued*

## Jigsaw Group—Volcanoes

| | |
|---|---|
| **Lesson Summary** | In this lesson, students participate in jigsaw groups to learn information and teach it to each other. They subsequently create a group slideshow, game, or other artifact to present their information. |
| **Materials** | ■ Textbook<br>■ Reference Materials |
| **Web Resources** | **Volcano World's Kids' Door**   http://volcano.und.nodak.edu/vwdocs/kids/kids.html<br>**Building Volcano Models**   http://volcano.und.nodak.edu/vwdocs/volc_models/models.html<br>**IKnowthat.com: Science Lab: Volcanoes**   www.iknowthat.com/com/L3?Area=Science Lab<br>**Internet Geography: Volcanoes**   www.geography.learnontheinternet.co.uk/topics/volcanoes.html<br>**Notes/Planning Template**   www.openc.k12.or.us/citeintro/elementary/process/docs/onlineplanner.pdf<br>**Self-Assessment**   www.sasked.gov.sk.ca/docs/elemsci/astemp2.pdf |
| **Lesson Activities** | 1. (a) Divide a textbook chapter or two into as many sections as you have members in a home group, or (b) Identify as many topics as there are members in a home group. (Example: if you have four home groups of six members each, you need six topics.) The examples in (a) depend on the chapter(s) you select and divide; the examples in (b) might include causes of volcanoes, locations of major volcanoes, important facts about major volcanoes, volcano disasters, and so forth. If you wish, you may use the Volcano World Web site listed in the Web Resources section above (and use various legends as topics), or the Landforms: Volcano Web site that deals specifically with the possible topics we listed for examples here in 1(b) .<br><br>2. Divide students into four to six diverse home groups and designate one student in each home group as captain. Each member of each home group will become an expert on a topic.<br><br>3. Home group members with the same topic jigsaw to become members of an expert group. Each expert group uses a variety of materials to research its topic.<br><br>4. Expert group members determine how they'll teach what they've learned to members of their home group.<br><br>5. Expert group members jigsaw back to their home group to teach what they've learned. Home group members take notes and listen as each member teaches.<br><br>6. Everyone is assessed on the topics taught by student experts. |
| **Technology Activity Options** | ■ Home group students can create a collaborative slideshow or brochure or other artifact to present their information.<br>■ Expert or home group students can create a *Jeopardy*-like or other game in presentation software, or a board game in Publisher. |
| **Differentiation/ Extension** | ■ More capable students may create a longer, more detailed artifact.<br>■ More capable students may create quiz questions or a game to augment their presentation.<br>■ Less capable students may be paired with a more capable student who serves as a mentor.<br>■ Less capable students may create fewer slides or a less detailed brochure. |
| **Evaluation** | Use rubrics to evaluate students on the following components. See sample rubric (Table 2.3):<br>■ Research notes<br>■ Completed product<br>■ Cooperative group<br>■ Effective team member |

TABLE **2.3** ■ Rubric for jigsaw group lesson plan

| Category | 4 | 3 | 2 | 1 |
|---|---|---|---|---|
| **Artifact** | Artifact is 100% complete. It includes all required elements and has no more than two spelling or grammatical errors. | Artifact is 85%–99% complete. It includes all but one required element and has three to four spelling or grammatical errors. | Artifact is 70%–84% complete. It's missing two required elements and has five to six spelling or grammatical errors. | Artifact is 55%–69% complete. It's missing three or more required elements and has more than eight spelling or grammatical errors. |
| **Content** | Shows 90%–100% understanding of the topic. | Shows 80%–89% understanding of the topic. | Shows 70%–79% understanding of parts of the topic. | Shows only 60%–69% understanding of the topic. Doesn't seem to understand the topic very well. |
| **Presentation** | Speaks clearly and distinctly 90%–100% of the time. Stands up straight and establishes eye contact with everyone in the room during the presentation. | Speaks clearly and distinctly 80%–89% of the time. Stands up straight and establishes eye contact with audience during the presentation most of the time. | Speaks clearly and distinctly 70%–79% of the time. Sometimes stands up straight and establishes eye contact. | Speaks clearly and distinctly only 60%–69% of the time. Often mumbles or cannot be understood. Slouches or does not look at audience during the presentation. |
| **Focus on Task/ Work Ethic** | Stays on task 90%–100% of the time to complete research. Very self-directed. | Stays on task 80%–89% of the time. Focuses on what needs to be done most of the time. | Stays on task 70%–79% of the time. Needs prodding from teacher or group members. | Stays on task only 60%–69% of the time. Doesn't complete all necessary research. |
| **Collaboration with Peers** | Supports the efforts of others in the group by listening to and sharing with others 90%–100% of the time. Tries to promote harmony within the group. | Supports the efforts of others in the group by listening to and sharing with others 80%–89% of the time. | Supports the efforts of others in the group by listening to and sharing with others 70%–79% of the time. May be disruptive at times. | Supports the efforts of others in the group by listening to and sharing with others only 60%–69% of the time and is disruptive. |

# R.A.F.T. Strategy

R.A.F.T., a third instructional strategy, is the acronym for **r**ole, **a**udience, **f**ormat, **t**opic. We like it because students are provided a guided structure for working on projects, and teachers can create many variations of the same theme simply by modifying the four elements of the acronym. Think about how you might use R.A.F.T. in your own classroom.

## Profile: *R.A.F.T.*

### Function

Initially, R.A.F.T.s were used as a reading reflection or reading comprehension strategy that involved written products. Today, teachers of all subjects rely on R.A.F.T.s to strengthen conceptual understanding using deep thinking and to allow for multiple product formats.

### Advantages

- The R.A.F.T. strategy is an extremely flexible differentiation tool because teachers can differentiate content, process, or product by interest, readiness, and learning profiles.

- The R.A.F.T. strategy may be used across curricular areas.

- The R.A.F.T. strategy forces students to consider a viewpoint different from their own, such as their teacher's, their parents', or another important person in their lives. It requires that they direct their response(s) to an audience that isn't their teacher or a family member. It entails the production of an artifact in a format different from what they might normally choose. These inherent elements foster creative thinking and imagination.

### Components

**Role**    Which role will the students take on in the production of the final artifact: Historical or literary figure? Politician or scientist? Writer?

**Audience**    To whom are the students writing or communicating: Friends or peers? Members of a local community or citizens of a nation? Another historical figure or character?

**Format**    What's the preferred format of the final product: An oral product? An art project? A written document?

**Topic**    Who, when, or what is the subject of the final artifact? (Use a strong verb to convey meaning; for example, use plead, convince, depict, argue, demand, predict, speculate, etc.)

### Steps to Create a R.A.F.T

1. Decide on the core concepts and essential ideas you want students to grasp.

2. Seek out electronic sources, printed sources, and other resources that will assist students in the research process, and steer students toward them.

3. Identify and be prepared to discuss with students:

   ■ possible roles for them to take on when preparing the final product,

   ■ a range of audiences for the product,

   ■ an assortment of formats for the product,

   ■ an array of topics for the product.

4. Determine how to differentiate the R.A.F.T. (by interest and readiness, by readiness only, etc.).

5. Show students a sample R.A.F.T. assignment, and review the key components together.

6. Design a rubric that you'll use to assess final products, and review it with your students.

7. As students work on their R.A.F.T., circulate among them and help as needed. It's possible to use the R.A.F.T. technique with pairs, triads, or even quads, but it's a little more difficult with more students in a group (due to the fact that each group produces one product).

8. Have students share their creations and assess them.

## Related Technologies: *R.A.F.T. Lesson Plan*

### Kidspiration/Inspiration/Brainstorming Tools/ Graphic Organizers

**How graphic organizer software will be used in the activity**: In the lesson plan below, students will complete a prewriting graphic organizer to help prepare them to take on a particular role in their writing assignment.

**Implementation challenges**: Although it's not difficult to learn, you'll need to show your students how to use various graphics and tools first. You'll need to also allow for some practice sessions.

### Paint and Draw Software

**How Paint and Draw software will be used in this activity**: Students will generate a picture of the character or person whose role they assume in their writing assignment.

**Implementation challenges**: Even children with little experience seem to warm up quickly to draw and paint software. It takes some practice to become familiar and adept with the drawing tools, and it doesn't allow for much fine detail.

### Word Processing Software

**How word processing software will be used in this activity**: Students will type their written assignment (a letter) in Word or another word processor.

**Implementation challenges**: In most cases, word processing templates are very user friendly. Sometimes misalignment problems might occur, or students will forget to save their documents or changes to them.

## Lesson Plan

### R.A.F.T. — The Chalk Box Kid

| | |
|---|---|
| **Grade** | 2 |
| **Subject Area** | Language Arts/Reading |
| **Curriculum Standards** | **NCTE and IRA Standards addressed:**<br><br>1. Students read a wide range of print and nonprint texts to build an understanding of texts, of themselves, and of the cultures of the U.S. and the world: to acquire new information; to respond to the needs and demands of society and the workplace; and for personal fulfillment. Among these texts are fiction and nonfiction, classic and contemporary works.<br><br>2. Students apply a wide range of strategies to comprehend, interpret, evaluate, and appreciate texts. They draw on their prior experience, their interactions with other readers and writers, their knowledge of word meaning and of other texts, their word identification strategies, and their understanding of textual features (for example, sound-letter correspondence, sentence structure, context, graphics).<br><br>3. Students adjust their use of spoken, written, and visual language (for example, conventions, style, vocabulary) to communicate effectively with a variety of audiences and for different purposes.<br><br>**National Educational Technology Standards for Students (NETS•S) addressed:** (see appendix for full list)<br><br>1. Creativity and Innovation: 1.a., 1.b.<br>2. Communication and Collaboration: 2.a., 2.b. |
| **Lesson Summary** | In this lesson, students read *The Chalk Box Kid,* complete a R.A.F.T. activity, and write a letter from a personal point of view. |
| **Materials** | ■ *The Chalk Box Kid,* by Clyde Robert Bulla<br>■ Copies of a R.A.F.T. graphic organizer<br>■ Paint, Kid Pix, or similar drawing program<br>■ Word processing, desktop publishing, or presentation software program (optional template) |

*continued*

## R.A.F.T. — *The Chalk Box Kid*

| | | |
|---|---|---|
| **Web Resources** | Clyde Robert Bulla's Web page | http://mowrites4kids.drury.edu/authors/bulla/ |
| | *The Chalk Box Kid* links and puzzle | www.gpschools.org/ci/depts/eng/k5/second/chalk.htm |
| | Come Aboard a R.A.F.T.! | www.geocities.com/writingprocess/R.A.F.T.choices.htm |
| | Reading Strategies with R.A.F.T. | www.greece.k12.ny.us/instruction/ela/6–12/reading/Reading Strategies/R.A.F.T..htm |

**Lesson Activities**

1. After finishing the book, ask students to complete a R.A.F.T. prewriting graphic organizer.

2. Distribute copies of the organizer and pair students to complete the organizer as a prewriting activity.

3. Ask students to choose either the role of Gregory (Option 1) or the role of one of the students in the new school he will be attending (Option 2). You might suggest that one student in each pair choose the role of Gregory and the other choose the role of another student.

4. After they complete their R.A.F.T., ask students to write their letters.

5. Ask students to generate a computer image of Gregory or themselves.

6. Ask students to print their graphic and assemble it with their letter.

7. After letters and images are completed, student pairs can share their products with one or more student pairs.

| Role | Audience | Format | Topic |
|---|---|---|---|
| Gregory | Students | Letter | Write a letter to tell students your feelings about coming to a new school. Describe your feelings. |
| Student | Gregory | Letter | Write a letter to Gregory to welcome him to your school. Describe your school and what he'll be able to do at your school. |

**Technology Activity Options**

- Students choosing Option 1 should draw a picture of Gregory in Paint, Kid Pix, or a similar program and label it "Gregory."
- Students choosing Option 2 should draw a picture of themselves in Paint, Kid Pix, or a similar program and label it with their own name.
- Students can print their image and paste or attach it to their letter.

**Differentiation/ Extension**

- More capable students who know basic keyboarding may type their letter into a word processor or publishing or presentation software program.
- Students who know how to insert their saved image into their document may do so on their own or with guidance.
- Less capable students may be paired with a more capable student, or upper elementary students could be assigned to work as mentors with second-grade pairs.

**Evaluation**

Use rubrics to evaluate students on three (or four) components:

- Completed, accurate R.A.F.T. graphic organizer
- Letter
- Computer image
- Typed letter + image (optional)

## WebQuest Strategy

A fourth strategy to consider is the WebQuest. WebQuests have been around for only a few years, but they're becoming increasingly popular. As the name implies, a WebQuest is a research project during which students use the Internet for resources.

### Profile: *WebQuest*

### *Function*

Investigating, synthesizing, and assessing mostly Internet-based resources to grapple with complex or open-ended questions.

### *Advantages*

There are many benefits to WebQuests. A well-constructed WebQuest:

- Enables a strong link between classroom activities and real-life situations, experiences, and skills.
- Improves understanding of the Internet and technology skills.
- Boosts collaboration and inspires learners.
- Permits interaction with authentic resources, such as historical documents.
- Offers interaction with real world experts and mentors in the field.
- Cultivates interdisciplinary skills.

### *Components*

WebQuests have six steps commonly referred to by the names, or a variation of them, listed below.

1. **Introduction:** Each WebQuest opens with a succinct but clear paragraph or statement that supplies background information, such as the rationale for and significance of the WebQuest. Perhaps the most important feature of step one is to prompt excitement and to motivate the students to undertake the principal task of the WebQuest.

2. **Task:** A description of the students' end goal or objective. Often, a WebQuest centers on a problem students must solve or a question they must answer.

3. **Process**: A summary of approaches students might draw on and the activities they might complete to fulfill the task.

   - These strategies might include individualized or cooperative activities.
   - You might choose to embed your key links right into this section.

4. **Information Resources**: A possible listing of Internet-based sources students might use to help complete their task.

   ■ You need not rely solely on Internet links. You may choose to accompany your links with other resources, such as maps, books, videos or DVDs, software, guest speakers or mentors, and field trips.

   ■ It's also helpful to provide some organizational tools (such as checklists and other graphic organizers) to help students sort the information they collect.

   ■ All of the resources, regardless of their type, are often included in a "Process" section.

5. **Evaluation Criteria**: This step spells out your expectations (with examples) for the end product, and might include:

   ■ Checklists

   ■ Scoring guides

   ■ Rubrics

   ■ Self-, peer, teacher, and/or mentor or expert assessment

6. **Conclusion or Wrap-up**: A concise synopsis or reflection about what students accomplished. Students will benefit if you link their in-class experience with the WebQuest to other curricular areas and the real world.

### Steps to Create a WebQuest

As is the case with the components of a WebQuest, the steps you follow to create one are fairly standard, but you might encounter some variation.

1. **Brainstorm ideas:** If at all possible, involve your students in the selection of the WebQuest's main theme's subtopics, ones that intrigue them or that they may even feel passionate about. As a substitute for brainstorming, or as a supplemental activity, you might choose to use a checklist, questionnaire, survey, KWL chart, or interest map to help with the identification of these topics of interest.

2. **Search for Web links and other resources to support the big idea of the WebQuest:**

   ■ Determine the task students will complete after your brainstorming session or interest inventory. As mentioned in the previous "Components" section, the task will require that they solve a problem or answer a question, or something similar.

   ■ Then, begin to investigate the Internet for suitable links and consider other useful resources that aren't Web-based.

3. **Identify student roles**: Upon completion of your search for resources, think about potential roles students might assume during the WebQuest. Here are four possible ways to group students based on the roles they take on:

   ▪ Establish groups according to learning styles, multiple intelligences, or some other means. (Each group crafts a unique product such as a skit, a letter, or a journal entry.)

   ▪ Divide students into homogeneous groups made up only of geographers, scientists, writers, artists, and so forth.

   ▪ Form heterogeneous groups in which each student assumes a different role. The groups might consist of journalists, biographers, environmentalists, governors, or members of other professions.

   ▪ Build groups according to interest areas or subtopics of the broad theme.

4. **Determine if the WebQuest warrants your time and energy**: If you believe your students would benefit from the task and you find appropriate resources that support it, move to step No. 5.

5. **Complete the WebQuest**:

   ▪ Create the Web page.

   ▪ Set up scaffolding.

   ▪ Formulate rubrics.

**NOTE**: the following lesson plan relies upon an existing WebQuest created by Lianne Zuber. You *do not* need to design *any* portion of the WebQuest. The most challenging portion of a WebQuest from a teacher's standpoint is the actual creation of the Web page, which is listed in step No. 5. However, several resources make this task much easier than ever before.

In the WebQuest lesson plan, we've listed resources such as QuestGarden, which actually generates a WebQuest with Web pages for you. (You follow prompts for information, and voilà! QuestGarden produces an attractive Web page with tasks, scaffolding, and rubrics designed to your specifications.)

In addition, you could construct your own WebQuest using FrontPage, Word, or Publisher. Completed Word and Publisher files can be easily converted into HTML documents, while FrontPage actually converts your characters into HTML as you type. We'll walk through the creation of a sample WebQuest in chapter 8.

# Related Technologies: *WebQuest Lesson Plan*

### Web Research Tools

**How Web research tools will be used in the activity**: In the WebQuest lesson plan, students will use Web links to learn about cryptograms.

**Implementation challenges**: Depending on team dynamics, it can be tricky to keep all teams on task and finish in a timely manner.

### Web Page Creation Tools

**How Web page creation tools will be used in the activity**: Students will complete a WebQuest that has already been created. The author of the WebQuest used Web page creation tools to generate her WebQuest.

**Implementation challenges**: Students need to be(come) comfortable with clicking on the appropriate or suggested URLs for research or information to complete their main task, and to know how to return to the main WebQuest page.

| Resources for Web Page Creation Tools | |
|---|---|
| **Description** | Programs that allow you to create, edit, or upload Web pages. |
| **Where to find the tools** | Programs such as Publisher and Word come with your computer. FrontPage comes with certain versions of Microsoft Office. Other Web page creation tools such as Quest Garden are found on the Web. |
| **Where to get help** | FrontPage has a built-in help feature with searchable contents. If you can't find the answer to your question, check the resources below. Web-based resources such as QuestGarden have help links on their Web sites. |
| | **Microsoft FrontPage Help and How-to** |
| | http://office.microsoft.com/en-us/frontpage/FX100647001033.aspx |
| | **FrontPage How-to Articles: Tutorials & Tips** |
| | www.Webworkshop.org/frontpage/ |
| | **Kent School District's Staff Development Course Page on FrontPage 2003** |
| | www.kent.k12.wa.us/KSD/IT/wwwdev/frontpage/ |

### *Puzzle Creation Tools*

**How puzzle creation tools will be used in the activity**: Students will solve sample cryptograms that have been created by a puzzle creation tool, and they'll design their own using a puzzle creation tool.

**Implementation challenges**: You must teach students how to use the puzzle creation tool. Practicing with a few sample puzzles might be beneficial.

| Resources for Puzzle Creation Tools | |
|---|---|
| **Description** | Programs that allow you to create a variety of puzzles. |
| **Where to find the tools** | One of the most frequently used is Discovery School's Puzzlemaker at http://puzzlemaker.school.discovery.com |
| **Where to get help** | Online at the Discovery Schools Puzzlemaker site listed above. |

This lesson uses a teacher-constructed WebQuest. If it doesn't apply to your grade level, you can make one of your own using QuestGarden (www.questgarden.com).

## Lesson Plan

### *WebQuest—Math: Multiplication and Cryptography*

| | |
|---|---|
| **Grade** | 3 |
| **Subject Area** | Math: Multiplication/Cryptography |
| **Curriculum Standards** | **NCTM Math Standards addressed (as per creator):**<br><br>MA1, MA3, MA4, CA3, CA5; Goal 1(all); Goal 2.1, 2.2; Goal 3.1, 3.2<br><br>Mathematics: In mathematics, students will acquire a solid foundation that includes knowledge of:<br><br>1. Addition, subtraction, multiplication, and division; other number sense, including numeration and estimation; and the application of these operations and concepts in the workplace and other situations<br><br>2. Data analysis, probability, and statistics<br><br>3. Patterns and relationships within and among functions and algebraic, geometric, and trigonometric concepts<br><br>Communication Arts: In communication arts, students will acquire a solid foundation that includes knowledge of and proficiency in:<br><br>1. Reading and evaluating nonfiction works and material (such as biographies, newspapers, technical manuals)<br><br>2. Comprehending and evaluating the content and artistic aspects of oral and visual presentations (such as storytelling, debates, lectures, multimedia productions) |

*continued*

## WebQuest—Math: Multiplication and Cryptography

| | |
|---|---|
| **Curriculum Standards** (continued) | **National Educational Technology Standards for Students (NETS•S) addressed:** (see appendix for full list) <br> 1. Creativity and Innovation: 1.a., 1.b. <br> 2. Communication and Collaboration: 2.a., 2.b. <br> 3. Research and Information Fluency: 3.a., 3.b., 3.c., 3.d. <br> 4. Critical Thinking, Problem Solving, and Decision Making: 4.b. |
| **Lesson Summary** | In this WebQuest, students play a role, investigate cryptograms, practice solving a cryptogram, practice multiplication, and create an original cryptogram using a puzzle maker. |
| **Materials** | ■ Scrap paper, library books on codes (if available) |
| **Web Resources** | **Build the Code WebQuest**      http://w4.nkcsd.k12.mo.us/~lzuber/wq/code/ <br> **Build the Code WebQuest: Teacher Info**      http://w4.nkcsd.k12.mo.us/~lzuber/wq/code/teacher.html <br> **QuestGarden**      http://questgarden.com/author/overview.htm <br> Register, read the overview, and follow the prompts to make a free WebQuest. Look at others for examples and ideas. <br><br> **The WebQuest Place**      www.thematzats.com/Webquests/page1.html <br> Benefits, how-to make a WebQuest, key elements, resources, and so forth <br><br> **The WebQuest Place Collections**      www.thematzats.com/Webquests/collections.html <br> **The WebQuest Page Training Materials**      http://Webquest.sdsu.edu/materials.htm <br> Training materials and examples |
| **Lesson Activities** | 1. Students learn about cryptography using the Web. <br> 2. Students solve sample cryptograms. <br> 3. Students learn how to create a cryptogram using multiplication facts. <br> 4. Students evaluate their work based on a rubric. |
| **Technology Activity Options** | ■ Use the Web for research and practice. <br> ■ Use a puzzle maker to create a cryptogram. |
| **Differentiation/ Extension** | ■ Some students may need scaffolding with this project. <br> ■ Students who really enjoy math and puzzles may want to create additional cryptograms. |
| **Evaluation** | ■ All tasks are completed versus the rubric provided at the following link: <br> http://w4.nkcsd.k12.mo.us/~lzuber/wq/code/eval.html <br> ■ Students might also use a self-reflection journal to record their experiences with this project. |

## Resources for Chapter 2

| When You Need... | Resources | |
| --- | --- | --- |
| **A list of online experts** | Collaboration: Ask-an-Expert | http://eduscapes.com/tap/topic14.htm |
| **A method to identify students' interests** | Read•Write•Think Webbing Tool | http://interactives.mped.org/view_interactive.aspx?id=127&title |
| | Ask students to create an interest map using Inspiration or Kidspiration, or supply a ready-made template. | |
| | Zoomerang (survey creation) | www.zoomerang.com |
| | Existing personal interest surveys | http://scclc.sancarlos.k12.ca.us/plp/Personal_Interest_Survey.pdf |
| **A note-taking form** | Read•Write•Think Notetaker | http://interactives.mped.org/view_interactive.aspx?id=722&title |
| | NoteStar (free, registration required) | http://notestar.4teachers.org |
| | An online planner | www.openc.k12.or.us/citeintro/elementary/process/docs/ onlineplanner.pdf |
| | Create a form using a Word table (see our template) | |
| **A way of citing resources** | Noodle Tools (free) | www.noodletools.com |
| | Citation Machine | http://citationmachine.net |
| **A way to help students find facts in nonfiction materials** | Read•Write•Think: Fact Fragment Frenzy | www.readwritethink.org/student_mat/student_material.asp?id=13 |
| **A tool to generate a timeline** | Our Timelines | www.ourtimelines.com |
| | Read•Write•Think: Interactive Timeline | www.readwritethink.org/materials/timeline/ |
| | TimeLiner software (Tom Snyder Productions) | www.tomsnyder.com/products/product.asp?SKU=TIMV50 |
| **A way to publish students' research** | Read•Write•Think: Printing Press | http://interactives.mped.org/view_interactive.aspx?id=110&title |
| | Use Word, PowerPoint, or Publisher, or similar software. | |
| **Teacher-created I-Searches or Web inquiry projects for student use or as models for your creations** | Web Inquiry Projects: Examples | http://edWeb.sdsu.edu/wip/examples.htm |
| | Ms. Turnbull's Room: Best I-Searches of 2003 | http://turnbull.Weblogger.com/stories/storyReader$17 |
| **An interest-based research graphic organizer** | Printable form | www.eduref.org/Virtual/Lessons/Information_Literacy/ IF00205c.pdf |
| **An interview form** | Worksheet | www.geocities.com/fifth_grade_tpes/interview_prewrite.html |

*continued*

## Resources for Chapter 2 *(continued)*

| When You Need... | Resources | |
|---|---|---|
| **An online tool to build a WebQuest** | QuestGarden authoring tool (free) | http://questgarden.com/author/overview.htm |
| **Detective tools and printable pages to carry out an investigation theme** | PBS's History Detectives Kids | http://pbskids.org/historydetectives/ |
| **Teacher-created WebQuests for student use** (or as models for your own WebQuests) | Theme-based collection | www.yesnet.yk.ca/schools/wes/Webquest_collection.html |
| | K–3 WebQuests | http://eduscapes.com/sessions/travel/k3Webquests.htm |
| | Grades 3–6 WebQuests | http://eduscapes.com/sessions/travel/36Webquests.htm |
| | WebQuest Search | http://Webquest.org/search/ |
| | Literature-based WebQuests | http://eduscapes.com/ladders/themes/Webquests.htm#1 |
| | Locate and Evaluate WebQuests | http://eduscapes.com/tap/topic4.htm#3 |
| | WebQuest Evaluation and Use | http://eduscapes.com/sessions/travel/use.htm |

Now that you've become better acquainted with four strategies—I-Search, jigsaw groups, R.A.F.T., and WebQuests—for using technology to differentiate by interest and have looked over some sample lesson plans, we hope that you're ready to test them out in your own classroom. While teachers still determine the core concepts that students need to comprehend and take ownership, we empower students to determine the topics that resonate with their individual curiosities. In turn, all partners benefit (parents and administrators, too!), because a vested interest in a particular topic motivates students to learn and remember.

These four inquiry-based strategies are powerful tools that bring out the detective in our students. The strategies permit a variety of flexible learning strategies and scenarios that marry nicely with differentiated instruction and technology. They promise to engage students and make for some exciting additions to your teaching repertoire.

## CHAPTER 3

# Using Technology *to* Differentiate *by* Readiness

*When the student is ready, the Teacher will appear.*

CHINESE PROVERB

How do you determine readiness in your students? At times it can be a struggle to accurately verify students' levels of comprehension in curricular areas. Before we begin a deeper investigation of using technology to differentiate by readiness, let's take a moment to consider a few interpretations of the interesting proverb above and look at how it relates to our topic at hand.

This proverb underscores the teacher's authority and implies the student must attain a certain level of readiness to reap the benefits of the teacher's wisdom and presence. At the same time, we can turn it around and consider the meaning of the adage from the student's perspective.

Perhaps "Teacher" refers to something that comes from within, after a person has prepared, undergone intense training, and gained insight and wisdom through life experiences. Regardless of the interpretation you choose (or might come up with yourself), we've concluded that confirming precise levels of student readiness is a challenging feat! As teachers who practice differentiated instruction, we embrace student involvement as well as the unique gifts that have impacted the distinctive ability levels of our students.

# Differentiating by Readiness

Differentiating by readiness means tuning into your students' varying degrees of ability in order to create activities that match their skills and levels of understanding. At the same time, you want to challenge them to move beyond their learning comfort zones to even greater successes.

Based on this definition, you might be asking yourself how differentiation by readiness today is any different from our strategies of days past. It seems that prior to differentiated instruction, teachers often delivered one level of instruction to the whole group of students in nearly every subject area except reading. Do you recall the reading groups named for colors or animals that were popular in elementary school? After the first few weeks, how many times did students move out of the groups they started in at the beginning of the year, indicating progress had been made? Not often. While consistency is key, particularly in elementary grades, teachers must also be attuned to students' shifting needs when changes occur.

Assessment and observation are important tools that help us determine students' readiness levels. We'll talk more in depth about assessment in chapter 9. Teachers who practice DI evaluate the results of pre-, ongoing, and post-assessment instruments and then contemplate how they're going to teach their students in ways that meet their academic needs while encouraging them to forge ahead to the next stage of growth. DI theory is founded on the premise that instructors not only recognize the importance of adjusting tactics to better suit ever-changing classroom dynamics, but they also follow through with those modifications.

You may already differentiate by readiness in your classroom by means of one of the following tools or strategies:

- Tiering or tiered assignments (the focal point of this chapter)
- Curriculum compacting (coming in chapter 5)
- Graphic organizers
- Our favorite tool—technology!

Before we move to tiering, the strategy that's the main focus of this chapter, let's pause for a moment to recap the power of graphic organizers and technology in readiness differentiation.

It's easy to underestimate the effectiveness of graphic organizers (GOs) because we rely upon them so regularly. Mark Twain was right when he penned, "Familiarity breeds contempt." This saying might not be accurate all the time, but there's certainly some truth to it. In addition to high frequency of use, it takes just the push of a button to download a template with a GO from the Internet, or to insert a CD with graphics-based software, such as Inspiration or Kidspiration.

Because GOs have become a common part of our repertoire, sometimes we fail to think about *why* we use them. We have so many choices at our fingertips! Some of the more familiar categories of GOs are: semantic Webs, story Webs, concept maps, and flowcharts. However, many more are available, and they come in all shapes and sizes. Allow us to share a top 10 list of some of the many reasons that GOs are beneficial for you *and* your students. GOs

1. assist students who don't react well to textbooks or "wordy" materials that might be too formal, culturally inappropriate, or exceptionally grade specific; such materials might also contain vocabulary that's overly complex;

2. can function to preview or reexamine concepts;

3. enhance students' ability to make predictions;

4. facilitate visualization of key content;

5. foster logical thinking and help sequence data and establish relevancy of details;

6. help struggling students concentrate on critical elements and see the structure of the material clearly;

7. help students distinguish and classify core concepts, consequences, and cause and effect;

8. enable students to understand significant data, timelines, and abstract ideas;

9. help teachers plan and evaluate lessons as well as compose rubrics, study guides, note-taking guides, checklists, and many other administrative materials;

10. link new material to past material and highlight interrelationships between important concepts.

Teachers can use a variety of technology tools to address the needs of their students. In fact, technology is so powerful a tool that many teachers underestimate its capabilities to help differentiate instruction.

How can technology help differentiate instruction? First, technology is a patient, accommodating teacher that can "tutor" students until they learn. Second, technology can also bring exciting real-world projects into the classroom. Third, technology can provide scaffolds and tools to support and enhance learning.

In the case of differentiating by readiness, technology is unsurpassed because it allows learning to be personalized. Here are some ways teachers can use technology to differentiate by readiness:

- Teachers can use technology to create or access a survey tool to determine readiness.

- Teachers can use technology with flexible grouping so that like students can employ software appropriate to their readiness level. For example, reading software can be structured to meet the needs of individual learners who are reading at different levels of understanding.

- Teachers can use technology to create tiered assignments and compact instruction.

- Teachers can use technology as a delivery strategy for subject matter content. For example, a WebQuest or Internet search can be designed with struggling, at-level, and above-level students in mind.

- Teachers can use technology as an independent learning tool. Software programs such as 2Create A Story or Early Learning Tools (both products by 2simple) have been designed with young children in mind. Their navigation tools are straightforward and similar in each of the company's programs. These software programs are great for independent learning if children are given a task (create a story and make a picture to fit with the story) and shown how to save their work.

- Teachers can use technology to create and tailor KWL charts or graphic organizers to match the level of readiness of individual students or groups of students.

Have we piqued your interest for differentiating by readiness? Before walking you through the process of tiering a lesson, let's examine a special tool that will assist you with readiness differentiation regardless of the strategy you employ.

This tool is called the "Equalizer" and was developed by DI guru Dr. Carol Tomlinson (2001) to permit modification of a number of instructional elements based on students' levels of readiness.

## The Equalizer

If you're like many experienced teachers we know, you're able to adjust your lessons to accommodate different levels of students without hours of painstaking work and reflection. Many educators are gifted with an intuitive ability that enables them to pinpoint students' strengths, weaknesses, and overall levels of comprehension.

If modification of your plans has become second nature to you, you might not use specific terminology to refer to the instructional elements you fine-tune based on students' levels of readiness. However, we're certain that several of these instructional variables will be familiar to you.

Dr. Tomlinson cleverly likened teachers' attempts to adjust eight instructional elements that are based on students' levels of readiness to sliding the levers of a graphic equalizer (see Fig. 3.1). You probably know that a graphic equalizer is a component of an audio system having several buttons or controls that permit the listener to modify different frequency bands affecting sound quality. Of course, the main purpose of a graphic equalizer in the music world is to help make beautiful noise or achieve optimal output. Such is the case with the musical pieces we create in our own orchestra pit: the classroom. As teachers, we conduct and improvise in the classroom in order to craft melodies that promote learning in ways that benefit the members of our ensembles.

Tomlinson's rationale for designing the Equalizer tool was to supply a means to "monitor the effectiveness of differentiated curriculum" by readiness. Her rendition of this instrument offers concrete continua to adjust to help us in our effort to best meet our students' needs. As you look over Tomlinson's visual model of the Equalizer, you'll notice that the levers move horizontally instead of vertically. Nonetheless, both a graphic equalizer, which is used for audio control, and Tomlinson's DI Equalizer share a similar objective. By adjusting the Equalizer's controls from right to left or left to right, teachers can fine-tune a customized learning experience for individual pupils.

See Figure 3.1 on the following page for our visualization of Tomlinson's Equalizer, along with some short descriptions of the range the variables represent. Let's take a look at its eight settings in more depth to see how they might assist us in differentiating by readiness. Keep in mind that the left-hand side of each variable represents a less intense or minimal range of output, while the right-hand side corresponds to a more intense or maximum range of output.

By adjusting the Equalizer's eight settings from right to left or left to right, teachers can fine-tune a customized learning experience for individual pupils.

Tomlinson's model is a concrete visual aid that can confirm whether you're appropriately challenging your upper-level students. It can also verify whether you're properly modifying below-level students' coursework so that they, too, are stretched and experience achievement. If the Equalizer is unfamiliar to you, or seeing eight variables all at once seems intimidating, begin with one "lever" at a time.

Also keep in mind that the Equalizer is a tool that's designed to simplify your planning rather than complicate it. It's a useful conceptual tool for planning and for reflecting on your instructional practices, but you can successfully differentiate without it. In fact, you probably modify some or all of the eight continua instinctively. *You* know your students best!

If you're ready to forge ahead to the creation of a tiered lesson, we'll show you how you can have your cake and eat it, too.

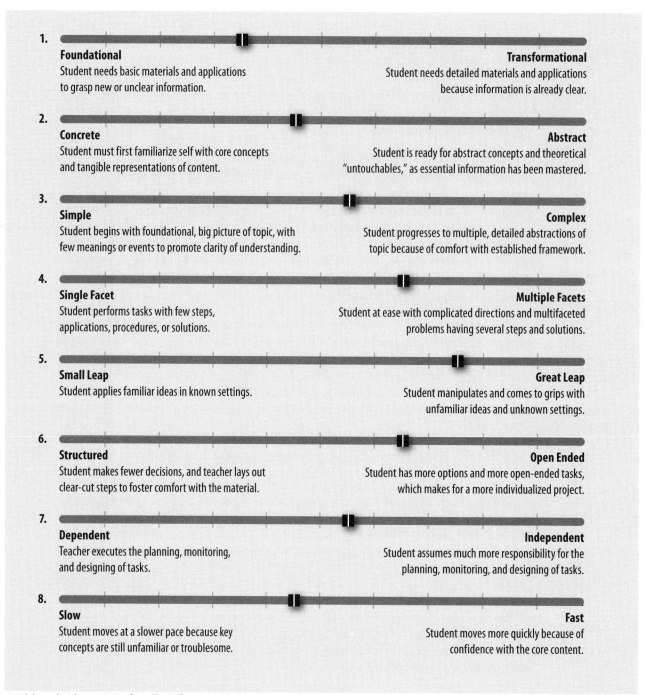

**1.**

**Foundational**
Student needs basic materials and applications
to grasp new or unclear information.

**Transformational**
Student needs detailed materials and applications
because information is already clear.

**2.**

**Concrete**
Student must first familiarize self with core concepts
and tangible representations of content.

**Abstract**
Student is ready for abstract concepts and theoretical
"untouchables," as essential information has been mastered.

**3.**

**Simple**
Student begins with foundational, big picture of topic, with
few meanings or events to promote clarity of understanding.

**Complex**
Student progresses to multiple, detailed abstractions of
topic because of comfort with established framework.

**4.**

**Single Facet**
Student performs tasks with few steps,
applications, procedures, or solutions.

**Multiple Facets**
Student at ease with complicated directions and multifaceted
problems having several steps and solutions.

**5.**

**Small Leap**
Student applies familiar ideas in known settings.

**Great Leap**
Student manipulates and comes to grips with
unfamiliar ideas and unknown settings.

**6.**

**Structured**
Student makes fewer decisions, and teacher lays out
clear-cut steps to foster comfort with the material.

**Open Ended**
Student has more options and more open-ended tasks,
which makes for a more individualized project.

**7.**

**Dependent**
Teacher executes the planning, monitoring,
and designing of tasks.

**Independent**
Student assumes much more responsibility for the
planning, monitoring, and designing of tasks.

**8.**

**Slow**
Student moves at a slower pace because key
concepts are still unfamiliar or troublesome.

**Fast**
Student moves more quickly because of
confidence with the core content.

Adapted with permission from *The Differentiated Classroom: Responding to the Needs of All Learners*, by Carol Ann Tomlinson. Alexandria, VA: ASCD (1999).

FIGURE **3.1** ■ **Visualization of Tomlinson's Equalizer showing the range of the variables**

# Tiered Assignments to Support Differentiated Instruction by Readiness

Sometimes teachers don't know how to get started with tiering an assignment, let alone adding technology to the assignment or lesson. To help you begin tiering, try this: in your mind's eye, scan the faces of the children in your classroom. Invariably, they'll fall into three groups: below-level learners, at-level learners, and above-level learners.

If scanning makes you uncomfortable, look at assessment results. Once you have the groups in your head or on paper, think about how you can offer three versions of an assignment, one for each level of learner.

Imagine we're in the kitchen preparing a cake with multiple layers. The preparation of a solid base provides the foundation upon which to add additional layers. If this base isn't stable, it can't support them. At the same time, the first layer is not the most fancy. It doesn't have the intricate decorations the top layer has. Each layer adds to the one before it.

So it is with instructional tiering. We begin with a foundational tier, and then build upward to create additional levels that require more sophisticated cake-decorating skills. As you can see, tiering really is a piece of cake!

To help you visualize, we'll walk you through a seven-step process to create a tiered assignment.

1. List the grade level content expectations (GLCEs) for the content area.

2. Determine the outcomes; that is, decide what students should know, understand, or be able to do.

3. Pre-assess or think about which students are working at grade level, below grade level, or above grade level. Consider their learning styles and interests.

4. Select or create a common launching activity for the whole group that requires high-level thought and will provide opportunities for students to use one or more key skills to understand a big idea.

5. Think about the range of possible activities, from low skill and low complexity of understanding to high skill and high complexity of understanding. Match or assign students to the activity level that challenges them most.

6. Add technology in the shape or form that best fits the need(s) of the learner.

7. Assess learning.

## Profile: *Tiering*

### Function

To vary the depth of a lesson that centers on specific concepts, big ideas, and skills to meet students' diverse interests, learning profiles, and levels of readiness.

### Advantages

- Permits multiple options for adjustment or customization of a lesson or activity to match varying levels of readiness.
- Allows for differentiation according to content, product, or process by readiness, learning profile, or interest.
- Solidifies knowledge of identical essential concepts and skills while challenging students to move forward.
- Increases student motivation by encouraging individual success.
- Minimizes frustration and boredom by designing tasks compatible with students' levels of readiness, whatever they may be.
- Complements instruction, pre-assessment, and assessment. Note: pre-assessment is key to formulation of groups, scaffolds, and tiers.

### Components

**A.** Identification of learning objectives, goals, outcomes, and content mastery expectations for unit of study.

**B.** Determination of essential concepts, key facts, and skills based on the goals and objectives selected in step 1 in Steps to Create a Tiered Lesson.

**C.** Assessment of student readiness levels as well as a survey of interests and favored learning styles. If assessment is complete, reflect upon the results.

**D.** Development of core activity to enable a common experience for all tiers and student levels.

**E.** Modification of core task (designed in step 4) to enable differentiation and assignment of students to appropriate versions of the tiered lesson.

**F.** Integration of technology.

**G.** Assessment.

### Steps to Create a Tiered Lesson

**1.** For component A, look at your grade level curriculum expectations, standards, and benchmarks for the current grade, the grade below, and the grade above in the desired content area and strand

2. For component B, consider the Equalizer and go over Bloom's taxonomy of learning domains.

3. For component C, consider the following possibilities:

   - Go over any formal or standardized testing results you have for your students.

   - Examine any past tests, achievements, and products completed in class.

   - If teacher support or help is available, ask your aide or volunteer to do some informal assessment of students as needed.

4. For component D, decide on a group task that will open the unit.

   - The activity should require a high level of thinking and application of skills to help students focus on a big or overarching concept.

   - Make sure to hook your students to foster interest in the topic.

5. For component E:

   - Glance at the Equalizer buttons again to remind yourself of the continua that we modify for students to challenge them at the appropriate level, as well as the range of options they offer.

   - Review Bloom's cognitive domain descriptors to help you begin to think about differentiating by readiness.

6. For component F, search out appropriate software, Web links, printable worksheets, and graphic organizers that help students master the selected skills and concepts.

7. For component G, choose the method(s) of assessment you wish to use for each tier.

## Related Technologies: *Tiering Lesson Plan*

### Web-based Games and Flash Simulations

**How Web-based games and flash simulations will be used in the activity**: In the following Money Unit lesson plan, students will build and master skills via Web-based games and flash simulations. To complete this activity, students must know how to use the Internet. You must select a number of activities in which students will participate for each tier.

**Implementation challenges**: If you decide to use Web-based games, there's always the possibility a server or Web site could be down. If the appropriate plug-ins for the online games or movies you choose have not been downloaded prior to the activity, the browser will prompt you to download them to play the games or view the movies.

| Resources for Web-based Games and Flash Simulations | |
| --- | --- |
| **Description** | Web-based games and simulations depend heavily on multimedia plug-ins. Plug-ins are software components that "plug-in" to your browser to allow it to transmit more detailed information, such as video and audio files. There are hundreds of plug-ins, but some of the most common are RealPlayer, QuickTime, Adobe Acrobat, Windows Media Player, Flash Player and Shockwave Player. Macromedia Flash is actually a software application that's often used by Web designers to create movies and interactive games. You use Flash Player or Shockwave Player to view or interact with that media. |
| **Where to find resources** | Usually, if you visit a Web site that requires a particular plug-in, your browser will let you know if a specific one is needed. Once you download the plug-in, it will automatically start itself anytime you visit a site that requires that plug-in. |
| **Where to get help** | **Adobe Flash Player Support Center**<br>www.adobe.com/support/flashplayer/<br><br>**Macromedia Shockwave Player Support Center**<br>www.adobe.com/support/shockwave/ |

### Math Skills and Drills Software

**How math skills and drills software will be used in this activity:** In the associated lesson plan, students will build and master skills via software. To complete this activity, students must be familiar with the software you choose.

**Implementation challenges:** Questions may arise about the software, so be prepared to make yourself available to your students to help troubleshoot.

## Build a Tiered Lesson Plan in a Table

In our experience, the easiest way to build a tiered assignment is to map it out in a Word table or on paper. Using seven steps, we show you how we build a table for differentiating a tiered assignment.

1. **GLCEs:** Always start with your grade level content expectations (GLCEs). Keep in mind national, state, and local standards, which can differ in many ways.

   Look at your GLCEs in a given content area for what at-level learners should be able to accomplish. In the tiered assignment table, we chose to use, for demonstration purposes, the money strand for the Grade 2 mathematics GLCEs. Grade 2 information is reflected in the middle column of the table. Next, look at the GLCEs for the grade level below and the grade level above for the same strand. Doing so will help you visualize three levels of learners and develop appropriate activities for each of them.

**Tiered Assignment Table** ▪ Money Unit Lesson Plan Tiered by Readiness, Interest, and Learning Profile for Grade 2 Students

| 1. Grade Level Content Expectations (GLCEs) for Money (Mathematics) | | |
|---|---|---|
| **Below-level Learners** | **At-level Learners** | **Above-level Learners** |
| ▪ Grade 1 or below<br>▪ Work with money.<br>▪ Identify the denominations of coins and bills.<br>▪ Match one coin or bill of one denomination to an equivalent set of coins or bills of other denominations; for example, 1 quarter = 2 dimes and 1 nickel.<br>▪ Tell the amount of money in cents up to $1, in dollars up to $100. Use the symbols $ and ¢.<br>▪ Add and subtract money in dollars only or in cents only. | ▪ Grade 2<br>▪ Record, add, and subtract money.<br>▪ Read and write amounts of money using decimal notations; for example, $1.15.<br>▪ Add and subtract money in mixed units; for example, $2.50 + 60 cents and $5.75 - $3 but not $2.50 + $3.10. | ▪ Grade 3<br>▪ Solve measurement problems.<br>▪ Add and subtract money in dollars and cents.<br>▪ Solve applied problems involving money, length, and time. |

2. **Outcomes:** Determine the desired outcomes or goals for the money unit/ lesson. In this case, you've determined that students should be easily able to use bills and coins in daily situations requiring transactions. Add this goal to the tiered assignment table.

| 2. Outcomes. Decide what students should know, understand, or be able to do. |
|---|
| Students should be easily able to use bills and coins in daily situations that require transactions |

3. **Think:** Next, think about your students. You can pre-assess them to determine their strengths and weaknesses, but you may also want to consider their interests and learning styles and offer choices. Ask your-selves what concepts each level of learner can grasp. How many learners fit each level? Add this information to the tiered assignment table.

| 3. Think about students' conceptual understandings and abilities. | | |
|---|---|---|
| # of Below-level Learners = 8<br>Working at Grade 1 or below<br>Little knowledge of money concepts and value | # of At-level Learners = 12<br>Working at Grade 2<br>Can identify coins and bills | # of Above-level Learners = 4<br>Working at Grade 3 or above<br>Can identify coins and bills<br>Can make accurate change |

4. **Common Experience:** This activity launches the unit or lesson with the whole group. Use a high-level thinking activity that will offer opportunities for students to apply their skills in order to understand a big idea for the money unit. For example, if a read-aloud book about money might help stir up interest in the unit, add it to the lesson.

| 4. Use a common experience for the whole group that requires high-level thought and will provide opportunities for students to use one or more key skills to understand a big idea. |
| --- |
| Read aloud to the students *Pigs Will Be Pigs: Fun with Math and Money*, by Amy Axelrod. Use some of the author's questioning strategies located at www.amyaxelrod.com/pwbp.html <br><br> … or use a lesson plan from the U.S. Mint <br><br>     www.usmint.gov/kids/index.cfm?FileContents=/kids/teachers/LessonView.cfm&LessonPlanId=94 |

5. **Think about activities:** Think about the range of activities that can be used to help students build and master skills. Consider low skill and low complexity of understanding as well as high skill and high complexity of understanding. Next, create versions of activities to challenge learners. This section of the table shows some potential learning activities for each tier.

| 5. Think about a range of activities for below, at, and above grade level learners. | | |
| --- | --- | --- |
| **Group A**<br>**Below-level Learners** | **Group B**<br>**At-level Learners** | **Group C**<br>**Above-level Learners** |
| ■ Learn to recognize coins and bills in a Concentration-type game.<br><br>■ Use flashcards.<br><br>■ Learn to count money and add it.<br><br>■ Work with groups B and C partners (mentors and modeling).<br><br>■ Use coin and bill manipulatives to solve problems.<br><br>■ Create "Riddle Your Team" problems. | ■ Learn to write money in decimal form.<br><br>■ Learn to add and subtract money in mixed units using facsimiles of real money.<br><br>■ Learn how to read a cash register receipt that shows the cost of several items.<br><br>■ Work with group A partners to mentor and group C partners on shared activities.<br><br>■ Create a money booklet or slideshow using a template.<br><br>■ Create "Riddle Your Team" problems. | ■ Learn the real-life experience of running a school supplies or snack store.<br><br>■ Learn how to price items.<br><br>■ Learn to use calculators to check transactions.<br><br>■ Work with groups B and C.<br><br>■ Create a money board game.<br><br>■ Create "Riddle Your Team" problems. |

6. **Add technology via software, Web sites, and printable worksheets:**
Some Web sites may support teachers (T). Others are for students to practice their money skills. The actual links for the Web sites are listed at the end of the chapter. On your own, investigate two or three of these opportunities and decide which are appropriate for your students at each level. Have your students use them independently or in a group situation with partners. Some of the Web sites and software provide tracking features.

| 6. Add technology | | |
|---|---|---|
| Basic Money Worksheets (T)<br>Money Worksheets (T) | Coin Clip Art (T)<br>Printable Coins (T) | Money Poetry (T)<br>Printable Money Worksheets (T) |
| **Group A**<br>**Below-level Learners** | **Group B**<br>**At-level Learners** | **Group C**<br>**Above-level Learners** |
| **Web sites** | **Web sites** | **Web sites** |
| ■ Coin and Money Related Crafts and Activities<br>■ Counting Money Activity<br>■ Graphing Organizers in Kidspiration<br>■ Math Games<br>■ Max's Math Adventures<br>■ Money Concentration<br>■ Money Equivalents Game<br>■ Money Match<br>■ Money to Build A Robot | ■ Adding Dollars, Dimes, and Pennies<br>■ Adding Money Amounts<br>■ Buy It with the Little Farmer<br>■ Change It Money Practice<br>■ ChangeMaker<br>■ Coin Recognition/Counting Coins<br>■ Counting Change Flash Cards<br>■ Counting Money<br>■ Discovering Coin Values<br>■ Learn to Count Money<br>■ Let's Compare<br>■ Match–em Up<br>■ Piggy Bank | ■ Add Money<br>■ Change Due<br>■ Checking Account<br>■ Ed's Bank<br>■ Lemonade Stand Game<br>■ Let's Go Shopping: Counting Money<br>■ Little Fingers: How Many Cents?<br>■ Printable Play Money<br>■ Subtract Money |
| **Software** | **Software** | **Software** |
| ■ Money Math<br>■ The Penny Pot | ■ Coin Critters<br>■ Money Challenge<br>■ The Penny Pot | ■ Coin Critters<br>■ Math Missions Grades 3–5: The Amazing Arcade Adventure<br>■ Mighty Math Calculating Crew |
| **Graphic Organizers** | **Create Artifacts** | **Create Artifacts** |
| ■ Graphic Organizer (Kidspiration) | ■ Using a teacher-made Publisher template, create a book about money. | ■ Using a teacher-made Publisher template, create a book about money.<br>■ Using a teacher-made template, create a board game about money. |

**7.** Assess students to determine what has been learned:

| 7. Assess Learners | | |
|---|---|---|
| **Below-level Learners** | **At-level Learners** | **Above-level Learners** |
| ■ Paper and pencil unit assessment from textbook | ■ Paper and pencil unit assessment from textbook | ■ Paper and pencil unit assessment from textbook |
| ■ Software assessments created by software publisher | ■ Software assessments created by software publisher | ■ Software assessments created by software publisher |
| ■ Teacher-created assessments using Word, Publisher, or similar software products | ■ Teacher-created assessments using Word, Publisher, or similar software products | ■ Teacher-created assessments using Word, Publisher, or similar software products |
| ■ Self-Reflection | ■ Self-Reflection | ■ Self-Reflection |

Perhaps you're a visual or auditory learner who memorizes important information using acronyms. To help you recall the seven steps to build a tiered assignment in a table, remember GOT CATE.

**G:** List the Grade Level Content Expectations (GLCEs) for the content area.

**O:** Determine the outcomes; that is, decide what students should know, understand, or be able to do.

**T:** Think about students' abilities and conceptual understandings.

**C:** Use a common experience for the whole group that requires high-level thought and will provide opportunities for students to use one or more key skills to understand a big idea.

**A:** Think about a range of activities for below, at, and above grade level learners.

**T:** Add the technology tool to fit the learner.

**E:** Assess (or evaluate) learning.

While dialogue about students' differing levels of readiness is common, differentiated instruction offers us some effective strategies to help adjust our plans to meet students where they are. If you're just beginning to differentiate by readiness, you might choose to start with something simpler, such as the incorporation of a graphic organizer or two into your plans. If you're a seasoned veteran, try your hand at developing a tiered assignment for your students. Regardless of the readiness strategy you choose, we're convinced it will reap positive results in your classroom.

### Visit the U.S. Mint!

You might be asking how you can do some of these activities. Along with the ideas in the table, here are some others to get you started:

1. Visit the US Mint—Kids' Version at www.usmint.gov/kids/. If you haven't seen all the great materials now available for both teachers and students, you're in for a treat. It really is H.I.P.! There are lesson plans, coloring pages, images, history, a glossary, and more. Older students can design their own coins in the Making Change game. It's outstanding. Younger students will enjoy the Coin Memory game. The Quarter Explorer is fantastic for students who are studying states and regions. The site's other 12 games are fun, too!

2. Find some money clip art. Did you know that the images at the U.S. mint are in the public domain and can be used in classrooms? Here's an idea for students who are learning to differentiate coins. Insert images of coins into Word or Publisher, enlarge the images, and print them. Laminate and cut the coins apart. If you have a magnetic board, affix tiny magnets on the back of each coin. Pose problems for students and have them come up to the board to move the coins around to solve the problem while students at their desk work on the same problem.

The Web sites in the Resources 3 section offer practice for students to become fluent in making change and using money. Investigate a few to see which sites meet the needs of your students. You may want to create a Tic-Tac-Toe card with a site in each cell for students to mark off as they move through sites. The card can be created by inserting a 3 x 3 table into Word. It can be printed so that they type in the URLs, or even better, make it digital so that students can click the links in the cards (Fig. 3.2). You can see a downloadable example at www.everythingdi.net.

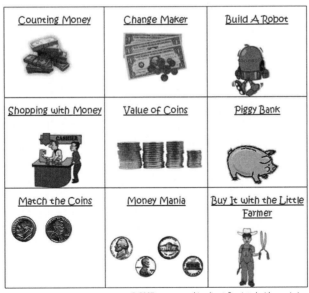

FIGURE **3.2** ■ Sample Tic-Tac-Toe Board: Let's Practice Our Money Skills

© 2007 www.everythingdi.net. Reprinted with permission.

## Resources for Chapter 3

| Money-Based Resources for Teachers | Basic Money Skills: Elementary Money Lessons | www.moneyinstructor.com/skills.asp |
|---|---|---|
| | Coin Clip Art | www.busyteacherscafe.com/Coin Clipart.htm |
| | Money Poetry | www.teachingheart.net/moneyp.htm |
| | Money Worksheets | www.teach-nology.com/worksheets/math/money/ |
| | Printable Money | www.moneyinstructor.com/wsp/pages.asp |
| | Printable Play Money | www.moneyinstructor.com/play.asp |
| Tiering Resources and Graphic Organizers | Tiered Assignment Plan—Blank Template | www.dcmoboces.com/dcmoiss/staffdev/oinit/dile/tact1.doc |
| | Planning a Tiered Activity Blank Template (PDF) | www.wilmette39.org/DI39/dipdf/planningtieredtemplate.pdf |
| | Tiered Curriculum Project | http://ideanet.doe.state.in.us/exceptional/gt/tiered_curriculum/welcome.html |
| | Education Place Graphic Organizers | www.eduplace.com/graphicorganizer/ |
| Money-Based Resources for Below–Grade Level Students | Coin and Related Money Craft Activities | www.enchantedlearning.com/crafts/money/ |
| | Counting Money Activity | http://teach.fcps.net/trt1/Counting_Money/counting__money.htm |
| | Graphic Organizer in Kidspiration | www.edina.k12.mn.us/concord/studentlinks/kidspiration/kidspiration.htm |
| | Math Games | www.e-ledesma.com/games.htm |
| | Max's Math Adventures | http://teacher.scholastic.com/max/icecream/ |
| | Money Concentration | www.quia.com/cc/4918.html |
| | Money Equivalents Game | www.fi.edu/pieces/knox/online/valuematch1.htm |
| | Money Match | www.harcourtschool.com/activity/con_math/g03c07.dcr |
| | Money Math Software | www.dositey.com/math/ls20/107/demomenu.htm |
| | Money to Build a Robot | www.harcourtschool.com/activity/money_build_robot/ |
| | The Penny Pot Software | http://sunburst.com |

*continued*

## Resources for Chapter 3 *(continued)*

| | | |
|---|---|---|
| **Money-Based Resources for At– Grade Level Students** | Adding Dollars, Dimes, and Pennies | www.aaamath.com/B/add211x5.htm |
| | Adding Money Amounts | www.aaamath.com/B/add45ax1.htm |
| | Buy It with the Little Farmer | www.lizardpoint.com/fun/java/buyit/BuyIt.html |
| | Change It Money Practice | www.mrsbogucki.com/aemes/resource/apps/change/ |
| | ChangeMaker | www.funbrain.com/cashreg/ |
| | Coin Critters Software | www.nordicsoftware.com/web/product_index/coin_critters/ |
| | Coin Recognition/Counting Coins | http://fi.edu/pieces/knox/onlineactiv.htm |
| | Counting Change Flash Cards | www.quia.com/fc/4918.html |
| | Counting Money | www.hbschool.com/activity/counting_money/ |
| | Discovering Coin Values | www.toonuniversity.com/flash.asp?err=569 |
| | Learn to Count Money | www.playtolearn.com/countmoney/count_money_main.asp |
| | Let's Compare | www.hbschool.com/activity/lets_compare/ |
| | Match 'em Up | http://fi.edu/pieces/knox/online/valuematch1.htm |
| | Money Challenge Software | www.gamco.com/product_info.php?products_id=37 |
| | Money Mania | www.mathplayground.com/MoneyLevel1.html |
| | Piggy Bank | http://fen.com/studentactivities/Piggybank/piggybank.html |
| | The Penny Pot Software | http://sunburst.com |
| **Money-Based Resources for Above– Grade Level Students** | Add Money | www.aaamath.com/B/mny45ax2.htm |
| | Change Due | www.aaamath.com/mny313-coins-for-change.html |
| | Checking Account | www.hbschool.com/teacher_resources/math/grade_05/ g5_checking.html |
| | Coin Critters software | www.nordicsoftware.com/web/product_index/coin_critters/ |
| | Ed's Bank | www.practicalmoneyskills.com/english/pop/games/ p_ed_bank.html |
| | Ice Cream Truck software | www.sunburst.com |
| | Lemonade Stand Game | www.lemonadestandgame.com |
| | Let's Go Shopping: Counting Money | www.superkidz.com/counting.html |
| | Little Fingers: How Many Cents? | www.little-g.com/shockwave/cents.html |
| | Math Missions Software | www.tomsnyder.com/products/product.asp?SKU=MMIMMI& Subject=Math |
| | Mighty Math Calculating Crew Software | www.Riverdeep.net |
| | Printable Play Money | www.moneyinstructor.com/play.asp |
| | Subtract Money | www.aaamath.com/B/mny45ax2.htm |

## CHAPTER 4

# Using Technology *to* Differentiate *by* Learning Profile

In today's classrooms, we find a considerable range of diversity that's remarkable yet challenging. Every day, many teachers work with 25 to 30 or more students, each with a unique, multidimensional learning profile. Students' learning profiles, shaped by many factors, suggest their preferred learning style or "customary" method of learning. Learning profiles include four general components, which Tomlinson calls "learning profile factors" (2001).

1. **Intelligence Preferences** refer to the brain-based predispositions we all have. Brain-based predispositions include analytic, creative, verbal/linguistic, interpersonal, and the like. Current models include the theory of multiple intelligences offered by Howard Gardner (1993) and the triarchic intelligences suggested by Robert Sternberg (1999).

2. **Learning-Style Preferences** include intelligence preferences, cognitive styles (auditory, visual, kinesthetic, or tactile), and environmental factors (noise level, temperature, light, classroom arrangement, space, etc.).

3. **Gender-based Preferences** refer to intelligence preferences, group preferences, and cultural factors that influence learning "personalities" typical of each gender, such as competitive versus collaborative styles, group versus individual styles, and analytic versus creative styles.

4. **Culture-influenced Preferences** suggest students' group preferences, their view of time, and whether they incline toward whole-to-parts or parts-to-whole instruction. In addition, several "emotional" traits that stem from students' cultural backgrounds shape their learning profile factor. These traits include tendencies toward a reserved or expressive learning personality, a contemplative versus spontaneous learning personality, a conventional or imaginative learning personality, a subjective or more personal approach to subject matter versus an objective or more impersonal approach to subject matter, and so forth.

We can use a number of strategies to manage and attend to our students' very diverse learning profiles. In our experience, the most effective approach is Gardner's multiple intelligences theory. In the following sections, we'll provide a bit of background on the theory itself and suggest ways to apply multiple intelligences (MI) in your classroom with the help of instructional technologies

## Background: Multiple Intelligences Theory

Gardner, a Harvard psychologist, offers pathways to learning in the style of the learner. He says, "It is of the utmost importance that we recognize and nurture all of the varied human intelligences, and all of the combinations of intelligences. We are all so different largely because we all have different combinations of intelligences. If we recognize this, I think we will have at least a better chance of dealing appropriately with the many problems that we face in the world" (1993, p. 12).

Gardner might say that learning styles are recognized approaches to learning that students use in and out of school. Walter McKenzie (2002), author of *Multiple Intelligences and Instructional Technology,* adds that intelligences are more than learning style or talents and aptitudes. McKenzie views intelligences as "legitimate conduits of cognition that can be flexibly applied across the curriculum in varied contexts by all learners" (p. 1).

We'll provide a more detailed description of the nine intelligences later in this chapter, but briefly, they're grouped into three broad categories: **Analytical Intelligences** (logic smart, music smart, nature smart), **Interactive Intelligences** (body smart, people smart, word smart), and **Introspective Intelligences** (wonder smart, picture smart, and self smart).

Noted practitioner Thomas Armstrong (2000) clarifies some key points of Gardner's theory:

- Each person possesses all nine intelligences in varying degrees.
- Most people can develop each intelligence to an adequate level of competency.

- Intelligences usually work together in any number of complex ways.
- There are many ways to be intelligent within each category; that is, each intelligence offers varied ways in which people demonstrate their gifts *within* the intelligence as well as *between* intelligences.

Making use of the multiple intelligences in the classroom enhances students' opportunities for learning and gives them more options for how they learn. When students are provided with choices, they almost always respond positively. Taking responsibility for their own learning is highly motivating to students.

## Multiple Intelligences Theory in Practice

We can begin to meet the needs of multiple and very distinct learning profiles by using insights gleaned from teachers who apply MI concepts in their classrooms.

First, we can explain MI theory to our students in ways they can understand. Sometimes teachers are tempted to believe that it's easier to simply apply certain theoretical techniques and practices without explaining all the jargon to students. While this may be true in some cases, we prefer to involve our students in the decision-making process to maximize their learning experiences.

Depending on your students' age levels, you might use words, symbols, or pictures to clearly illustrate the intelligences that best support a learning connection. You might show the naturalist intelligence by a picture of a tree, flower, or bird. The logical-mathematical intelligence might be illustrated by images of numbers or puzzle pieces. If we involve students in our approaches and our terminology, we often see higher levels of motivation and comfort with our tactics.

By the way, a really engaging, ready-to-go-activity that you can print and use with your students is Pick an Alien (appropriate for Grades 3–8) at www.ncwiseowl.org/kscope/techknowpark/LoopCoaster/eSmartz1.html. The site includes directions, a printable graph to record the intelligences in your class, and other materials.

We can expand our teacher tool kit by modifying instruction according to various learning profile factors. Obviously, our students don't necessarily learn in the same way we do, nor do all of them respond to our particular teaching styles. As we stretch our students beyond their comfort zones, we, too, need to make changes and try out varied techniques that touch auditory, visual, and kinesthetic learners. Perhaps one of the most positive aspects of making use of the multiple intelligences theory is that doing so allows students to work with and strengthen their highly developed intelligences while it challenges them to develop their weaker ones.

Although you're responsible for many students, we're confident that you have a fairly good idea as to your students' learning preferences. Teachers are usually gifted with an intuitive ability to know and read their students. If you're uncertain about a few of your students or want to make sure that your judgments are on target, you can use pre-assessment tools to determine your students' preferred intelligence areas. You might use a questionnaire, survey, or inventory to do this. (See the resources section at the end of this chapter for additional information.)

We've found that our students appreciate it when we ask for their input and are excited to share their talents, gifts, likes, and dislikes. In addition, simple observation of our students during classroom activities can speak volumes about their stronger and weaker areas of intelligence, as well as their preferred learning styles and gender-based and culture-influenced preferences.

We can use technology. Technology easily complements activities based on multiple intelligences and allows teachers to support students with distinct learning profiles. Technology offers a wide range of choices, including Web research, databases, spreadsheets, software (such as interactive, drill and practice, group decision or collaborative, movie-making, robotics, multimedia, and concept-mapping), handheld computers, and WebQuests. Additional options include word processing, desktop publishing, digital cameras, audio files, online projects, collaborative Web sites, tutorials, journals and diaries, and electronic portfolios.

Teachers can draw on MI as a basis for choosing software and Web sites to use in the classroom or computer lab. Spreadsheets and logic games are a natural for the logical-mathematical intelligence, and word processing software is a terrific match for the verbal-linguistic intelligence. Draw and paint software goes well with spatial intelligence, and music software, of course, fits with the musical intelligence.

Students with bodily-kinesthetic intelligence benefit from Lego/Logo construction kits as well as simulation games such as flight simulators. Those with naturalist intelligence enjoy nature simulation activities and explorations, and students can use their intrapersonal intelligence with software and Web sites where they can make personal choices, role play, and self-pace.

Finally, interpersonal intelligence can be supported via e-mail, blogs, two-player games, and similar activities in which students can interact with others.

Teachers can use the Web to connect their students with multiple intelligences activities. At www.everythingdi.net, we 've constructed Web pages with resources for each of the nine intelligences. A section of each resource page includes student links to activities that support that intelligence (Fig. 4.1).

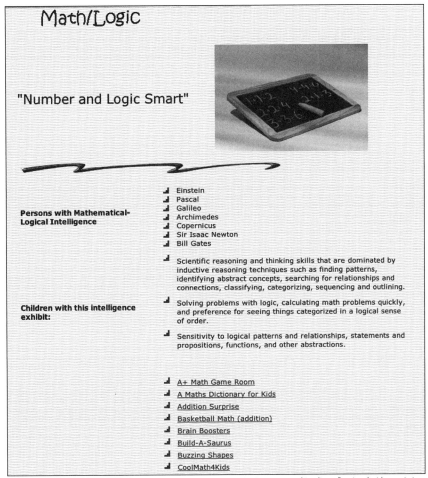

**FIGURE 4.1** ■
Sample
resource page

Before we attempt to connect MI with our core curricula, we first need to familiarize ourselves with the key traits of the nine intelligences. To help you better distinguish between each type, we've prepared a table of examples (Table 4.1).

Let's imagine that we've chosen nine students to work on a pizza-making activity, plan a Valentine's Day party, or coordinate a field trip to a historic place. Based on their strengths in one of the nine intelligences, they've selected a specific task or focus relative to the cooking endeavor, Valentine's Day celebration, or historical outing.

Glance at Table 4.1 to expand your understanding of the intelligences and view how each "theme" brings the array of intelligences to life.

TABLE **4.1** ■ Multiple intelligences and their traits, with examples

| Intelligence Type | Description/ Key Traits | Pizza Maker's Focus | Valentine's Day Party Planner's Focus | Field Trip Guide's Focus |
|---|---|---|---|---|
| **Bodily-Kinesthetic** | Expression through movement. Handles objects dexterously. Learns by doing. | Responsible for developing deep dish, hand-tossed, traditional round, and flavored crusts. | Creates new Valentine's Day dance or party game. | Prepares seating arrangements for bus portion of tour and luncheon area. If possible, "walks" the tour ahead of time. |
| **Existential** | Likes to totally immerse self in a project. Wonders about philosophical questions, values, and history. | Reflects upon history of pizza, its creator, and its role in modern-day culture. | Ponders the origin of Valentine's Day and the legends associated with it. | Mulls over the key or worthwhile exhibits students should visit. |
| **Interpersonal** | Focuses on others and relationships and is intuitive in regard to others' moods and motives. Prefers collaborative work. | Surveys friends as to possible meeting locations and then selects appropriate facility, with kitchen and inviting, private dining atmosphere. | Personalizes and distributes invitations for party. | Arranges tour time based on participants' schedules, and tells them by note or in person. |
| **Intrapersonal** | In tune with self and emotions. More introspective and reserved. Prefers working alone and in a quiet environment. | Free-writes in a diary about worries: will there be enough pizza for all, will the pizza be tasty enough, will everyone like the pizza? | Journals about apprehension relative to potential love interest who will attend party. | Escapes to a quiet place to bite nails and review note cards for presentation of tour. |
| **Logical-Mathematical** | Bent toward numbers, logic, and patterns. Prefers well-organized, strategic-type activities. | Calculates cost per serving. Organizes shopping list, with number of items and categories for purchase. | Calculates how much is spent per year on chocolates and flowers. | Determines how much to charge per person and whether a group discount can be offered. |
| **Musical** | Prefers to express self through activities such as dance, singing, and/or playing of instruments. | Pens a jingle or slogan to market and sell creation to the school cafeteria. | Selects dance music and serves as disc jockey. | Provides music as guests eat lunch and converse. |

*continued*

TABLE **4.1** ■ **Multiple intelligences and their traits, with examples** *(continued)*

| Intelligence Type | Description/ Key Traits | Pizza Maker's Focus | Valentine's Day Party Planner's Focus | Field Trip Guide's Focus |
|---|---|---|---|---|
| **Naturalist** | Enjoys science experiments and observational activities. Loves to be outdoors and to study the natural world. | Searches out natural ingredients and locates regional products. | Brings naturally scented candles and fresh-cut flowers for centerpieces. | Beautifies meeting location and lunch area by planting or flowers. Includes nature on the tour. |
| **Verbal-Linguistic** | Strong listening, reading, writing, and speaking skills. Takes pleasure in activities such as storytelling, debate, and word-based games. | Presents monologue to defend superiority of own creation over Domino's, Little Caesar's, Pizza Hut, and those of other pizza giants. | Recites famous love poems, or writes and shares valentine riddles or limericks. | Tells a story associated with history, buildings, and/or people. |
| **Visual-Spatial** | Prefers charts and graphs over verbal or written instructions and activities. Sensitive to pictures and images relative to color, shape, line, form, and space. | Attends to aesthetic appearance of pizza; for example, placement of toppings, neatness, and variety of color. | Responsible for wall hangings and decorations. | Prepares map of tour route and various stops. |

As we look over the table of possibilities and reflect on our own experiences as students, we may lament that MI theory didn't exist during our school years. MI empowers students to work to their strengths and to further develop their weaker intelligences in a positive way. If only physical science and geometry could have been so engaging! How much more attractive and useful it would have been to improve our levels of comprehension through activities drawing on musical or interpersonal intelligences. Perhaps our distaste for certain subjects might have decreased a bit if a well-rounded, multifaceted strategy such as MI had been available when we were students.

Let's examine how we can connect MI and instructional technology with our core curricula.

# Connecting MI and Instructional Technology with Core Curricula

Students in Grades 3–5 in the United States study the original 13 colonies. In the majority of classrooms we've observed, students read books about how the New England, Middle, and Southern colonies came into being. Students learn about Colonial people, places, and things during a timeframe from about 1600 to 1763. They color maps, read biographies, and make timelines.

Sometimes students are divided into three groups. One group studies, and later shares, information about the New England colonies; a second group studies and shares information about the Middle colonies; and a third group studies and shares information about the Southern colonies. In other classrooms, students work in pairs or triads to study one of the 13 colonies. After learning about their colony from mostly text-based resources, students report information either orally or in writing.

In general, most classrooms use verbal-linguistic activities to learn about the 13 original colonies, but not all students excel in the verbal-linguistic intelligence. We believe that adding a range of MI activities to the usual print-based information engages students in their own learning and makes learning about the colonies more interesting and fun. In the tables that follow, we show how teachers can add MI to any unit or theme.

Many of you probably know that technology marries nicely with multiple intelligences theory (and countless other instructional strategies as well). One of the simplest ways we can begin to introduce technology into our MI-based activities is to provide practical links from the Internet for each task. Using Table 4.1 as a starting point, we've included Web enhancements for the Colonial American theme. Take a glance at Table 4.2 and the links it provides to see how we can add research assistance from the Web.

TABLE **4.2** ■ Web resources for MI activities connecting Colonial America with core curricula

| Intelligence | Math/Science | Language Arts/Social Studies |
|---|---|---|
| **Bodily-Kinesthetic (Body Smart)** | Create the pieces and learn how to play Nine Men's Morris, a Colonial game. Teach your classmates how to play.<br><br>http://noahWebsterhouse.org/games.html (history)<br><br>www.1771.org/cd_nine.htm (printable)<br><br>www3.sympatico.ca/pesullivan/merrelles (interactive) | Write and act out a play about an early Colonial event or create a quiz show for your class.<br><br>www.history.org/kids/games/foundingFather.cfm<br><br>Game samples, a blank Jeopardy game template, and directions are available at<br><br>Hardin County, Kentucky, schools<br><br>www.hardin.k12.ky.us/res_techn/countyjeopardygames.htm<br><br>Internet4Classrooms<br><br>www.Internet4classrooms.com/online_powerpoint.htm |
| **Existential (Wonder Smart)** | What if you were Benjamin Franklin? Which new invention would you make? Why?<br><br>Check out Ben's inventions at<br><br>www.pbs.org/benfranklin/l3_inquiring_little.html<br><br>www.libertyskids.com/arch_who_bfranklin.html<br><br>Use Paint or another drawing tool to design your next invention. | If you were Colonial leader X, what would you have done differently? Reflect about your life, then write a letter to your children or grandchildren in which you share this information.<br><br>www.foundingfathers.info/<br><br>http://earlyamerica.com/earlyamerica/notable/notable2.html<br><br>www.whitehouse.gov/history/firstladies/<br><br>Use word processing software or the online letter generator at<br><br>http://readwritethink.org/materials/letter_generator/ |
| **Interpersonal (People Smart)** | Investigate, with a group or partner, common Colonial occupations. Make a chart of the occupations and describe each trade's range of skills.<br><br>http://eev.liu.edu/KK/colonial/resources.htm#Trades | Write a dialogue about a Founding Father or Mother. (One partner or group member acts as a reporter, and another plays the Founding Father or Mother.)<br><br>www.foundingfathers.info/<br><br>http://earlyamerica.com/earlyamerica/notable/notable2.html<br><br>www.whitehouse.gov/history/firstladies/<br><br>www.colonialhall.com/biodoi.asp |
| **Intrapersonal (Self Smart)** | Construct a timeline of foods Colonists ate by date. Describe some of their unusual foods.<br><br>www.foodtimeline.org<br><br>www.apva.org/exhibit/eats.html<br><br>www.apva.org/ngex/xfood.html<br><br>Create a timeline in TimeLiner software or online at<br><br>http://teachers.teach-nology.com/Web_tools/materials/timelines/ | Describe your life as a child in Colonial times. Write a diary entry as if you were that person.<br><br>Use a word processor or publishing software to create a diary entry or use an online journal tool at<br><br>http://teacher.scholastic.com/activities/our_america/colonial/ |

*continued*

TABLE **4.2** ■ Web resources for MI activities connecting Colonial America with core curricula   *(continued)*

| Intelligence | Math/Science | Language Arts/Social Studies |
|---|---|---|
| **Logical-Mathematical (Number/ Reasoning Smart)** | Graph the New England, Southern, or Middle Colonies in terms of origin, size, products, and founder.<br><br>Use kid-friendly spreadsheet software or an online site such as<br><br>http://nces.ed.gov/nceskids/createagraph/ | Measure the number of miles from Williamsburg and Boston to Philadelphia. Calculate how long it would take riders on horseback to travel from Williamsburg and Boston to Philadelphia, the largest city at the time. Make a comparison chart.<br><br>www.imh.org/imh/kyhpl3a.html |
| **Musical (Music/ Rhythm Smart)** | Learn how to dance the steps of the Virginia reel or a minuet and teach your classmates.<br><br>http://homepages.apci.net/~drdeyne/dances/vareel.htm<br><br>www.stratfordhall.org/ed-music.html?EDUCATION | Compose a rap or song about Colonial life. Use some Colonial words in your music.<br><br>You can listen to some Colonial tunes at<br><br>www.contemplator.com/america/<br><br>www.plimoth.org/learn/education/kids/talk.asp<br><br>You can make music at<br><br>www.sfskids.org/templates/musicLabF.asp?pageid=15 |
| **Naturalist (Nature Smart)** | Which plants did the Colonists use for medicinal purposes? Investigate some of them and make a chart or brochure to share the most interesting ones.<br><br>www.history.org/history/teaching/plants.cfm<br><br>www.history.org/history/teaching/medtn.cfm<br><br>MyBrochureMaker<br><br>www.mybrochuremaker.com | Create a postcard. On the front, sketch some of the "new" animals and plants Colonists observed and used. Write a message on the back about your sketch and address the postcard to one of your siblings.<br><br>www.plimoth.org/learn/education/kids/homeworkHelp/growing.asp#col<br><br>www.plimoth.org/learn/education/kids/homeworkHelp/dinner.asp#col<br><br>MyPostCardMaker<br><br>www.mypostcardmaker.com |
| **Verbal- Linguistic (Word Smart)** | What did Ben Franklin contribute as a scientist? Using word processing software, write a description of some of his unique inventions and include images or original art.<br><br>http://sln.fi.edu/franklin/scientst/scientst.html | After studying Ben Franklin's maxims, create some of your own in word processing software.<br><br>www.sacklunch.net/poorrichard/ |
| **Visual-Spatial (Picture Smart)** | Learn about some early Colonial tools and invent a new one to help you do work; use Paint or another drawing program to draw your tool.<br><br>www.history.org/Almanack/life/tools/tlhdr.cfm<br><br>www.memorialhall.mass.edu/activities/tools/<br><br>www.apva.org/ngex/xtools.html<br><br>Design a period home interior at<br><br>http://teacher.scholastic.com/activities/our_america/colonial/ | Sketch a model of a Colonial home or Colonial clothing using Paint or another drawing program. Describe your drawing.<br><br>www.memorialhall.mass.edu/activities/architecture/wellsthorne_ell.html<br><br>www.hfmgv.org/education/smartfun/colonial/intro/<br><br>http://library.thinkquest.org/J002611F/clothing.htm<br><br>www.history.org/history/clothing/intro/index.cfm<br><br>www.memorialhall.mass.edu/activities/dressup/<br><br>www.plimoth.org/learn/education/kids/homeworkHelp/clothing.asp#col |

In Table 4.2, one of the naturalist activities is to create a postcard. On the front, sketch some of the "new" animals and plants Colonists observed and used. Write a message on the back about your sketch and address the postcard to one of your siblings. How can this activity be updated using technology? Here are two methods to consider:

## Method 1

1. Have students use Paint or a similar program to draw their animal.

2. Ask students to save their animal file in My Pictures or in another place they can find their saved file.

3. Go to MyPostCardMarker online at www.mypostcardmaker.com.

4. Follow the directions for uploading and framing the picture, typing the message, and printing it.

## Method 2

1. Use Publisher, Word, or similar word processing or publishing programs.

2. Ask students to create a text box that's the size of a postcard.

3. Insert images to match the assignment.

4. Show students how to copy the text box, paste it, and align it exactly with the first text box.

5. In the second text box, remove the images and write the message on one half. (Depending on your program, students may have to create two text boxes and align them.) Address the card in the other half of the textbox.

6. Print the postcard. Fold it in half so that the images are on one side of it and the message and address are on the other. Glue the folded paper with a glue stick.

We hope you're feeling a bit more comfortable with pairing up the nine intelligences with Web links to explore and investigate ways students can round off each task. Before sharing a detailed lesson plan, let's consider the types of tools technology itself offers for differentiating learning.

## Technology Tools and Multiple Intelligences

Have we mentioned that flexibility is yet another positive feature of MI theory? You can take any K–5 learning theme or content area and add tech tools to enhance the multiple intelligences.

In Table 4.3, we list a selection of tech tools that you might use with MI to further enrich your activities and pique your students' interests. These tools are grouped into three categories: **Analytical Intelligences** (logic smart, music smart, nature smart); **Interactive Intelligences** (body smart, people smart, word smart); and **Introspective Intelligences** (wonder smart, picture smart, and self smart). Table 4.3 may be helpful for pulling ideas to use with a Tic-Tac-Toe Board in which you ask students to make choices from each of the categories.

How might you use the ideas in Table 4.3? You might create your own table following this same format with its nine cells. In each cell, list a student activity. As an anchor activity, or in free time, students choose a cell and do that activity. When they've completed three activities to make a Tic-Tac-Toe, they've completed the choice board.

We've also seen teachers require their students to complete all nine activities in the choice board. However, these students may choose the order in which to do the activities. If all the activities are online, make the choice board available in digital format so that students can click directly on the link.

Let's say you want logic-smart students to use online resources that complement their analytic intelligence. Depending on the student's grade level, choose one or more of the math activities at Illuminations (http://illuminations.nctm.org/ActivitySearch.aspx).

You can do a search by grade level and then drill down to the one or two activities that would most benefit your students. List the exact Web link for the activity in the choice board. Or, if you have access to the Early Learning Toolkit by 2Simple USA, try 2graph. Students may wish to do a simple survey, such as finding out which sports are most popular with classmates, then graph the results (see Fig. 4.2). Or perhaps verbal-linguistic students would like to play word games. Visit Learning Vocabulary Can Be Fun (www.vocabulary.co.il/) and decide which game or games would be best for your students.

TABLE **4.3** ▪ Ideas to create a Tic-Tac-Toe Board

| Analytic Intelligences | Interactive Intelligences | Introspective Intelligences |
|---|---|---|
| **Logic Smart**<br>Databases<br>Excel, Graph Club/2graph (2simpleUSA) spreadsheet software<br>Illuminations site<br>Logic and problem-solving software<br>Strategy-based software and games | **Body Smart**<br>Claymation and movie software tools<br>Handheld computers<br>Interactive software<br>Lego/Logo, robotics/construction software<br>Manipulatives and probes | **Wonder Smart**<br>All About Me Scavenger Hunt<br>If You Were President<br>The Little Prince Online<br>Online encyclopedias and similar resources<br>Philosopher's Island |
| **Music Smart**<br>Juice Bottle Jingles<br>Multimedia software with sound<br>Music Ace/music software<br>Musical Pattern Builder<br>Music sound bytes<br>Online piano<br>Play Music<br>Sing Along Tunes and Lyrics | **People Smart**<br>Collaborative software and Web sites<br>Group decision software (Tom Snyder's Geography Search software)<br>Telecommunications projects such as Flat Stanley or Monster Exchange<br>WebQuests and ThinkQuests with collaborative elements | **Picture Smart**<br>Inspiration/Kidspiration/Webbing software<br>Matisse for Kids<br>Neighborhood Map Machine/mapping software<br>Paint/drawing-painting software<br>PowerPoint/presentation software<br>Sanford Art Edventures |
| **Nature Smart**<br>Digital and video cameras<br>Environmental research and simulations<br>Probes and microscopes<br>Nature-related software | **Word Smart**<br>Publisher/desktop publishing<br>Word/word-processing<br>Word-related games, puzzles, and riddles | **Self Smart**<br>Diaries<br>Electronic portfolios<br>Independent tutorials<br>Journals |

Your picture-smart students will enjoy using Paint or other drawing software to create original art. Let's say that your students are writing original poems for celebrating Mother's Day. Using drawing software, students can create original portraits of their mothers and insert them into a word processing or publishing document to highlight their poetry.

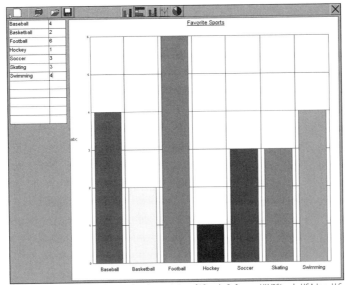

FIGURE **4.2** ■ Author-created graph of favorite sports using 2Simple USA

Reprinted with permission of 2Simple Software, UK/2Simple USA Inc., U.S.

FIGURE **4.3** ■ Mother's Day portrait created by fifth grade student

Created by Kamala K.

Created by Casey W.

FIGURE **4.4** ■ Mother's Day portrait created by fifth grade student

Now that you have become acquainted with Howard Gardner's multiple intelligences theory and learned how you can apply the theory to classroom activities, you're ready to review a sample lesson plan that includes technology to help differentiate MI-based tasks. We continue with our Colonial America theme and rely upon MI and technology tools to assist us in our challenging endeavor to differentiate by learning profile.

# Lesson Plan

## *Colonial America*

| Grade | 5 |
|---|---|
| **Subject Area** | Social Studies—with connections to other core curricula |
| **Curriculum Standards** | **Social Studies Standards (National Council for the Social Studies) addressed:** (available at http://cnets.iste.org/currstands/cstands-ss_ii.html) |

**II. Time, Continuity, and Change**

Social studies programs should include experiences that provide for the study of the ways human beings view themselves in and over time so that the learner can

- demonstrate an ability to correctly use vocabulary associated with time, such as past, present, future, and long ago; read and construct simple timelines; identify examples of change; and recognize examples of cause and effect relationships;

- compare and contrast different stories or accounts about past events, people, places, or situations, identifying how they contribute to our understanding of the past;

- identify and use various sources for reconstructing the past, such as documents, letters, diaries, maps, textbooks, photos, and others;

- use knowledge of facts and concepts drawn from history, as well as elements of historical inquiry, to inform decision making concerning public issues and how to take action regarding them.

**National Educational Technology Standards for Students (NETS•S) addressed:** (see appendix for full list)

1. Creativity and Innovation: 1.a., 1.b.
2. Communication and Collaboration: 2.a., 2.b.
3. Research and Information Fluency: 3.a., 3.b., 3.c., 3.d.
4. Critical Thinking, Problem Solving, and Decision Making: 4.b.
6. Technology Operations and Concepts: 6.b.

| **Lesson Summary** | In this lesson, students choose and use technology activities based on a multiple intelligences Tic-Tac-Toe Board for the study of Colonial America. |
|---|---|
| **Materials** | <ul><li>Copies of the Colonial America Tic-Tac-Toe Board</li><li>Paint, Kid Pix, or similar computer drawing software</li><li>Word processing, desktop publishing, presentation software</li><li>Printer</li></ul> |
| **Web Resources** | Internet access<br>Access to online encyclopedias (optional) |

*continued*

## *Colonial America*   (continued)

| | |
|---|---|
| **Lesson Activities** | 1. After completing research, ask students to independently choose three activities to complete a Tic-Tac-Toe Board. |
| | 2. Distribute copies of the Tic-Tac-Toe Board and discuss the choices. |
| | 3. Ask students to Think-Pair-Share. |
| | 4. Ask students to (Think) choose activities that complete a three-in-a-row Tic-Tac-Toe that uses all three-column categories (only diagonal cells or horizontal rows). |
| | 5. In the handout, students can write a sentence stating why an activity would be an appropriate choice, why it matches the student's intelligence, or why it would serve to strengthen that particular intelligence. |
| | 6. Ask students to Pair-Share their choices. |
| | 7. Collect the handouts, read the choices, and determine whether any changes need to be made. For example, if students have made an unwise decision, talk with them about change. |
| | 8. Create a chart that shows which students have selected each activity and construct a timeline for when each activity is due. Post the chart or provide copies. |
| | 9. Create guidelines and rubrics for each activity so that students know what's required. |
| | 10. Meet with the students doing each activity and assign a group leader who can troubleshoot problems before they come to you. |
| | 11. Ask students to start on the first activity. In the case of group work, you'll need to help organize where students work and how they use classroom and building resources. |
| | 12. After the activities or products are completed, students share information with a small group or the class. You may choose to organize the presentations so that either all students who chose product No. 1 meet together and share or all students who chose product No. 2 meet together and share, or you may decide to have students share their work in pairs or with the full class. |
| **Technology Activity Options** | ■ If computers must be shared, pair students to work on activities. |
| | ■ If a lab is available, students should organize their notes and prioritize their time in the lab. |
| **Differentiation/ Extension** | ■ More capable students who know basic computer skills can expand any assignment beyond the requirements. For example, they can create original art to embellish their product. They can research additional information to add to their product. They can create games, puzzles, or riddles to accompany their product. |
| | ■ Less capable students may be paired with a more capable student, or upper elementary students could be assigned to work as mentors with these students. During paired learning, the more capable student becomes the tutor and assists the less capable student in learning new skills. At the same time, the more capable student hones explanation and communication skills as knowledge is shared. |
| **Evaluation** | Use rubrics to evaluate students on the following components: |
| | ■ Completed products |
| | ■ Independent work or group work |
| | ■ Reflection on learning activities |

## Colonial American Tic-Tac-Toe Board Using MI and Technology

**Directions:** Choose three activities in a diagonal or horizontal line to make Tic-Tac-Toe.

| Analytic Intelligences | Interactive Intelligences | Introspective Intelligences |
|---|---|---|
| **Logic Smart**<br><br>**Technology:** Internet and Word.<br><br>**Product:** A comparison chart between Wampanoag and Colonists in daily life in 1621. Visit "You Are the Historian" at Plimouth Plantation and "Daily Life in 1621" to learn more. | **Body Smart**<br><br>**Technology:** Publisher.<br><br>**Product:** Construct a game that Colonial children used and show classmates how to play it. | **Wonder Smart**<br><br>**Technology:** Publisher or Word.<br><br>**Product:** A letter to your children or grandchildren 50 years after Colonists discovered you were a spy. Print the product to share. |
| **Music Smart**<br><br>**Technology:** Music composing software or an online program such as Music Ace or 2Simple Music Toolkit.<br><br>**Product:** Original song or rap to tell a story about a person or event during Colonial times. Save the file so that you can play it for the class. Type the words into PowerPoint to project on the computer screen or distribute. | **People Smart**<br><br>**Technology:** Liberty's Kids research tools (online), Publisher, or My Newsletter Maker. Visit Colonial Williamsburg for some ideas.<br><br>**Product:** A one-page newsletter with two articles about your colony. With a partner, tell about school, work, games, toys, trades, farming, or other ways people share and help each other in daily life. Print it! | **Picture Smart**<br><br>**Technology:** Computer drawing software such as Paint.<br><br>**Product:** Portrait of a Colonial person. Label the portrait with date, name, and key information. Print the portrait and mount it on construction paper. Save the file for sharing. |
| **Nature Smart**<br><br>**Technology:** Kidspiration or graphic organizer or chart.<br><br>**Product:** Compare and contrast the daily life of the Wampanoags and the Colonists. Use Scholastic's First Thanksgiving site for information. | **Word Smart**<br><br>**Technology:** Publisher.<br><br>**Product:** Poster advertising a Colonial event. Product shows who, what, where, when, why, and how and includes clip art or original art. Print the product to share. | **Self Smart**<br><br>**Technology:** Publisher or Word.<br><br>**Product:** Four personal diary pages that reflect a young person's thoughts about an important event or daily life during Colonial times. Print the product to share with the class. |

### Tip: Create Peer Tutors!

If you plan to teach a new computer skill or program, teach a small group of students first. When you're ready to teach the whole group, the previously taught students can serve as your assistants to help others in the class. Be sure to alternate students so that everyone has a chance to be a star helper.

## Technology Steps

How would you set up one of these activities? Let's take the People Smart suggestion and look at the steps.

1. Determine the research topic and ask students to visit Liberty's Kids online at www.libertyskids.com/archive.html (or another site of your choice).

2. Students take notes about their topic and write their news article, proofread it, and make changes.

3. To create the newsletter, use what's available at your school. Word and Publisher can be used to put news into newsletter format. An online tool, My Newsletter Maker (www.mynewslettermaker.com), is great for those who don't have software.

4. Students can use images from Liberty's Kids or draw their own in Paint.

5. After creating their newsletters, the final step is print and share.

TABLE **4.4** ▪ Sample product rubric for self-smart activity in Tic-Tac-Toe Board

| Diary Pages | Beginning (1) | Developing (2) | Accomplished (3) | Exemplary (4) |
|---|---|---|---|---|
| Number of pages/ Organization | One diary page with date | Two diary pages with dates | Three diary pages with dates | Four diary pages with dates |
| Information about a real event | One detail | Two to three details | Four to five details | Six or more details |
| Opinion about the event | No opinion stated | Opinion stated | Opinion stated with two supporting details | Opinion stated with three or more supporting details |
| Mechanics | Six or more spelling, punctuation, or grammatical errors | Four to five spelling, punctuation, or grammatical errors | Two to three spelling, punctuation, or grammatical errors | Zero to one spelling, punctuation, or grammatical error |
| Technology Integration | Used Word or Publisher for diary pages | Used Word or Publisher for diary pages and included one clip art image | Used Word or Publisher for diary pages, included two clip art images | Used Word or Publisher for diary pages and included original image(s) drawn in Paint |

Perhaps the most advantageous aspect of employing multiple intelligences coupled with technology is that there are so many ways to combine them. Together, they afford endless choices to our students. As K–5 teachers, you should keep in mind that younger or less able students will need more structured choices and that older or more able students generally will need less structured choices.

We've found that the best way to combine technology with multiple intelligences is to start with one or two additions, like getting your big toe wet, and then jumping in until your whole body is submerged. Take the plunge! The MI + Tech water is great!

## Resources for Chapter 4

| MI Pre-Assessment Tools | Pick an Alien | www.ncwiseowl.org/kscope/techknowpark/LoopCoaster/eSmartz1.html |
|---|---|---|
| | MI Test for Children | www.mitest.com/omitest.htm |
| *These tools can be used online or printed to determine students' MI traits.* | MI Tests for Teachers | http://surfaquarium.com/MI/inventory.htm |
| | | www.literacyproject.org/DL/MultipleIntelligencesSurvey.htm |
| | | www.lvarv.org/el-civics/More EE PDF Files/Intros/MISurvey.pdf |
| | | www.swadulted.com/workshops/lessonplan/LP HandoutsPDF.pdf |
| | Printable form for recording students' intelligences by category | www.ncwiseowl.org/kscope/techknowpark/LoopCoaster/MIRecord.html |
| **MI Resources** | All About Me Scavenger Hunt | www.dampier.wa.edu.au/Room13/scavhunt.htm |
| *These sites can be matched with students' MI traits.* | Flat Stanley | http://flatstanley.enoreo.on.ca/ |
| | Juice Bottle Jingles | www.lhs.berkeley.edu/shockwave/jar.html |
| | Illuminations | http://illuminations.nctm.org/ActivitySearch.aspx |
| | If You Were President | www.scholastic.com/kids/president/game.htm |
| | Matisse for Kids | www.artbma.org/education/matisse_kids_frame.html |
| | Monster Exchange | www.monsterexchange.org |
| | Musical Pattern Builder | www.hbschool.com/activity/pattern/pattern.html |
| | Play the Piano Online—Java Piano | www.pianoworld.com/fun/javapiano/javapiano.htm |
| | Philosopher's Island | www.portables2.ngfl.gov.uk/pmpercival/philosophy/ |
| | Play Music | www.playmusic.org |
| | Sanford Art Edventures | www.sanford-artedventures.com/play/play.html |
| | Sing Along Tunes and Lyrics | www.niehs.nih.gov/kids/musicchild.htm |
| | The Little Prince Online | www.angelfire.com/hi/littleprince/ |
| **Colonial America Links** | Colonial Williamsburg | www.history.org/media/index.cfm#trad |
| | … and Tour the Town | www.history.org/visit/tourTheTown/index.cfm |
| | Jamestown Rediscovery | www.apva.org/jr.html |
| | Liberty News | www.libertyskids.com/lnn.html |
| | Daily Life in 1621 | http://teacher.scholastic.com/thanksgiving/daily_life/ |
| | Plimoth Plantation | www.plimoth.org/OLC/index_js2.html |
| | Talk Like a Pilgrim | www.plimoth.org/learn/education/kids/talk.asp |
| | Thanksgiving Challenge | http://teacher.scholastic.com/thanksgiving/voyage/ |
| **Rubrics and Rubric Generators** | RubiStar | http://rubistar.4teachers.org |
| | TeAch-nology | www.teach-nology.com/Web_tools/rubrics/ |
| | Tech4Learning | http://myt4l.com/index.php?v=pl&page_ac=view&type=tools&tool=rubricmaker |
| **Compare/ Contrast Tools** | Compare/Contrast Diagram | www.readingquest.org/pdf/compare.pdf |
| | Interactive Venn Diagram | www.readwritethink.org/materials/venn/ |

## CHAPTER 5

# Using Technology *to* Differentiate *by* Content

Content is the "stuff" of teaching; it's the information and concepts we want students to learn and the materials through which they learn. As we help to provide access to content, we empower students to take ownership of it. When we differentiate by content, we vary what we teach as well as how we teach it.

As educators strive to fulfill an ever-growing number of diverse job tasks and reach our "wired" students, we must become increasingly more resourceful and innovative. Although these responsibilities seem overwhelming at times, may we offer a fresh perspective to encourage you?

You might begin to think about content as the "infotainment" center in a classroom. Your Content Infotainment Center houses access to all the information and concepts you want students to know for each subject you teach.

There are seven shelves in the Infotainment Center. Each shelf provides storage for important resources and aids.

**Shelf 1:** Media, access to the Internet, and software

**Shelf 2:** Printed texts and resource materials

**Shelf 3:** Manipulatives and related activity tools for understanding concepts

**Shelf 4:** Paper, drawing tools, crayons, and related supplies

**Shelf 5:** Headsets, recorders, and tapes for listening activities

**Shelf 6:** Bulletin boards, strings, clothespins, and tacks for displaying student artifacts

**Shelf 7:** Certificates, awards, stickers, and similar products for honoring students' progress

You stand before your Infotainment Center, with its keys in your hand. You decide when to open its doors and which shelf you'll use to help students understand the content before them. Which shelf or shelves will you draw from today? How will you decide? In the process of making this decision, reflect on the following Chinese proverb: "Learning is a treasure that will follow its owner everywhere."

## Matching Content to Learners

To help students understand why learning is a treasure, we have to engage them. To engage them, we have to understand them and their needs. Knowing how to differentiate content is based on our understanding of the learners in our class-room. When we've figured out how to match content with learners or learners with content, we open the door to understanding.

To build on your ability to differentiate by content, this chapter will offer some useful strategies for differentiating content by readiness, interest, and learning profile. We'll review the fundamentals of differentiating content by these three student traits, explore some strategies that correspond to each trait, and, finally, put technology to work as we pull out some exciting tools from our Infotainment Center to communicate content to our students in an effective manner.

## Differentiating Content by Readiness

Readiness is a student's entry point in relation to a particular concept or skill. More able students who are capable of complex or open-ended activities need advanced materials and enough time to investigate topics in depth. Less able students need more opportunities for practice or direct instruction, simpler materials, and more structured activities.

How do you know which students are ready for advanced skills and which aren't? Many teachers use their powers of observation to determine students' readiness. However, some teachers use pre-assessments of the content to be taught, prior report-card grades, anecdotal records, conversations with a previous teacher, or a combination of these indicators. Whatever your method, your students will prob-ably fit into one of three categories with respect to the content they need to master for your grade: at grade level, below grade level, or above grade level. Happily, there are some useful strategies to use with students at varying levels of readiness.

## Compacting Curriculum for More Able Students

When I (Grace) taught sixth-grade language arts and reading, a number of students in my classes had previously mastered the content. They were excellent writers, possessing fine grammar skills as well as superb reading and comprehension skills. You've probably experienced similar students in your classes. An important question is: What do teachers do with these students?

In most cases, school curriculum builds on, and actually repeats, previous content. In language arts, for example, students may have learned about sentence elements in Grade 2 or 3, again in Grade 4, and yet again in Grade 5. While some students—those who haven't grasped the concept of how sentence elements work together—need more teaching and practice to understand, others don't need a repeat or three-peat. It makes sense for teachers to address both kinds of learners: those who have mastered the concepts and those who haven't. Curriculum compacting, then, is a strategy for streamlining curriculum to allow more able students to work at a faster pace so that they can pursue an alternate topic or investigate an area of study in greater depth.

The idea for curriculum compacting was developed by Joe Renzulli, professor and director of the National Research Center on the Gifted and Talented at the University of Connecticut. Renzulli's research indicates that by compacting curriculum, we avoid teaching students what they already know. We can offer differentiated and challenging learning opportunities to more able students, and we can provide opportunities for new, enriched, and accelerated learning. Information about Renzulli Learning, a project of the University of Connecticut's Research & Development Corporation, is online at www.renzullilearning.com.

By compacting curriculum, teachers offer three benefits to students. We can 1) reduce boredom and its related issues of distraction, discipline, and under-achievement; 2) foster the challenging environment that DI supports; and 3) permit students to work at an appropriate pace. Compacting curriculum is useful for any curriculum or grade level because it's a strategy designed to make suitable modifications to content so as to match learners' abilities to instructional tasks.

At this point, you might be asking yourself how to compact your own curriculum. We recommend starting off with one or two responsible students, selecting appropriate content, and trying a variety of methods to determine student mastery.

Here are the steps recommended by Dr. Renzulli and his research team:

1. Pre-Assess
   - Identify the content goals and outcomes; that is, the learning objectives or goals for a particular unit of study.
   - Pre-assess students on the identified objectives before teaching the content. Students who consistently finish tasks early and correctly are usually good candidates for compacting. Scores on previous tests, assignments, and participation in the classroom will serve as indicators of ability. Pretests, such as end-of-the-unit tests for specific objectives or other informal or formal assessments, should also be used.

**2.** Modify Learning Activities

- Identify which students have mastered the learning objectives.

- Decide whether the identified students need enrichment or accelerated activities.

- Create replacement activities for students who have met the objectives that are about to be taught. Examples of learning activities include independent or self-directed learning, student-created projects, alternative textbooks, peer teaching and coaching, and research projects. Replacement activities can be differentiated by interest, readiness, and learning profile.

**3.** Manage

- Develop a plan with students to determine what they'll do while others work on regular lessons. Create guidelines, timelines, work rules, and assignments for content not mastered.

- Evaluate student performance.

Renzulli and his staff have developed a guide for compacting. The "compactor" tool consists of a three-column form that captures the compactor's three categories:

**1.** Curriculum Areas to Be Considered for Compacting

**2.** Procedures for Compacting Basic Material

**3.** Acceleration and/or Enrichment Activities

Information about the categories and a copy of the form may be viewed and printed at www.gifted.uconn.edu/siegle/CurriculumCompacting/section7.html.

Once you've determined whether a student would benefit from compacting, you can substitute accelerated or enrichment activities for basic skills work that the rest of the class is performing. Ideas for substitutions are found throughout this chapter.

## Learning Contracts

Learning contracts go hand in hand with compacting curriculum. Although the term *contract* sounds like an inflexible term, such is not the case in differentiated classrooms. Learning contracts provide for a mix of both required and self-selected tasks. Technology assists students and teachers in many ways when it comes to such opportunities for new, enriched, independent, and accelerated learning. Learning contracts are an exciting, flexible strategy that you may use alongside other DI techniques and tools. Because they're such a valuable strategy, we wish to devote more time and space to them in chapter 10, "Using Technology to Manage Your Differentiated Classroom."

## Profile: *Curriculum Compacting*

### Function

To streamline curriculum in order to offer students alternatives instead of holding them to basal or grade level curricular objectives that they may have already mastered. An excellent article about curriculum compacting is available at www.gifted.uconn.edu/sem/pdf/Curriculum_Compacting.pdf.

### Advantages

- Decreases boredom, distraction, underachievement, and discipline issues.
- Cultivates the challenging environment that DI supports.
- Is useful for any curricular framework or school configuration and is not constrained by grade level.
- Allows students to work at an appropriate pace.

### Components

**A.** Pre-assessment

**B.** Modification of learning activities

**C.** Management

### Steps to Compact Curriculum

1. Pre-assessment

   - Identify the content goals and outcomes; that is, the learning objectives or goals for a particular unit of study.

   - Pre-assess students on the identified objectives before teaching the content. Students who consistently finish tasks early and correctly are usually good candidates for compacting. Scores on previous tests, assignments, and participation in the classroom will serve as indicators of ability. Pretests, such as end-of the-unit tests for specific objectives or other informal or formal assessments, should also be used.

2. Modification of Learning Activities

   - Identify which students have mastered the learning objectives.

   - Decide whether the identified students need enrichment or accelerated activities.

- Create replacement activities for students who have met the objectives that are about to be taught. Examples of learning activities include independent or self-directed learning, student-created projects, alternative textbooks, peer teaching and coaching, and research projects. Replacement activities can be differentiated by interest, readiness, and learning profile.

**3.** Management

- Develop a plan with students to determine what they'll do while others work on regular lessons. Create guidelines, timelines, work rules, and assignments for content not mastered.

- Evaluate student performance.

## Differentiating Curriculum for Less Able Students

We've addressed a strategy for more able students. What, though, can we do to differentiate content for less able students? Elementary teachers have always used scaffolding, a support strategy for helping students gain the skills needed to do coursework more effectively. Scaffolding means doing some of the work for the student who isn't quite ready to accomplish a task independently. Similar to the supports that construction workers use on buildings, scaffolding is meant to be temporary. Scaffolding is "applied" to aid the completion of a task; then, over time, it's removed. We'll talk more about scaffolding in chapter 10, "Using Technology to Manage Your Differentiated Classroom."

Teachers also use small-group learning and specific activities to help students develop skills and master learning objectives. Content materials written at simpler reading levels, graphic organizers, and materials with multisensory components appeal to, and are more appropriate for, less able students. Many teachers also create learning centers at which students can work on specific skills. Additional strategies include varied time allotments, supplementary print resources, and varied computer programs.

## Differentiating by Readiness with Technology

In the last few years, skills practice software and online learning sites have become readily available as new tools for learning and practice. Recent software programs such as Splish Splash Math, Earobics, StudyDog, and similar interactive programs help students work with content as they build skills in a fun and motivating way. Multimedia software programs and online skills-building sites personalize learning and can help struggling students master core skills and achieve significant gains. Online sites offer opportunities for more able students to explore content in depth and investigate topics of interest.

Table 5.1 shows some examples of the plethora of software and online learning tools currently available. Depending on the readiness of the student, the product may be appropriate for reinforcing concepts or challenging skills. The resources section at the end of this chapter includes Web sites for learning about these tools.

TABLE **5.1** ■ Software and online learning tools

| | K–2 | 3–5 |
|---|---|---|
| **Language Arts** | Earobics | Book Central |
| | The Literacy Center | FactMonster Biographies |
| | StudyDog | Make Your Own Book |
| | World Build and Bank | Merriam-Webster Word Central |
| **Math** | Ghost Blasters | Are You a Math Magician? |
| | Speed Grid Subtraction Challenge | Mad Math Minutes |
| | Splish Splash Math | That's a Fact: Math Facts |
| | Understanding Numeration | Understanding Math |
| **Social Studies** | Ben's Guide to U.S. Government | Geography Search |
| | Harriet Tubman and the Underground RR | Plimoth 1621 |
| | Neighborhood Map Machine | TimeLiner |
| | White House Kids | Trades at Colonial Williamsburg |
| **Multiple Content** | 2Simple Software | BrainPop |
| | Game Goo Learning | Discovery Education *unitedstreaming* |

Many other resources and strategies are also available to assist us in our effort to differentiate content by interest. Let's turn now to differentiating content by the curricular element that's closest to our students' hearts: interest.

## Differentiating Content by Interest

Differentiating content by interest refers to topics students choose to explore because they're eager to learn about them. Differentiating by interest is the hook we can use to engage students in learning.

Below are some ideas for differentiating content by interest in your classroom. The resources section at the end of this chapter contains links for information about these strategies. Remember that we also investigated a few of the following strategies in greater detail in chapter 2, "Using Technology to Differentiate by Interest."

Fortunately, most students are eager to talk to us about their specific interests and are also willing to complete an interest survey or questionnaire. Two ready-to-go student-interest surveys are available at the University of Connecticut Web site.

If I Ran the School is a primary interest inventory while the Interest-A-Lyzer is a short survey designed to help students think about and focus their interests. Although the Interest-A-Lyzer is geared toward older students, you could make a similar version for upper elementary students. Links to these tools are available in the Resources section at the end of the chapter.

Once you've received feedback from your students about their interests using a simple conversation or one or more assessment surveys, you might choose to differentiate content by interest through one or more of the following appealing strategies.

## Interest Centers

In many elementary classrooms, the most familiar approach to differentiating by content is to set up interest centers in the classroom. Each interest center represents a physical space within the classroom and contains a variety of materials grouped together by interest or theme. Materials and activities in each center represent a wide range of skill levels and can be used independently, with a partner, or in a small group.

A math center, for example, might include manipulatives, books about famous mathematicians, a computer with math software, math puzzles, tools to draw mathematical patterns, math challenges and problem solving, and math games.

A publishing center might include a computer with word processing and desktop publishing software, a printer, writing and illustrating tools, books about famous writers, blank books, fancy paper for final products, a dictionary and thesaurus, and related materials.

**Add Tech!**

**Adding a computer to any interest center** offers learners the opportunity to use technology to create an artifact or to pursue their interests using software or the Web. You might include a list of WebQuests or sites geared to interest. In our district, we started a Web page called Curious Kids (www.gpschools.org/ci/depts/library/ckids.htm) and posted links based on Dewey decimal categories that students use in the library. Organizing the categories in this way helps to reinforce library skills.

We created another page called Reading Rocks! (www.gpschools.org/ci/depts/library/reading.htm) for kids who enjoy reading and learning more about their favorite authors. This page provides links to a variety of familiar authors and series.

We also designed a variety of bookmarks, football and Olympics reading incentives, and reading achievement awards. Many of these are available at www.everythingdi.net.

### I-Searches

I-Searches are investigative reports that students conduct on a particular topic. Students choose a topic and complete a KWL chart on the topic. From the L in the chart, students develop research questions and make a list of resources they'll use to find answers to their questions. Next, students research information, take notes, and organize their findings. Finally, students write about and report on the five phases of the process: 1) my questions, 2) my search process, 3) what I learned, 4) my skills as a researcher, and 5) references used in my report.

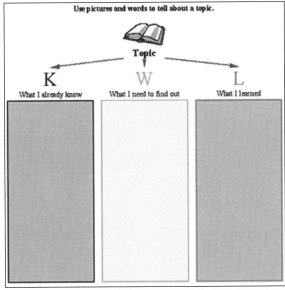

FIGURE **5.1** ■ Kidspiration software provides a ready-made KWL template that students can use for the I-Search process.

Diagram created in Kidspiration by Inspiration software. Reprinted with permission.

> **Add Tech!** **Adding a technology element** kicks I-Searches up a notch. Although I-Searches can be conducted using library materials, adding teacher-selected Web sites often increases learner motivation and enhances technology skills. We explored I-Searches in depth in chapter 2 and offered a sample lesson plan and profile page to familiarize you with this strategy.

### Online Explorations

Many Web sites are devoted to content that students want to investigate in more depth. You might consider developing a Web site or clickable document of URLs for kids to explore. The Curious Kids Web page lists a number of links children can explore. Many public libraries and museums also offer pages with topics of interest to children. Some of them are NGA Kids (www.nga.gov/kids/kids.htm), Matisse for Kids (www.artbma.org/education/matisse_kids_frame.html), and The Children's Museum of Indianapolis (www.childrensmuseum.org).

> **Add Tech!** Creating a starter list of links for kids to explore starts them off in the right direction and enhances their tech quest for knowledge. You can create a list of online links by typing them into a Web page, a Word or PowerPoint document, Kidspiration/Inspiration, or any software that allows hyperlinks.

The Kids Zone at the El Paso Public Library (www.elpasotexas.gov/kidszone/ kidszone_library/index.htm) is one of the best kid-friendly sites we've seen. Check out its spectacular, engaging graphics, and take at look at the Cool Sites and Games & Activities sections for ideas for your own list. Children's librarian and artist for the Kids Zone, Laurel Lynn Indalecio, offers insight into her design. She says, "I came up with the dinosaur theme because, hey…dinosaurs are just cool. In public libraries, dinosaurs have remained one of the most requested subjects over time. I wanted the home page image to show a library that looked fun…a parent reading to a child, toys, a computer, etc. The mountains in the background are the Franklin Mountains. The star on the mountain actually exists in lights and is turned on at least half of the year in the evenings. The landmark is instantly recognizable to the children of El Paso."

**FIGURE 5.2** ■ El Paso Public Library's Kids Zone page invites readers in with engaging graphics.

Graphics and Web site maintained by Laurel Lynn Indalecio for the El Paso, TX Public Library. Reprinted with permission.

### Software

Thousands of K–5 software programs have been developed for computers, the Internet, and handheld tools. How do you separate the wheat from the chaff? We like to use the *Children's Technology Review* (subscription-based) resources; the Codie educational software awards; Tech Learning reviews; and the California Learning Resources Network (CLRN), a free resource that requires registration. Codie award winners for 2005 included netTrekker, Kidspiration 2, Inspiration 7.5, and Thinking Reader. Award winners for 2006 included FASTT Math, Kidspiration 2.1, and netTrekker d.i.

netTrekker d.i. is an award-winning search engine for schools. Teachers and students can access more than 180,000 educator-selected online resources organized by readability level and aligned with state standards. Each resource has been assigned a readability measure based on Lexile ratings and other readability methods. A section of netTrekker d.i. resources is dedicated to teaching English as a second language. A dictionary/translation hot key is available to find the definition or translation for any word selected on a Web site. The Multicultural Pavilion offers resources on many different cultures. One of the coolest features is Read Aloud. Read Aloud allows text-to-speech functions for all information on netTrekker d.i. pages, text on Web resources accessed from any search result, and definitions accessed by using the Dictionary Hot Key. You can learn more about netTrekker d.i. by visiting www.nettrekker.com.

**FIGURE 5.3** ■
The netTrekker search engine for schools offers access to more than 180,00 educator-selected online resources.

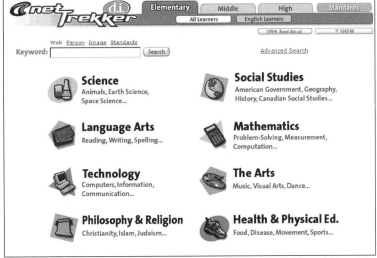

## WebQuests and Similar Projects

Another way to differentiate content by interest is to find or create a WebQuest that complements students' interests. WebQuests are interactive, interest- or research-driven tasks completed by teams or individuals who use the Web. Students often assume a specific role (scribe, historian, leader, and so forth) and work together to complete a product. San Diego State University hosts a WebQuest portal and offers the new QuestGarden, a free authoring tool (http://webquest.sdsu.edu). Detailed information about WebQuests also appears in chapter 2, "Using Technology to Differentiate by Interest," along with a sample lesson plan and a profile page.

> **Add Tech!**
>
> **If WebQuests aren't your specialty,** then create an original scavenger hunt or computer-related activity that intrigues kids. Maybe it's a mystery or a puzzle to solve. Maybe it's a historical event for students to interpret. Whatever you can do to enhance learning in a fun way will be popular and well regarded. Education World has an archive of Internet Hunts available at www. education-world.com/a_lesson/archives/hunt.shtml.
>
> Time for Kids has a fine example at
>
> www.timeforkids.com/TFK/class/pdfs/2005F/050902_wr3.pdf

## Differentiating by Interest with Technology

If you haven't yet experimented much with using technology to help differentiate by interest, you'll be pleased to learn that it's very accommodating. You can implement some simple solutions immediately, such as adding a computer to interest centers.

Computers offer learners the opportunity to use technology to create an artifact or pursue their interests through software or the Web. Although research-based projects such as I-Searches can be conducted using library materials, adding teacher-selected Web sites often increases learner motivation and enhances technology skills. Creating a starter list of links for kids to investigate as a part of inquiry-based tasks (such as I-Searches) or online explorations (of content that really fascinates them) starts them off in the right direction and boosts their tech quest for knowledge.

Although WebQuests provide an excellent way to use technology to differentiate by interest, they may not be your specialty. Instead, create an original scavenger hunt or computer-related activity that intrigues kids. Maybe it's a mystery or a puzzle to solve. Maybe it's a historical event for students to interpret. Whatever you can do to enhance learning in a fun way will be popular and well regarded.

## Differentiating Content by Learning Profile

Finally, we need to think about differentiating content by learning profile. All of our students come to us with unique backgrounds, learning styles, and preferences. As we endeavor to communicate key concepts and core material to them, differentiating according to learning profile is an essential and effective tool.

Students' learning profiles indicate their preferred method of learning. Teachers also have a preferred teaching and learning style, which may not be compatible with the preferred learning style of every student in their classroom. However, strategies can be used to reach students who don't match your style.

For example, we can provide information visually and orally to students by using PowerPoint slides, transparencies, or flip charts. We can create graphic organizers and diagrams to aid visual-spatial learners. We can create raps or songs to emphasize key points and offer multiple texts and resources to help students learn. We can share information by printed text, by digital text, by pictures and videos, by music, and by field trips. Finally, we can offer content that appeals to and strengthens the multiple intelligences.

Video streaming is one of the newest implementations of technology-driven content that appears to improve student learning. Discovery Education *unitedstreaming,* one of the largest providers, is a digital video-on-demand and online teaching service with videos aligned with U.S. and Canadian standards. Offering a collection of more than 50,000 video segments from among 5,000 full-length educational videos by award-winning producers, the company adds more than 1,000 new titles each year. Two recent research studies show that students who receive instruction in math, social studies, and science aided by videos show an increase in achievement over those who do not. Details about the studies are available on the Discovery Education *unitedstreaming* Web site at www.unitedstreaming.com/home/why.cfm?id=3/.

Videos address several of the multiple intelligences, particularly visual, kinesthetic, and musical learners. Videos with closed captions also appeal to text-based learners or those with verbal-linguistic intelligence. They can enhance classroom instruction by visually demonstrating an abstract concept or bringing history and literature to life through stirring reenactments.

| **Add Tech!** | The Multiple Intelligences and Technology Web site created by your authors (www.everythingdi.net) offers content and practice sites based on each of the intelligences. This site offers links for students of varying levels, interests, and learning profiles. Students can explore sites related to their strengths as well as investigate those that are less familiar. |
|---|---|

## Differentiating by Learning Profile with Technology

You've probably realized that combining multiple intelligences with technology is one of your authors' favorite ways to focus on students' unique learning profiles. The Multiple Intelligences and Technology site created by your authors (www.everythingdi.net) offers content and practice sites based on each of the intelligences. This site offers links for students of varying levels, interests, and learning profiles. Students can explore sites related to their strengths as well as investigate those that are less familiar We've also prepared a quick list to guide you in your attempt to encourage students to use technology that supports the multiple intelligences.

Now that you've upgraded your understanding of differentiating content by readiness, interest, and learning profile, let's view a sample lesson plan that includes technology to help differentiate content-based tasks. Since many states require the study of state history in Grade 4 or 5, in addition to the development of narrative skills in the genre of legends and tall tales, we elected to incorporate both into our lesson plan.

## Differentiating Content by Readiness, Interest, and Learning Profile with Technology

The Stretch-a-Long Michigan Tall Tale lesson plan integrates technology with language arts. Depending on your state's grade level content expectations, social studies standards may also apply. While the sample plan employs a tall tale from Michigan, a similar story from any state can be used.

This plan differentiates content and uses technology in the following ways:

### Readiness

- The plan makes use of varied text and resource materials, including Web-based resources rather than textbook resources.
- Tall tale examples can be matched to students' reading levels.
- Organizers can create structure for less able students.

### Interest

- Students can choose individual ways of expressing their tall tale.
- The Word document for creating the tall tale is a new form for expressing tall tales.

### Learning Profile

- Students can select Web, library, or other materials for gathering examples and ideas.
- Students can select organizers or take notes for creating their own tall tale.
- Students can select how they wish to create the head and feet of their tall tale.

## Lesson Plan

### *Stretch-a-Long Michigan Tall Tale*

| | |
|---|---|
| **Grade** | 4/5 |
| **Subject Area** | Language Arts |
| **Curriculum Standards** | **Language Arts (Writing) Standards (State of Michigan ELA Standards based on NCTE) addressed:**<br><br>W.GN.04.01: write a cohesive narrative piece such as a myth, legend, fantasy, or adventure creating relationships among setting, characters, theme, and plot.<br><br>W.PR.04.05: proofread and edit writing using appropriate resources (e.g., dictionary, spell check, grammar check, grammar references, writing references) and grade-level checklists, both individually and in groups.<br><br>W.GN.05.01: write a cohesive narrative piece such as a mystery, tall tale, or historical fiction using time period and setting to enhance the plot, demonstrating roles and functions of heroes, anti-heroes, and narrator; and depicting conflicts and resolutions.<br><br>W.PR.05.05: proofread and edit writing using grade-level checklists and other appropriate resources, both individually and in groups.<br><br>**National Educational Technology Standards for Students (NETS•S) addressed:** (see appendix for full list)<br><br>1. Creativity and Innovation: 1.a., 1.b.<br>2. Communication and Collaboration: 2.a., 2.b.<br>3. Research and Information Fluency: 3.a., 3.b., 3.c., 3.d.<br>4. Critical Thinking, Problem Solving, and Decision Making: 4.b.<br>6. Technology Operations and Concepts: 6.b. |
| **Lesson Summary** | 1. In this lesson, students create original tall tales with settings in Michigan.<br>2. Students write their tall tales, proofread and edit them with a partner, and then enter their stories in column format into a word processing document.<br>3. After proofreading and making revisions with their partner, students print a final document.<br>4. Next, students cut the columns apart and tape or glue them together as a single column (to make a "long" tall tale).<br>5. Using construction paper and crayons or markers, students create and add the head and feet of the tall tale's main character. Students write the title of the tall tale and their name on the character's feet. These very tall tales can then be hung in the classroom for students to read. |
| **Materials** | ■ Proofreading or editing pencils<br>■ Original tall tale<br>■ Construction paper<br>■ Glue or glue stick and transparent tape<br>■ Crayons or colored markers |

*continued*

## Stretch-a-Long Michigan Tall Tale   (continued)

| Web Resources | **Michigan History and Geography Resource Links** | |
|---|---|---|
| | Kids' Stuff from the Michigan Historical Museum: Choose Settling a State, Lumbering, or Rural Michigan 1865–1900 | www.michigan.gov/hal/0,1607,7-160----,00.html |
| | Michigan History for Kids | www.michiganhistorymagazine.com/kids/mag_topics.html |
| | Where Is the Green Gold? | http://americanepic.org/greengold/GreenGoldFlash1.html |
| | Lumbering in Michigan | www.michiganepic.org/lumbering/lumbering.html |
| | Michigan Cities and Towns | www.merriam-Webster.com/cgi-bin/nytmaps.pl?michigan |
| | **Proofreaders' Checklists and Symbols** | |
| | Correcting and Proofreading Checklist | www.teachers.net/gazette/JUL03/images/proofreading.pdf |
| | Proofreading Checklist | www.ettc.net/writing/PDFfiles/Proofreading Checklist.pdf |
| | Common Proofreading Symbols | http://wwwold.ccc.commnet.edu/writing/symbols.htm |
| | Common Proofreading Symbols | www.geocities.com/fifth_grade_tpes/Proof.html |
| | **Tall Tales Examples Online** | |
| | Great American Tall Tales | www.turner.k12.ga.us/users/tholmes/tales.html |
| | Michigan Folktales | http://americanfolklore.net/folktales/mi2.html |
| | Paul Bunyan | www.paulbunyantrail.com/talltale.html |
| | Paul Bunyan | www.animatedtalltales.com/en/paulb/thanks.php |
| | Pecos Bill | http://pbskids.org/lions/pecos/ |
| | State and Regional Folktales | www.americanfolklore.net/ss.html |
| | Tall Tales Arizona Style | www.kyrene.k12.az.us/schools/brisas/sunda/talltale/talltale.htm |
| | **Tall Tales Writing Tools** | |
| | Tall Tales Checklist | http://artsedge.kennedy-center.org/content/2267/2267_talltales_checklist.pdf |
| | | www.kent.k12.wa.us/curriculum/tech/K6/3/tall_tales/unit_plan_3talltales.doc |
| | Tall Tales T-Chart | www.readwritethink.org/lesson_images/lesson327/chart.pdf |
| | Tall Tales Writing Rubric | www.readwritethink.org/lesson_images/lesson327/rubric.pdf |
| **Prewriting Activities** | Students will have previously read some examples of tall tales and learned how to write similes. | |
| | Students will be familiar with word processing software and know how to use Web links. Students will know how to use MS Paint or another graphic design program. | |

*continued*

## *Stretch-a-Long Michigan Tall Tale* (continued)

**Lesson Activities**

### Lesson 1: Pre-Assessment and Prewriting

1. Discuss tall tales. Ask students to describe how tall tales got started. (Settlers in the wilderness made up stories to pass the time and exaggerated the stories to "one-up" each other.) Name some famous tall tale characters (Paul Bunyan, Pecos Bill, and so forth).

2. Pre-assess students (or discuss with the class) using the vocabulary terms (see Key Vocabulary for Language Arts section). The key point is to determine students' familiarity with the characteristics of tall tales.

3. Ask students to brainstorm (prewrite) a tall tale that takes place in Michigan during pioneer days or another time. Students can use the Web sites, their social studies textbook, or library resources for ideas.

4. Ask students to use the Tall Tales Activity Sheet or take notes to list the characteristics and the special powers of the main character, such as superhuman strength, speed, or intelligence. Think about some problems the main character can solve by using special powers. List the events in the tall tale in order.

### Lesson 2: Drafting and Revising

1. Ask students to look at their list of the main character's characteristics and special powers in the Tall Tales Activity Sheet.

2. Ask students if they have exaggerated their main character's characteristics and special powers enough. Have they really stretched out the exaggerations? Ask students to think of some juicy similes to describe their main character.

3. Ask students to write their draft and share it with a partner. If students are having trouble, use a fill-in-the-blanks paragraph to start off the first paragraph and then continue writing. (Note: There's an example of a fill-in-the-blanks story at www.hasd.org/Faculty/DHietpas/Index.htm#writeatale/)

### Lesson 3: Create a Tall Tale Document in Word Processing Program (Create the steps as a handout, or project the steps on the wall for students to follow as you walk through them.)

1. Open a blank document in Microsoft Word.

2. Choose Page Setup from the File menu.

3. Select the Margins tab.

4. Set 0.5 for the top, bottom, left, and right margins.

5. Go to the Format menu and click Columns.

6. Click 3 Columns.

7. Choose Verdana or another font specified by the teacher.

8. Change your font size to 16.

9. Type the tall tale and spell-check it.

10. Save the document and print it.

*continued*

## Stretch-a-Long Michigan Tall Tale   *(continued)*

| | |
|---|---|
| **Lesson Activities** *(continued)* | **Lesson 4: Proofread, Edit, and Construct**<br><br>1. Ask students to proofread their tales and make any changes. (You may want students to proofread and make changes to printed copies first.)<br>2. Ask students to work with a partner to proofread their partner's tale.<br>3. Ask students to make revisions to their document.<br>4. Ask students to revise and then print a final copy and carefully cut the columns apart.<br>5. Ask students to carefully tape or glue the columns together to make a "long" tale.<br>6. Ask students to create a head and feet (to match the description of the main character) out of construction paper and crayons or colored markers.<br>7. Glue the head and feet to each end of the tale. Students may also use "magazine" heads, Paint-created heads and feet, three-dimensional products, yarn, and other means of expression.<br>8. Ask students to write the title of their tale and their name on the feet.<br><br>**Lesson 5: Tall Tales Celebration!**<br><br>1. As a culminating activity, students share their tall tales with other students (or circulate them round-robin).<br>2. Students read others' tales. (Optional: Write comments to the author and clip them onto the back of the tall tale.)<br>3. Students self-reflect on the tall tale process.<br>4. Students take the post-assessment. |
| **Differentiation/ Extension** | ■ More capable students who know basic computer skills can expand any assignment beyond the requirements.<br>■ Less capable students may be paired with a more capable student. |
| **Technology Activity Options** | ■ If computers must be shared, pair students to work on activities.<br>■ If a lab is available, students should organize their notes ahead of time and prioritize their time in the lab. |
| **Evaluation** | **Pre-Assessment**<br><br>Pre-assess the class using the vocabulary terms (see Key Vocabulary for Language Arts section). The key point is to determine students' familiarity with tall tales terminology.<br><br>**Scoring Criteria**<br><br>Use 10 vocabulary terms. If you choose to record the pre-assessment, each right answer counts as 10 points. Adjust the rubric below to fit the selected theme and students' skill levels. Use your current grading scale to determine a letter grade.<br><br>**Post-Assessment**<br><br>1. Use the same pre-assessment to determine what students have learned.<br>2. In addition, if necessary, modify the rubric below to fit more closely with the tall tale theme. Use the rubric to assess the final product.<br>3. Students self-reflect on their experience in producing a tall tale in their learning log or in a written paragraph. (Alternate: Group discussion.) |

*continued*

## *Stretch-a-Long Michigan Tall Tale* (continued)

| | |
|---|---|
| **Key Vocabulary for Language Arts** | **Audience**—The people most likely to be interested in your writing. |
| | **Character**—A person in a story. |
| | **Description**—Writing that paints a picture of a person, place, thing, or idea. |
| | **Exaggeration**—Making something or someone greater or bigger than it really is; words that stretch the truth. |
| | **Narrator**—The person or character telling the story. |
| | **Protagonist**—The hero or heroine of the story. |
| | **Setting**—The time and place of the story. |
| | **Simile**—A figure of speech that makes a comparison using the words like or as. |
| | **Storyteller**—the person who tells, or narrates, a story. |
| | **Tall Tale**—A story with a superhuman main character who solves a problem in a funny way. Details are exaggerated to describe things and people as greater than they really are. |
| **Key Vocabulary for Technology used in this lesson** | Blank document |
| | Columns |
| | Copy/Paste |
| | File menu |
| | Font |
| | Format |
| | Insert |
| | Margins |
| | Page setup |
| | Spelling checker |

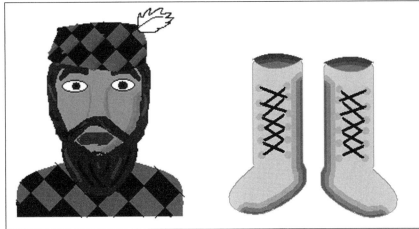

FIGURE **5.4** ■
**Paul Bunyan head and feet, created for the Tall Tale lesson by a fifth grade student**

Created by Kamala K.

TABLE **5.2** ■ Michigan Tall Tale rubric

| | Excellent 4 | Good 3 | Developing 2 | Beginning 1 |
|---|---|---|---|---|
| **Appeal to the Audience** | The tall tale has exceptionally attractive formatting and well-organized information. | The tall tale has attractive formatting and well-organized information. | The tall tale has well-organized information. | The tall tale's formatting and organization of material are confusing to the reader. |
| **Head and Feet (Construction Paper)** | Head and feet go well with the tall tale.\n\nThe title and author's name are listed on the feet. | Head and feet go well with the tall tale.\n\nThe title and author's name are listed on the feet, but there's a misspelled word. | Head and feet go well with the tall tale.\n\nAuthor's name or title is missing from the feet. | Head and feet do not go well with the tall tale.\n\nAuthor's name or title is missing from the feet. |
| **Exaggeration** | The tall tale has three or more exaggerations. | The tall tale has two exaggerations. | The tall tale has one exaggeration. | The tall tale has no exaggeration. |
| **Spelling** | There are no spelling errors. | There are one to two spelling errors. | There are three to four spelling errors. | There are five or more spelling errors. |
| **Writing: Grammar** | There are no grammatical mistakes in the tall tale. | There are one to two grammatical mistakes in the tall tale. | There are three to four grammatical mistakes in the tall tale. | There are five or more grammatical mistakes in the tall tale. |
| **Writing: Mechanics** | Capitalization and punctuation are correct throughout the tall tale. | There are one to two capitalization and punctuation errors in the tall tale. | There are three to four capitalization and punctuation errors in the tall tale. | There are five or more capitalization and punctuation errors in the tall tale. |
| **Technology Skills** | Technology tasks are correct throughout the tall tale. | There are one to two technology errors, such as incorrect revisions, misaligned text, or no spacing between paragraphs. | There are three to four technology errors, such as incorrect revisions, misaligned text, or no spacing between paragraphs. | There are five to six technology errors, such as incorrect revisions, misaligned text, or no spacing between paragraphs. |

## Tall Tales Activity Sheet

| Category | Who/What | Description/Characteristics |
|---|---|---|
| **Narrator**<br>**(Who is telling the story?)** | | |
| **Main Character** | | |
| **Location/Place in Michigan** | | |
| **Year/Time of Year** | | |
| **Other Characters** | | |
| **First Exaggeration** | | |
| **Second Exaggeration** | | |
| **Third Exaggeration** | | |
| **Conclusion** | | |

Remember the analogy of the "infotainment" center from the introduction to this chapter? We're confident that your Content Infotainment Center is now brimming over with resources and aids—particularly tech-enhanced ones—that you can access to help students make sense of the content before them. Since you know and understand your students' interests, levels of readiness, and learning profiles—the three student traits—you are best equipped to effectively differentiate content for them.

Experiment with some of the strategies we've reviewed in this chapter to differentiate content, using the three student traits, as well as technology, during the differentiation process. Although teachers still ultimately choose the content that's communicated to students, the "shelves" that we draw from provide a number of appealing means to assist students in their effort to take ownership of that content. Are some shelves in your Content Infotainment Center dusty from lack of use? We challenge you to clear the "cobWebs" and share the treasure!

## Resources for Chapter 5

| | | |
|---|---|---|
| **Content Tools Based on Readiness** *These Web sites and software may be helpful in determining students' readiness.* | Are You a Math Magician? | http://oswego.org/ocsd-Web/games/mathmagician/maths1.html |
| | Compactor | www.gifted.uconn.edu/siegle/CurriculumCompacting/section7.html |
| | Earobics | www.earobics.com |
| | Game Goo | www.earobics.com/gamegoo/gooey.html |
| | Ghost Blasters Mathhtml | www.oswego.org/ocsd-Web/games/Ghostblasters1/gbcd. |
| | The Literacy Center | www.literacycenter.net/lessonview_en.htm# |
| | Mad Math Minutes | http://staff.wssd.k12.pa.us/awillis/games/math.htm |
| | | http://www.mrsbogucki.com/aemes/resource/apps/madmath/ |
| | Speed Grid Subtraction Challenge | www.oswego.org/ocsd-Web/games/SpeedGrid/Subtraction/ urikasub1res.html |
| | Splish Splash Math | www.swexpress.com/home.nsf/tit_www_cat!readform&RestrictTo Category=Math+-+Basic+Skills |
| | StudyDog Reading | www.famlit.org/studydog/ |
| | That's a Fact | www.harcourtschool.com/activity/thats_a_fact/english_K_3.html |
| | TimeLiner | www.tomsnyder.com/products/productextras/TIMV50/ |
| | Trades at Colonial Williamsburg | www.history.org/Almanack/life/trades/tradehdr.cfm |
| | 2Simple Software | www.2simple.com |
| | World Build and Bank | www.readwritethink.org/materials/wordbuild/ |
| **Content Tools Based on Interest** *These Web sites are great for helping students explore their interest* | Children's Museum of Indianapolis | www.childrensmuseum.org |
| | Curious Kids | www.gpschools.org/ci/depts/library/ckids.htm |
| | El Paso Public Library Kids Zone | www.elpasotexas.gov/kidszone/kidszone_library/ |
| | Interest Surveys at UConn | www.gifted.uconn.edu/siegle/CurriculumCompacting/section11.html |
| | KidsClick! | http://sunsite.berkeley.edu/KidsClick!/ |
| | Matisse for Kids | www.artbma.org/education/matisse_kids_frame.html |
| | NGA Kids | www.nga.gov/kids/kids.htm |
| | QuestGarden and the WebQuest Page (requires a nominal fee to build WebQuests) | http://Webquest.sdsu.edu |
| **Content Tools Based on Learning Profile** *These Web sites offer help with assessing multiple intelligences.* | Discovery Education *unitedstreaming* | www.unitedstreaming.com |
| | Multiple Intelligences software ideas | www.chariho.k12.ri.us/curriculum/MISmart/MISoftwr.html |
| | Multiple Intelligences Survey | www.lvarv.org/el-civics/More EE PDF Files/Intros/MISurvey.pdf |
| | Multiple Intelligences and Technology | www.everythingdi.net |
| | Printable form for recording students' intelligences by category | www.ncwiseowl.org/kscope/techknowpark/LoopCoaster/MIRecord.html |
| | SurfAquarium | http://surfaquarium.com/MI/ |
| | Technologies by Intelligence | http://surfaquarium.com/mediaselection.pdf |
| | *unitedstreaming* Student Achievement Research | www.unitedlearning.com/streaming/evaluation.cfm?id=315 |

## CHAPTER 6

# Using Technology *to* Differentiate *by* Process

Teachers of today are multifaceted professionals, and we always have been. It's no secret that we wear many hats as we serve in our classrooms. Some of the hats you might wear are actor, counselor, coach, orchestra conductor, cheerleader, guide, or parent. It's fairly common to hear colleagues talk about the different roles we fill as we share classroom experiences and strategies.

As we think about differentiating by process, we encourage you to add another metaphor to your understanding of a teacher's role: a bridge. Read this inspirational quote from Marion Shumway, written when she was a teaching assistant at Brigham Young University:

> *In my experience as a teaching assistant in organizational behavior, I have often felt much like a bridge. I feel a responsibility to support unsteady travelers and to provide passage into previously unexplored realms. Although I do not minimize the responsibility of the student in the learning process, I do feel, as a bridge, the weight of the responsibility to not "turn around" (Shumway, 1993, Summer, p. 4).*

In this chapter, we offer strategies for using technology to differentiate by process, the "bridge" between content (input) and product (output). We'll examine Cubing, ThinkDots (a cousin to Cubing), and Flexible Grouping, and we'll offer some technology resources to support these strategies in the classroom. Before we investigate the specifics of these strategies, let's review the basics of differentiation by process.

# Differentiating by Process

To differentiate by process, teachers use sense-making activities with students to enable comprehension of content. Differentiating by process involves giving students opportunities to explore key concepts that constitute an essential part of the input side of the equation (content). As we mentioned above, it's helpful to think of process as a bridge.

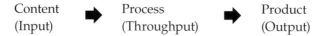

Content (Input) → Process (Throughput) → Product (Output)

Differentiation by process gives our students the chance to come to grips with the material they've been learning—to play with it, twist it, experiment with it, and test it. The activities that you design as a part of the process phase offer possibilities to manipulate the content in such a way that allows students to take ownership of the material. As students grasp the core material, they begin to make progress across the bridge to their destination, the output side. When learners engage in cooperative activities, they, too, become bridges that support one another along the path to learning.

We can differentiate by process according to each of the three student traits that guide DI. First, differentiating process according to student interest provides for student choice about facets of a topic on which to focus and facilitates a link between a personal interest and a sense-making goal. Jigsaw and interest groups or centers are effective ways to differentiate process by interest, and we examined those in chapters 2 and 5. Literature circles are another popular means to differentiate process by interest, and we'll discuss them in this chapter.

Differentiating process according to student learning profile means helping students make sense of an idea in a preferred way of learning (visually, kinesthetically, by means of multiple intelligences, and so forth). In chapter 4, our lesson plan illustrated how students could choose and use technology activities based on a multiple intelligences Tic-Tac-Toe Board for the study of Colonial America.

When we differentiate process according to student readiness, we match the complexity of an activity or task to a student's current level of skill and understanding. Tiering (or tiered assignments), which we investigated in chapter 3, allows us to vary the depth of a lesson and to permit multiple options for adjustment or customization of a lesson or activity.

You may already differentiate by process in your classroom using flexible groups, because this strategy is quite popular in elementary classrooms. However, we don't want to overlook the importance of this cornerstone of collaborative learning in the DI classroom just because it seems so familiar to us. Therefore, in this chapter, we'll revisit flexible grouping because it's so vital to DI's success.

We'll then move on to Cubing and ThinkDots. If you're well versed in these strategies, feel free to go directly to the profile pages to review the basics, and then turn to the sample lesson at the end of the chapter.

## Differentiating by Process Using Flexible Groups

During my years of classroom experience, I (Stephanie) have been kidnapped by pirates, lived in a jungle hut, become the queen of an imaginary country, and won the World Cup (for women's soccer). These are just a few of the comical events that students chose to write about as they penned my biography over the years as part of a flexible group assignment driven by student choice.

I've often used this assignment to help my students gain a better understanding of the preterit and imperfect tenses in Spanish. Students choose their own groups, and each group creates its particular version of my biography. When all groups are finished, I redistribute the documents to other groups for peer editing without revealing the writers' identities, and I look them over to correct errors that might impede comprehension.

Once the groups have prepared their final drafts, I pass them out again to students in other groups and read them aloud to the class, still keeping the writers' identities secret. Then I post them, coded by number, in an area of the classroom or sometimes in the hallway or on a class Web site so that students can vote for their favorite biography. The winning group gets some sort of Spanish-related prize or a treat with me, such as an ice cream cone at our student union.

It's a fun exercise with many laughs, and the students learn even more about the preterit and imperfect because they're thrilled to have the chance to invent outrageous stories about their instructor.

If you're an experienced teacher, we're certain that some of your flexible grouping assignments have brought positive results similar to those described above. If you're a preservice teacher, anticipate some exciting outcomes in your classroom as you put this great strategy to work! Flexible grouping is a more recent term for arranging students into teams according to their interests, readiness levels, and learning profiles, or by random selection or student choice. Grace has a number of very practical group tasks that she's used over the years that involve one or more curricular areas. We'll share them with you later in this chapter.

Perhaps the greatest advantage of using flexible groups (also called "cooperative groups" or "student teams") in your differentiated classroom is that learning goes beyond the mere academic. In a sense, these pairs, triads, and quads, or other small groups of varying size, mimic some of the social and work relationships that students will someday have to negotiate, and they allow them to practice future job-related skills. When students are on the job in the real world, they'll need to organize, evaluate, design, and manage their own responsibilities and plans. They must be able to negotiate and cooperate with others to accomplish shared goals whether they truly like the people that are a part of their teams or not. Flexibly grouped students learn how to solve problems and encourage others while they're actively taking ownership of content.

## Countdown to Powerful Flexible Grouping

Since flexible grouping is so critical to DI's success, let's take a few moments to examine two preliminary tasks we must complete to better prepare our students for this strategy. If your students aren't accustomed to flexible grouping, these activities will ease the transition and also help foster a spirit of community in your classroom.

### *Preliminary Task No. 1: Establishing Ground Rules*

You already know that differentiated instruction strategies are built on student choice and active involvement in the learning process. In the differentiated classroom, students also assist in the development of ground rules that govern behavioral expectations. Although guidelines for student conduct are not usually received with much enthusiasm, you might encounter a more favorable reaction because you're allowing students to participate in the process. Ground rules fend off problems and help provide an escape route when trouble starts. Due to the wide span of comfort levels, grade levels, and behaviors, ground rules will vary from one classroom to another.

When you and your students team up to create ground rules, you might want to use a computer and projector system to record the ground rules. If you don't have access to the necessary equipment, just write the rules on a flip chart or poster board and hang them in the classroom. Once they're complete, reorder them as needed and then print copies for the classroom and for each student. Student copies could be printed in checklist form using Word or another word-processing program. Some printers have a poster feature that allows for the printing of enlarged documents by section, which you could then glue or tape together and post in your classroom.

Following are some prompts you may use to guide your students toward the development of ground rules:

1. All ideas are valid.
2. Clean up after yourself.
3. All students participate.
4. Keep hands, feet, and objects to yourself.
5. Respect others by keeping quiet when they talk.
6. Listen to understand.

**7.** Do not interrupt.

**8.** Respect different viewpoints and be considerate.

**9.** Use school-appropriate language.

**10.** Move and work quietly.

### *Preliminary Task No. 2: Decision or Consensus Making*

Flexible grouping assignments cannot be realized if decision- or consensus-making skills are absent. Decision or consensus making is based on balance, mutual respect, and team building. While all group members have the chance to express their thoughts and opinions, everyone must agree to a final decision.

Before you work through the consensus-making process with students, you might choose to prepare a graphic organizer in mapping software, PowerPoint, Publisher, or Word, or print one from an Internet link. (See the Resources section.) If you don't have one in your classroom, request an Elmo or a computer and projector system for this exercise. In addition, you'll need to come up with a possible problem or opportunity with which your students can come to terms. See the vignettes at the Making Decisions: Grades 4–6 Web site (www.acde.org/educate/46plan2.htm) for fresh ideas.

If you haven't used decision or consensus making, or a similar technique, look over the sample steps we suggest here:

**1.** Introduce a problem or opportunity to students, such as whether school uniforms should be required of all students in your building.

**2.** Have students work through the problem or opportunity individually. Ask them to restate the problem or opportunity and record their options for resolving it in a graphic organizer of your choice. Make sure they also list the consequences of the options. It might be helpful to them to think in terms of pros and cons. Students might write about the fact that while uniforms eliminate their freedom to choose their own style of clothing they could also reduce the amount of money spent on clothes. Ask them to consider the principal's or school district's perspective.

**3.** Next, place the students into small groups to discuss their ideas with classmates. When students become more comfortable and capable, you may be able to omit the small group step and invite them to discuss their thoughts in a large-group setting. Then, have the whole class formulate a consensus decision.

**4.** Reiterate the problem or opportunity that necessitates a decision and present it on the board, a flip chart, an overhead transparency, a poster board, an Elmo projector, or a computer and projector.

**5.** List the different alternatives in the graphic organizer.

6. Ask students to enumerate various actions that can be taken. Record them in the organizer. Students will recognize absolute options, such as banning school uniforms or requiring them, but encourage them to generate possibilities that might allow for a compromise, such as wearing uniforms 4 days a week and having a free day on Fridays.

7. Consider how the different choices affect the participating students as well as those outside of the decision-making group. (What will happen to _____ if this choice is made?) Here, students can talk about how uniforms will not only affect them, but their parents and other students as well. They might mention that their parents won't have to spend as much money on school clothing if uniforms are mandated. They might think about whether there's fighting or jealousy between classmates as a result of the brand or style of clothing that some people have but others can't afford.

8. Lead the group to choose the option that's best for all.

9. Encourage the group to commit to the decision.

You may already be familiar with some standard learning group arrangements. If not, here are some possibilities you can try out in your classroom. Each group activity promotes collaboration among students and fosters decision and consensus building.

### Think-Pair-Share

Think-Pair-Share (or T-P-S) is a straightforward, uncomplicated technique you can use in any subject area. The teacher poses an open-ended or thought-provoking question. The students **think** independently (without raising hands) of a response and then pair with a classmate (nearby) to discuss responses. Finally, they share their responses with the whole class. (See the resources section for a blank T-P-S template and sample activity.)

### Literature Circles

In literature circles, students collaborate with one another during discussion of a common work of literature. These groups may be formed according to students' interest in a particular text or according to their levels of readiness, which would obviously impact the selection of the text.

They respond critically to the book through a conversation about characters, plot, setting, author's style, and, sometimes, how the novel relates to real life issues or experiences. Technology is easily incorporated into assignments correlated to literature circles. Students might use the Internet to research information about the author and the historical background of the plot or setting, or they might participate in an online collaborative project with other students who are across the globe. (See the Resources section at the end of the chapter for sample links.)

### *Job or Role Cards*

Job or role cards are extremely handy tools that benefit both the students and the instructor. When students work together in flexible groups, they must often fulfill a particular role. This is particularly true when students participate in WebQuests. How do students learn to execute the duties of their new job, especially when they're in the lower elementary grades?

As the teacher, you can either assign students a role or job or students can "draw" a role from a stack of laminated role cards. You might create your own role cards using Publisher, Word, or PowerPoint, or print them from an Internet site, such as Read•Write•Think's Team Member Job Cards (www.readwritethink.org/lesson_images/lesson218/jobcards.pdf).

Before students enact the role, model or explain each role so that students understand it, then describe what the job or role should include. In either case, students should have the opportunity to alternate roles so that they can carry out the responsibilities associated with each one. (See the resources section for sample sites.)

Once you believe your students are proficient in decision or consensus making and comfortable with the ground rules, move on to other flexible grouping strategies and combinations that are a little more complicated than the three listed above.

## Flexible Grouping Strategies and Combinations

A fairly simple way to set up groups rather quickly is to select groups at random. You could count off by number or use another arbitrary method, such as distributing cards or other manipulatives that invite students to search for partners or group members. You might also decide to give students the liberty to choose their group members based on friendships or other criteria.

Another alternative is to present a number of suitable options and let students determine their own mode of expression, interest area, or activity to be completed. I (Stephanie) often used this format with my Spanish students. When I teach a class in Spanish drama, novel, or short stories, occasionally I allow student groups to select among the following:

- a historical task (developing a timeline using Timeliner or another software or Web site that displays key events and figures during the time the piece was authored)

- a musical task (writing, performing, and recording a rap or some other type of song to help students recall important points)

- a performing/dramatic task (presenting a skit that might offer another conclusion to a play or presenting a significant dialogue or monologue from a novel or short story)

- a social/cultural task (synthesizing information about the sociocultural norms of the time in which the piece was written, and preparing a chart or table in Excel or Word for others to grasp major concepts)

- a visually artistic task (designing a mural or a set of character portraits, or building a scene from the text, perhaps using Paint)

- a writing task (creating poetry, a letter, or a diary or journal entry using Word or Publisher and writing from the protagonist's or antagonist's point of view)

Students appreciate the freedom to choose from a variety of options, and this format supplies a lot of creative ways to assimilate the material. You could simplify these tasks or adapt them for use in your own K–5 classroom with one of the core titles your students read.

Now let's take a deeper look at grouping students specifically by the three curricular elements: interest, learning profile, and readiness.

## Grouping Students by Interest

In order to deliberately group students by their **interests**, we have two major options:

**1.** sorting students by parallel interests

**2.** sorting students by unrelated interests

Flexible group tasks driven by interest can be formulated by content area (for example, literature, fine arts, technology, sciences) or mode of expression (artistic, written, oral, etc.).

When we put together a group of students with related interests, we give them a chance to carry out one or more tasks driven by their common passion. Related interest groups include specialty teams that investigate a topic, literature circles, and similar structures. When we establish a group of students with contrasting interests, our purpose might be to foster a multifaceted approach or multiple points of view. Contrasting interest groups are useful for debating controversial issues or national or world problems, or approaching a problem from different points of view.

## Grouping Students by Learning Profile

Arranging students by **learning profile** means that we consider our students' culture-influenced preferences, their gender-based preferences, and their learning styles. We also take into account our students' brain-based intelligences and use resources such as Sternberg's triarchic intelligences and Gardner's multiple intelligences. Once more, we have two basic choices:

1. grouping students who have comparable learning profiles

2. grouping students who have very disparate learning profiles

At times, we've found that students accomplish more when they're grouped with those who share similar preferences. It can also be advantageous to assemble groups of students with parallel learning profiles if they're working on similar projects, such as portfolios, slide shows, or booklets, or are charged with developing one aspect of a project or component that will later be combined with others. If we assign a task—a group presentation, for example—that requires several elements, such as multimedia, preparation of a classroom activity, visual aids, or written reports, we might decide to assemble groups of students with differing learning profiles.

## Grouping Students by Readiness

When we intentionally group students by **readiness**, our main alternatives are to

1. group students of the same level, or

2. group stronger students with weaker ones.

How do you decide when it's best to use one option over another? Advanced students who work with struggling students often take on a leadership role in the classroom. In addition, by explaining concepts to weaker students, stronger students may internalize their own knowledge and strengthen it. Struggling students benefit from one-on-one, personalized tutoring sessions from students who can explain concepts in a different way or style than the teacher's. Students at the same level who work together can help each other focus on the same topic or skill at a level that's appropriate for both.

## Sample Grouping Assignments that Link Content and Technology

I (Grace) have used flexible groups in language arts, art, social studies, reading, math, and technology classrooms. Here are some ideas for connecting flexible groups with content and technology:

### *Art or Foreign Language and Technology*

Divide students into pairs or triads as previously described, and assign or let students pick from a list of famous Hispanic personalities (artists, entertainers, athletes, historical figures, etc.). Students can produce biographical information about the legendary individual and a slide show gallery of the person's achievements, works, or contributions to history. Art teachers in our district use my slide show lesson to teach PowerPoint skills to third-graders.

FIGURE **6.1** ▪
Sample slide
created by
authors in
PowerPoint

**Variation:** Divide students into pairs or triads as previously described, and ask students to produce a slide show that's calendar based. For foreign languages, it might be as simple as designing a slide for each month, using clip art and key words associated with seasons, weather, and holidays. For art, students could select a famous artist's birthday for each month of the year. For each month, they could craft a slide with a picture, biographical information, and trivia about the artist who celebrates a birthday in that month. See Figure 6.1 for a sample PowerPoint slide in Spanish.

### Geography and Technology

Take digital pictures of a few neighborhood landmarks. Distribute the photos to students, who add the photos to their map in the correct locations.

**Variation:** Pair or triad the students as previously described. Each pair creates a map of their school or neighborhood using Paint, Publisher, or Neighborhood Map Machine.

### Language Arts and Technology

**Story Relay:** Prenumber each pair of students. Each pair is given 10 minutes to start a story and key it in. The first pair provides the title and places its pair number after the title. At the end of 10 minutes, students shift to the next computer and continue the story displayed on the screen. Each group adds its pair number after the previous pair's. At the end of 10 minutes, students shift again. The last group proofs the story, retitles it, ends it, and prints it. Depending on the age group, four to five shifts may be enough. After the marathon, the teacher collects the printed versions and duplicates them for distribution. In another session, each pair reads all the stories (optional: makes corrections) and votes for the winning story. The teacher polls the pairs and places votes on the board or overhead. The teacher or a student reads the winning story aloud to the class. [Note: Adjust time as needed.]

FIGURE **6.2** ■ Screenshot of a slide from 2Simple Software's 2Create A Story

Reprinted with permission of 2Simple Software, UK/2Simple USA Inc., USA.

**Variation:** Pair the students by interest, learning profile, readiness, or random pick. Each pair composes an original story and keys it into Word or Publisher, illustrates it using Paint or another graphic creator (or finds clip art), and prints and shares it with peers. Word or Publisher can be used to set up a booklet format.

**Primary Students:** A simplified version of this round-robin activity could be used with an appropriate software program such as 2Simple's 2Create A Story (www.2simpleusa.com). This software is a creativity program with virtual crayons and text windows. Its features include simple slide show capabilities, so an individual child or a pair of children could create one slide and a line of text, then move to the next computer in the same way described previously (Fig. 6.2).

### Math or Science and Technology

Pair or triad students as previously described and allow them to play the role of the teacher or peer tutor. Each group is responsible for writing a set of math "rules" or science truths or concepts that correspond to the unit you're studying. Students generate a slide show with an explanation of the rules or concepts and examples.

**Variation:** Each group produces a poster or slide show about a mathematician or scientist who made a significant contribution to the field of math or science. Offer a list of research topics, such as background, contribution, education, importance to the field, timeline, and related themes. This topic also works well with explorers and geographers.

### Reading or Math and Technology

Pair students to create booklets or PowerPoint slide shows with vocabulary or math problems or riddles.

**Variation:** Based on pre-assessment, each student uses software or online drills or games to practice or improve skills in a content area.

### Social Studies and Technology

Set up pairs as previously described. Assign a Revolutionary War landmark, historical figure, or artifact, or let each pair choose one from the proverbial hat. Students craft a bookmark in Paint, with a picture of their artifact, person, or landmark on one side and factual information about their topic on the other. You could do the same project with other wars or historical units.

**Variation:** Set up pairs or triads as previously described. Assign one of the 13 colonies or let each pair or triad choose a colony from the proverbial hat. Supply each group with a list of common research topics and have them develop a newsletter or slide show about their colony. You could do the same project with states or regions.

## Profile: *Flexible Grouping*

### Function

To challenge learners to take on new roles in work teams and to better prepare our students for relationships and cooperative projects in the real world.

### Advantages

- Aids in making sense of things through a small-group effort.
- Strengthens the classroom community through collaborative learning activities that enhance team-building skills and self-esteem.
- Permits differentiation by readiness, learning profile, and interest.
- Develops listening, research, planning, questioning, and presentation skills (depending on assignment).
- Reduces competitive element created by assignment of individual grades found in traditional classrooms.
- May be used across curricular areas.

### Possible Grouping Options

**1.** Random grouping by counting off by number or handing out matching cards or manipulatives to search for partner(s).

**2.** Grouping by student choice according to social or classroom working relationships students have formed.

**3.** Grouping by readiness into homogeneous groups (students at same level) or heterogeneous groups (mix of below-level, above-level, and at-level students).

4. Grouping by interest according to modes of expression (for example, artistic, oral, written) or interest areas (literature, fine arts, technology, sciences, etc.). Form homogeneous groups (learners share same interest area or modes of expression) or heterogeneous groups (learners have contrasting interests or modes of expression).

5. Grouping by learning profile into homogeneous groups (those with similar learning profiles) or heterogeneous groups (those with diverse learning profiles).

Baltimore County Public Schools offers some wonderful options for flexible grouping:

- Debate teams (exploring perspectives)

- Detective squads (problem solving)

- Integrative teams (linking learning to real-life experiences)

- Investigative clusters (alternative solutions)

- Mentor-guided teams (older students or volunteers)

- Performance teams (using arts)

- Supportive teams (building each others' skills)

- Tech-supported researchers (Internet research)

- Tournament teams (competitive)

The Baltimore County Public Schools' site has a superb document on differentiated instruction that can be viewed at www.bcps.org/offices/oit/ using techtodifferentiate/differentiatedinstruction.doc.

# Differentiating by Process
# Using Cubing and ThinkDots

Cubing and ThinkDots are related strategies that are extremely versatile and engaging. They both involve the use of a manipulative to perform tasks that "work out" their assignment. The ThinkDots strategy, developed by Kay Brimijoin, associate professor of education at Sweet Briar College in Virginia, is a spin-off of Cubing. While both fulfill the same function and share the same benefits and components, their physical formats differ slightly.

The term *Cubing* actually originates from a paper cube that students roll to work out their assignment. ThinkDots are six hole-punched cards joined together by a ring, yarn, string, or the like. Each card has a picture of one or more dots that correspond to the faces of a die (see Fig. 6.5). Instead of rolling a cube, students roll a die and complete the activity on the back of the card that matches the dot combination that appears on the face of the die.

Teachers often use a premade template for these strategies. Each face of the cube or back side of a ThinkDots card displays a different task, many of which involve a writing activity (see Fig. 6.6). These six key tasks encourage students to consider core concepts from six different perspectives. Task descriptions often contain a strong verb in the form of a command. We've compiled a list of possible suggestions you might use to describe your tasks. If you find some of the verbs are too complex for your K–5 students, just simplify them or choose some of the easier verbs.

**Describe It**

Example: Examine your topic closely and use descriptive words to tell about it. Name its shape, color, and size.

**Compare It**

Example: Is your topic similar to another? Is it different from another? Explain or give an example.

**Associate It**

Example: Does your topic remind you of something? It could be a feeling, a person, a place, or a thing.

**Analyze** It

Example: Identify the important parts of your topic.

**Apply It**

Example: What is the purpose of your topic? How can you use it?

**Argue For or Against It**

Example: Stand for or against your topic. Speak out in support of your topic or protest against it.

In the differentiated classroom, you may design different colored paper cubes for particular students or groups of students, as well as multiple variations of cards in a set of ThinkDots. The tasks on the cubes and cards are differentiated for individual students or groups based on interest, learning profile, or readiness.

To differentiate by interest or learning profile, create cubes or sets of cards, each of which has two or three identical faces. The remaining three or four faces could include tasks that correspond to dissimilar cognitive styles, interests, or multiple intelligences. For example, visual learners might draw a diagram or prepare a chart, while auditory learners might record a story or an interview. Students who are strong in verbal-linguistic intelligence might recite a poem, pen some riddles, or create a limerick. Learners who are passionate about history might complete tasks related to different time periods: ancient, medieval, Renaissance, Colonial, modern, and so forth.

To differentiate by readiness, you could prepare two or more different cubes or sets of cards with activities at varying levels of complexity. For example, perhaps you distribute orange cubes or cards to those who are at or below grade level in reading and writing, and purple cubes or cards to those who are above grade level in reading and writing. If you don't want to use colored paper, you could vary the color of the yarn you use to hold the cards together, or make only the dots a different color.

To physically prepare your students and your room for a ThinkDots or Cubing activity, organize the class in small groups at tables or desks with students who have cubes of the same color or identical card sets. You, the teacher, will first present a topic of focus. Students take turns rolling their cubes or dice, completing the tasks as they turn up. Tasks can be completed on a worksheet, on separate paper, or at a computer. If a roll turns up a task that they'd rather not do, you might give your students the option of "passing" on that task.

As students work on their tasks, you may decide to allow them to ask for help from their classmates. When the activity is over, you might ask students to share their ideas with the other members of their groups. Yet another alternative would be to use Cubing or ThinkDots as a review tool, in which one cube or set of cards is shared by a group of students. Each student has a turn to roll the cube or die and must complete the task that appears.

At first, it might seem that Cubing and ThinkDots don't maximize technology integration, perhaps because students manipulate a physical cube or card that is template-generated. However, you can easily design tasks that require technology-driven responses or products. Some examples are provided in the next section.

## Sample Cubing and ThinkDots Tasks that Link Content and Technology

Here are some ideas for connecting Cubing and ThinkDots with content and technology:

**Art:** Show the students a painting or other piece of art that will accommodate a discussion of some of the elements of art (the parts of a work that an artist plans; for example, color, value, line, shape, form, texture, and space), some of the principles of design (elements that help an artist plan his work and consider how the public might respond to it; for example, balance, contrast, proportion, pattern, rhythm, emphasis, unity, and variety), or a combination of the two.

Divide students into six groups and ask each group to talk about a particular element or principle, or both, of the painting, and then write their viewpoints using a word processing tool. Have each group make a short presentation of their perspectives to the class, and then have the class as a whole discuss the different perspectives.

**Foreign Language:** On the faces of each cube, type a different time of day or include pictures of differing clocks with a decipherable time. In addition, include a picture on the faces of each cube of 1) two people shaking hands, or of a handshake, to represent a greeting, or 2) of two people waving goodbye to one another, to represent a farewell.

Divide students into six groups and ask them to take at least one turn rolling the cube. (It doesn't matter if the same face of the cube appears more than once, because there are several phrases or words they may use to greet or take leave of one another.) Students must determine whether they have to generate a salutation or a goodbye based on the picture, and it must also be appropriate for the time of day that appears on the cube. They take turns recording their verbalizations of the farewells or greetings using RealPlayer or Sound Recorder (one of the accessories on most computers). Once the recordings have been completed, the group listens to them and decides whether each student's response matches the clues on the upturned face of the cube. (It's a good idea to have students identify themselves when recording.)

**Geography:** On the faces of each cube, write six landform terms. Divide the students into six groups and ask students to take one turn rolling the cube within their group. (Students roll again if their roll turns up a face revealing a term that has already appeared.)

FIGURE **6.3** ■
Sample image of a landform created by author in Paint

Students create a picture by hand, in Kid Pix or in Paint, to represent the landform that turns up on the face of the cube, and they must key in or write in the name of a concrete example of this landform (Fig. 6.3). After they've completed their pictures, they return to their groups, show the pictures, share the names of their landforms, and locate them on a map or globe. If you wish, you may paste their pictures to physical cubes, which can be hung in the classroom.

**Science:** This activity may be used to explore or review what a plant needs in order to grow.

On the faces of each cube, write six things a plant needs to grow. Divide the students into six groups and ask students to take one turn rolling the cube within their group. (Students roll again if their roll turns up a face revealing a topic that has already appeared.)

Students create a picture in Kid Pix or Paint to represent the plant's need that turns up on the face of the cube, and they may also key in a short textual explanation. After they've completed their pictures, they return to their groups, show the pictures, and explain why a plant must have that particular element to grow.

This activity may be modified and used with the life cycle of a plant or the parts of a plant.

**Social Studies and English Language Arts:** To focus more closely on the core democratic values of life and diversity, display a profound picture that shows children from another society or culture. Organize the students into six groups and ask each group to analyze the picture from one of the six points of view. Then ask groups to write their perspectives into a word processing document. Combine the six perspectives electronically or in printed form. Discuss the six perspectives with the whole group and ask each mini-group to share its perspective.

**Technology:** Show students a technical object (or a picture of one), such as a digital camera, MP3 player, electronic pointer, or scanner, and assign each student to one of six groups to chat and write their perspectives. Students might describe the function of the technical object or just report how and where they've seen someone using the object. Each group keys its perspective into a template. Next, print the combined templates for discussion and editing. To conclude, print and then paste each group's perspective of the technology object onto a physical cube, which is hung in the classroom.

Students usually respond quite positively to these strategies because they seem more like games than classroom work. Teachers are thrilled to find themselves in a neutral rather than oppositional position because the roll of the cube or the die determines the students' tasks for them. Cubing and ThinkDots work especially well across curricular areas and accommodate differentiation by each of the three curricular elements.

## Profile: *Cubing with ThinkDots Variation*

### *Function*

To empower students to consider a concept from several different viewpoints by means of a series of tasks, often writing based.

### *Advantages*

- Enables differentiation by readiness, interest, or learning profile.
- Removes teacher from oppositional (bad guy) position because students' tasks are determined by chance (roll of the cube).
- Provides opportunities for sharing with peers.
- Engages students in a physical activity that has game-like qualities they enjoy.
- May be used across curricular areas.

### *Components*

**A.** Identification of essential concept to be mastered.

**B.** Determination and description of key tasks students will perform.

**C.** Modification of tasks (designed in step 2 below) to enable differentiation and assignment of students to appropriate versions of the Cubing template.

**D.** Appropriate grouping of students by cube color in designated areas (at tables or clusters of desks).

  - Roll away!

### *Steps to Create a Cubing Activity*

**1.** For component A:

  - Choose an area of focus or review that's a part of your current unit of study (or a recent one).
  - Present a brief overview of the Cubing process so that students know how it works.

2. For component B:

- Create six tasks that provoke students to consider the essential concept from six unique perspectives.

- Start the written description of each task with a strong verb or command.

- Key description of tasks into a Cubing template (Fig. 6.4) as you prepare possible cubes for each group.

| *Cubing Template* | |
|---|---|
| Topic: | |
| Describe it | Compare it |
| Associate it | Analyze it |
| Apply it | Argue for or against it |

FIGURE **6.4** ■
Sample cubing
template

3. For component C:

- To differentiate by readiness, you could design two or more different cubes with tasks at varying levels of difficulty. For example, assign blue cubes to those who are above grade level in reading and writing and green cubes to those who are at or below grade level.

- To differentiate by interest or learning profile, you could create two or more different cubes, each of which has two or three identical faces. The remaining three or four faces could present tasks that correspond to differing interests, cognitive styles, or multiple intelligences. For example, students who are curious about history might have to develop a timeline using Time Liner software, examine a primary document at the National Archives site (www.archives.gov/historical-docs/), or write a journal or diary entry in Word as if they were living in a past era.

- Auditory learners might have to listen to an audio clip of a famous speech, interview, or song. A good resource is the Great Speeches section of History.com's Web site (www.history.com/media.do?action= listing&sortBy=1&sortOrder=A&topic=GREAT SPEECHES)

- Additionally, these learners would benefit from music CDs or a narrative of a story or poem, such as Janet S. Wong's stories and poems (www.janetwong.com/poems/index.cfm). Students who are strong in visual-spatial intelligence might have to draw a chart in Excel, graph or map in Graph Club or Map Maker's Tool Kit, or create a sketch using Paint.

- Cubing is a wonderful instrument for review. Each group shares a cube, and each student gets a turn to roll and answer the question that appears.

4. For component D:

- Circulate and assist students as they take part in the Cubing lesson.

- If desired, provide for a time of sharing of results within individual groups.

## Variation: ThinkDots Option

ThinkDots and Cubing are virtually identical strategies in terms of functions, advantages, components, and steps to follow. However, as mentioned previously, the ThinkDots strategy uses six hole-punched cards that are joined together by a ring, yarn, or string (or the like), and a die. Each card has a picture of one or more dots that correspond to the faces of a die. ThinkDots activities can be used in several ways and constructed according to readiness levels, learning styles, or interests.

To use a ThinkDots activity, each student (or pairs of students) is given a set of the ThinkDot cards and one die. Instead of rolling a cube, students roll a die and complete the activity on the back of the card that matches the dot combination that has appeared on the face of the die. Another variation is for students to complete any three short tasks.

ThinkDots sets can be constructed using a word processor. Here's how you set up your document.

1. Insert a table of two columns and three rows (portrait) or three columns and two rows (landscape).

2. In each cell on the front of the card, insert one dot on the first card, two dots on the second card, and so forth. You can use the black circles from the symbols menu and change the size to 36 or 40, using a font such as Comic Sans or Verdana.

3. Use the Enter and Space keys to move the dots to match the pattern of a die. You can also use the text alignment option, which can be found on the Tables and Borders toolbar, to align the dots within each cell.

4. For the back side of the cards, copy the table and paste it into page 2 of your document.

5. Move the dots to the top of each cell so that you have room to write the directions for each task in the table. Select the dots and change the size to 28.

6. If you're familiar with using tables in a word processor, you can try inserting a table in Publisher and using a circle autoshape for the dots. Once you get the size you want, fill a dot with color and copy it to make the correct number of dots in each cell.

7. You can color code ThinkDots if you use the circle autoshape in either Word or Publisher. You can also purchase colored dots in an office supply store and affix them to your cards before laminating. Color coding dots is helpful for grouping students by readiness.

8. Print and assemble the two pages of your document with the printed sides facing out. Laminate the cards and cut them into six sections.

9. Use a hole punch to make holes in the top left corner of each card. Place the six cards on a metal or plastic ring to make a set.

10. Some teachers like to make an activity sheet that corresponds with the ThinkDots cards. Activity sheets are useful for short tasks—reading, vocabulary, spelling, or math.

Figure 6.5 shows the front side of ThinkDot cards, and Figure 6.6 shows a sample ThinkDots activity for Grade 5 students who are studying American history. These cards are based on learning profile (multiple intelligences). Because students may not get their first choice on a roll of the die, you may allow them an extra roll so that they can choose between the two. You can also just let them choose the roll they would like to play.

FIGURE **6.5** ▤
Front side of
ThinkDots cards

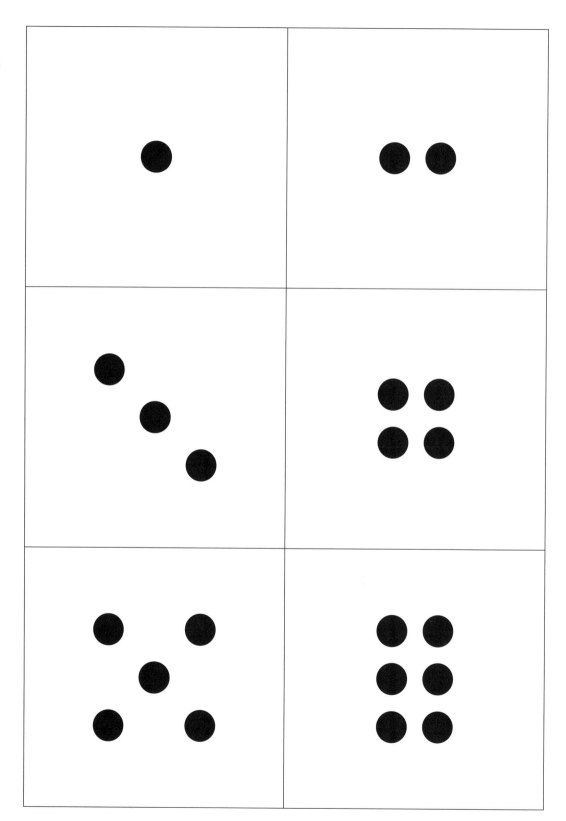

FIGURE **6.6** ■
Reverse side of
ThinkDots cards

You're an artist and publisher. Create a brochure about three women in the Revolutionary War. Make your own images in Paint and write original words about the women you choose. Research and include information about their childhood and heroism.

(visual-spatial and verbal-linguistic)

Teach your classmates a cumulative song from Colonial times called "The Rattlin' Bog." Then play "Greensleeves," one of the most popular tunes of the 16th, 17th, 18th, and 19th centuries, on the recorder. It was played over and over again, with many different sets of lyrics.

(musical-rhythmic and verbal-linguistic)

You're a Colonist who's angered by the various acts (Stamp Act, Sugar Act, Currency Act, Townshend Acts) created by the British Parliament to raise revenue and assert its authority over the Colonies. You have the opportunity to share your feelings over Colonial radio. Protest one of these acts over the airwaves, and use a microphone for your broadcast.

(bodily-kinesthetic and verbal-linguistic)

You're Nathanael Greene, one of General Washington's top generals. You're concerned about weapons for your soldiers. Create a set of sketches of the types of weapons your men use, as well as weapons you hope to obtain. Sign your sketches and present them to your superior or to General Washington.
http://members.aol.com/JonMaltbie/Biography.html

(visual-spatial and intrapersonal)

You're General Washington's quartermaster.
The general needs a report on the number and categories of supplies you had delivered to camp headquarters in the last year. He also wants to know how the supplies were moved and how much they cost. Use graphs in PowerPoint or Excel to show you're organized and spending money wisely.

(mathematical-logical and visual-spatial)

You're a spy who looks like an ordinary person so that you can mingle with the enemy and learn information. Put on your costume and mingle with your class to find out clues about the enemy's plans. Report your findings in a "speech" to the class.

(interpersonal and bodily-kinesthetic)

# Differentiating by Process with Technology

If we allow it to do so, technology affords us many opportunities to assist in our efforts to differentiate by process. First, let's focus on the tech options—Cubing and ThinkDots—we may use with flexible groups because these two options are the featured strategies of this chapter. Then, we'll brainstorm a few additional alternatives we could use to differentiate by process with other strategies as well.

### *Cubing and ThinkDots Resources*

You may easily convert the lesson resources on Cubing to a ThinkDots format, which is still a relatively new spin-off of Cubing.

**The Ball State University Teachers College instructional link on Cubing** (www.bsu.edu/gate/instruction/cubing.htm) contains a number of sample Cubing templates with prompts for various subject areas and grade levels. Some are appropriate for K–5 students, but others will need to be adapted. For younger children, see the link titled Bear Stories for Cubing tasks related to Corduroy, Winnie the Pooh, and Smokey the Bear.

**The Blank Cubing Template in Word** (http://jeffcoWeb.jeffco.k12.co.us/isu/ gifted/Cubing pattern.doc) offers a modifiable Word template to which you can add your own Cubing prompts. We've also included our own blank Cubing template (Fig. 6.4).

**The Character Cube Web** (www.babinlearn.com/pdf files/Cultivating Kids/ Character Cube.pdf) provides a printable version of an ELA cube in PDF format. The cube's faces display prompts that students answer about literary characters.

**The Cubing Anchor Activity** (www.mcps.k12.md.us/curriculum/enriched/ giftedprograms/docs/gradefive/unittwo/efivetwo.pdf) used in conjunction with Everyday Math in the Montgomery County Public Schools furnishes a PDF document with two possible Cubing activities that you may incorporate into your classroom.

**Cubing on the Great Lakes** (www.learningtogive.org/lessons/unit54/lesson3. html) contains a lesson titled Responsible Stewardship: The Saving of the Great Lakes. This lesson is the third of three on My Water, Your Water, Our Water. While its primary area of focus is science, it also includes social studies and ELA as additional subject areas. This lesson uses a Cubing activity in the Anticipatory Set and shows the prompts a teacher has created. In addition, the link provides a handout that you may give to students that includes a brief explanation of Cubing and the tasks on which students will work.

**Teaching All Our Students and Differentiated Instruction: What Is the Fit?**
(www.fssd.org/curriculum_profdev/Prof_Dev/DI_Day4(6–8)Imbeau.ppt) is a
lengthy but very helpful PowerPoint presentation. DI Slides 143–154 focus on
Cubing, and slides 175–183 deal with ThinkDots. An overview of each strategy is
presented, and examples are suggested.

**Walking Students through the Cubing Process** (www.glencoe.com/sec/
teachingtoday/downloads/pdf/cubing2.pdf) also supplies a printable handout you
may give to students that includes a brief explanation of Cubing, as well as a blank
fill-in sheet to use with the Cubing activity. If you wish to avoid preparing your
own blank fill-in sheet in Publisher, Word, or another program, you may use the
sheet provided here.

### *Flexible Grouping Resources*

Further resources for flexible grouping information and activities can be found in
the Resources section at the end of the chapter.

**The Cooperative Learning Center at the University of Minnesota**
(www.co-operation.org) provides an overview of cooperative learning, Q & A,
peacemaking, conflict resolution, assessment, and many other related topics.

**Differentiated Grouping Plan** (www5.esc13.net/gt/docs/Lesson_Grouping_Plan1.
pdf) offers a lesson-planning sheet for grouping. However, you may use Word or
another word processor to make your own.

**Flexible Grouping** (www.eduplace.com/science/profdev/articles/valentino.html)
discusses flexible groups and typical arrangements of student-led and teacher-led
groups.

**Grouping Strategies** (http://wblrd.sk.ca/~bestpractice/coop/process3.html,
http://wblrd.sk.ca/~bestpractice/coop/examples.html, http://wblrd.sk.ca/
~bestpractice/coop/process.html) features best practices for grouping, which offers
practical reminders about the effective use of cooperative groups.

**How to Thrive—Not Just Survive—in a One-Computer Classroom**
(www.educationworld.com/a_tech/tech/tech092.shtml) suggests helpful ideas
for the one-computer classroom.

**Printable Cooperative Group Worksheets** (www.teachnology.com/worksheets/
time_savers/grouping/) offers printable forms for organizing student groups of
three, four, or five via the use of random "tickets."

**Rotation Chart** (http://artsedge.kennedy-center.org/content/3801/3801_canUmea-
sureUp_rotate.pdf) may be used for flexible groups and rotating learning centers.
However, you could use Word or Publisher to make your own chart or table.

**Strategies to Enable More Independent Work at the Computer** (www.cdli.ca/%7Ejscaplen/integration/english/independent.html) offers recommendations to help students learn to work on their own at the computer.

### Additional Tech-based Options

Because the purpose of the process (throughput) stage is to explore and come to grips with core content, technology can offer new and more appealing variations on traditional, process-based activities. Today's students are visually and electronically driven, so sometimes the simple integration of computer work into an assignment makes our students respond more favorably. While it's possible to design detailed, more complex, tech-based tasks, we've found that even some simple activities involving technology excite students, too.

Some easy ways you can use technology to help you differentiate by process are:

**Option 1:** Create an image or document in Kid Pix, Paint, Kidspiration, Inspiration, or another software application you choose. In the following table, we've keyed in some suggestions for various subject areas. We've listed some possible documents or images that your students might generate as well as the objective behind the creation of that image or document. We think you'll find many of the documents and images aren't overly labor intensive.

TABLE **6.1** ■ Suggestions for technology integration into subject areas

| Subject Area | Possible Image or Document | Purpose |
| --- | --- | --- |
| **Art and Music** | Graphic creator | Identification of schools of art or music, particular artists or musicians, and their major works |
| | Publisher | |
| | Timeline | Invention or revision of artwork or piece of music |
| | Web or other graphic organizer | Journal or diary |
| | | Likeness of artist or musician |
| **ELA** | Bookmark | Bookmark |
| | Graphic creator | Describe or compare or contrast characters |
| | Publisher | Identify storyline |
| | Web or other graphic organizer | Journal/Diary/Log |
| | | Represent likeness of character or visualization of setting |
| **Foreign Language** | Diagram | Invitation, menu, ads, journal, or other short writing assignment |
| | Graphic creator | |
| | Publisher | Identification of target vocabulary |
| | Spreadsheet | Picture to assimilate target vocabulary |
| | | Survey results |

*continued*

TABLE **6.1** ■ Suggestions for technology integration into subject areas   *(continued)*

| Subject Area | Possible Image or Document | Purpose |
| --- | --- | --- |
| **Math** | Chart<br>Diagram<br>Graph<br>Spreadsheet | Data or statistics<br>Procedures |
| **Physical Education/ Health** | Chart<br>Database<br>Graph<br>Graphic creator<br>Graphic organizer<br>Spreadsheet | Cause-effect relationships<br>Data or statistics<br>Journal/Diary/Log<br>Survey results |
| **Science** | Bookmark<br>Chart<br>Database<br>Diagram<br>Door hanger<br>Graph<br>Graphic creator<br>Publisher<br>Spreadsheet<br>Web or other graphic organizer | Cause-effect relationships<br>Cycles<br>Data or statistics<br>Illustrations<br>Interrelationships between concepts<br>Lab work |
| **Social Studies** | Bookmark<br>Graphic creator<br>Publisher<br>Spreadsheet<br>Timeline<br>Venn Diagram or other graphic organizer | Bookmark<br>Comparison or contrast of places or people<br>Geographical or cultural data<br>Likeness of an important figure |

You might be wondering why our suggestions seem to advocate product rather than process because process-based differentiation is the focus of our present chapter. Please keep in mind, however, that there's some overlap between the differentiations of the three student traits.

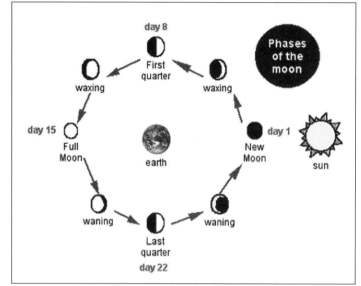

**FIGURE 6.7** ■
Sample science
cycle depicting
the phases of the
moon in
Kidspiration

Diagram created in Kidspiration by Inspiration Software. Reprinted with permission.

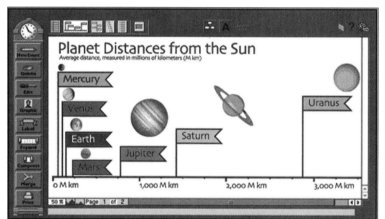

**FIGURE 6.8** ■
Science sample of
the distances of
the planets from
the sun, created
using TimeLiner

Reprinted with permission of Tom Snyder Productions.

The production of a simple artifact, such as an image or document, can play a significant role in the process phase. The creation of such images or documents may offer students alternative methods to digest or grasp the material they've been learning. Kinesthetic learners in particular respond well to these hands-on ways to experiment with content.

Also note that the ideas listed in the chart don't serve the same purpose as that of a final product, nor are they long-term projects. As we've repeated many times, the beauty of differentiation is that you can customize the strategies to fit your students' unique needs and interests!

**Option 2:** Students can key in answers to a Word document; a teacher-created form or survey; an online game, simulation, or activity (such as a Web-based treasure hunt or skills-based game); or a software-based task or drill. Figure 6.9 shows a screenshot of a sample game on decimals from the Fun Brain site.

Now that you've investigated some practical process-based strategies in depth, you may be ready to review a sample lesson plan that includes technology along with the Cubing strategy. For our sample lesson plan, we've selected a common second-grade science theme (insects), and we've also incorporated ELA as a secondary curricular area. (You might also choose to add math and measurement as a tertiary subject area.) In this lesson, you may elect to differentiate either by readiness or learning profile.

FIGURE **6.9** ■
**Example of Fun Brain's Power Football math game**

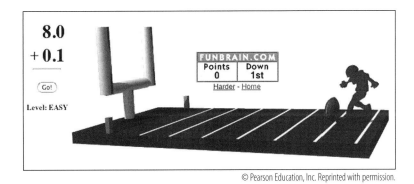

## Lesson Plan

### *Cubing and Technology: Insects*

| | |
|---|---|
| **Grade** | 2 |
| **Subject Area** | Science and Language Arts (Math/Measurement could be a third option) |
| **Curriculum Standards** | **National Science Standard addressed:**<br><br>Compare and contrast familiar organisms on the basis of observable characteristics.<br><br>NS.K-4.3 Life Science: As a result of activities in grades K–4, all students should develop understanding of:<br><br>■ The characteristics of organisms<br>■ Life cycles of organisms<br>■ Organisms and environments<br><br>**NCTE and IRA Standard addressed:**<br><br>Write an informational piece including a magazine feature article using an organizational pattern such as description, enumeration, sequence or compare/contrast that may include graphs, diagrams or charts to enhance the understanding of central and key ideas.<br><br>5. Students employ a wide range of strategies as they write and use different writing process elements appropriately to communicate with different audiences for a variety of purposes.<br><br>**National Educational Technology Standards for Students (NETS•S) addressed:** (see appendix for full list)<br><br>**1.** Creativity and Innovation: 1.a., 1.b.<br>**2.** Communication and Collaboration: 2.a., 2.b.<br>**3.** Research and Information Fluency: 3.a., 3.b., 3.c., 3.d.<br>**4.** Critical Thinking, Problem Solving, and Decision Making: 4.b.<br>**6.** Technology Operations and Concepts: 6.b. |
| **Lesson Summary** | Prior to Lesson: Students observe mealworms and waxworms (or two other insects of your choice) as they progress through their life cycle. They describe and record changes over several weeks.<br><br>Lesson: Students compare and contrast waxworm moths to mealworm beetles (or two other insects) through the use of Cubing. Students write an informational article about mealworm or waxworm behavior. |
| **Materials** | ■ Cubes based on readiness or student profile (see Fig. 6.10) |
| **Web Resources** | **Amazing Insects** — www.ivyhall.district96.k12.il.us/4th/kkhp/1insects/bugmenu.html<br>**Insect Images** — www.insects.org/entophiles/index.html http://classroomclip art.com/cgi-bin/kids/ imageFolio.cgi?direct=Animals/Insects/<br>**Insect Printouts** — www.enchantedlearning.com/subjects/insects/printouts.shtml<br>**Let's Talk About Insects** — www.urbanext.uiuc.edu/insects/01.html<br>**Virtual Insects** — www.ento.vt.edu/~sharov/3d/virtual.html |

*continued*

## Cubing and Technology: Insects *(continued)*

| | |
|---|---|
| **Lesson Activities** | 1. Students organize their notes on mealworms and waxworms or use completed KWL charts. <br><br> 2. Students work in pre-assigned pairs or triads based on readiness or student profile. <br><br> 3. Struggling learners use red cubes, at grade level learners use yellow cubes, and above grade level learners use green cubes, or cubes are based on learning profile such as multiple intelligences. |
| **Technology Activity Options** | ■ Create original illustrations in Paint or Kid Pix. <br> ■ Write a feature article in Stationery Studio or similar tool. <br> ■ Make a door hanger from a Publisher template (see Fig. 6.11). (Can include the original art from Paint and words from the feature article.) <br> ■ Create graphs in Graph Club or a similar program. <br> ■ Create a Venn diagram in Kidspiration 2 (see Fig. 6.12): www.teach-nology.com/Web_tools/graphic_org/venn_diagrams/. <br> ■ Create a Venn diagram in Word to compare/contrast two insects: www.rrcc.edu/teachered/sharon/turtle1_venndir.html. |
| **Differentiation/ Extension** | ■ More capable students can create a longer or more detailed artifact or product. <br> ■ Less capable students may create a shorter or less detailed artifact, and may need scaffolding. |
| **Evaluation** | ■ Use rubrics to evaluate students on research, writing, and technology components. <br> ■ Use a journal or other product for student self-reflection. |

The process stage of differentiation is an exciting one because it's student driven. It affords us the opportunity to try out strategies that captivate students, such as Cubing and ThinkDots.

Flexible grouping, one of the hallmark strategies of differentiated instruction, plays a key role in the process phase, and it allows for countless variations on assignments and organization of multiple types of student groups. If teachers are flexible and willing, these differentiation strategies will easily accommodate tech-based tasks and will offer students the chance to take ownership of the material.

Do you recall the bridge analogy that we used in the introduction to this chapter? The process stage is perhaps the most critical of all, because it's here where we potentially lose students as they "fall off of the bridge." Those students who don't have ample time or opportunity to experiment with and test the content we've communicated to them may arrive late (or not at all) to their destination, the output side of the bridge. Watch for those students who seem to stumble as they begin the trek across the bridge, and support their journey with some of these absorbing strategies!

FIGURE **6.10** ■
**Sample cube**

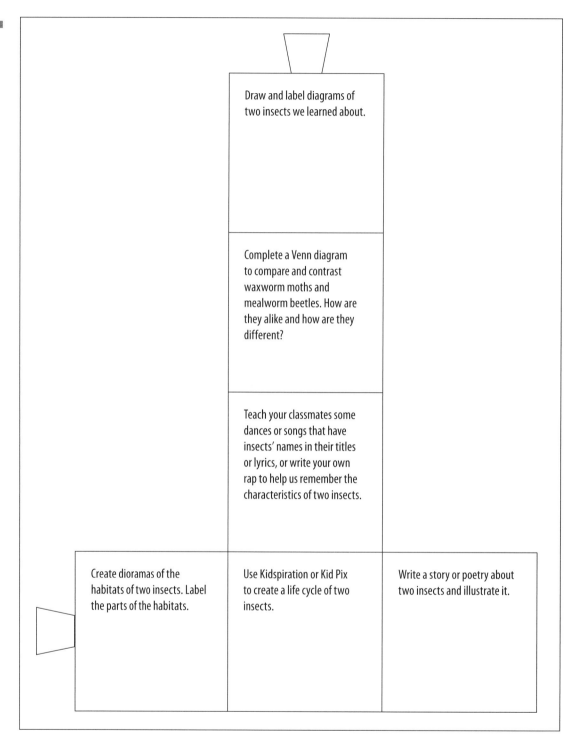

Draw and label diagrams of two insects we learned about.

Complete a Venn diagram to compare and contrast waxworm moths and mealworm beetles. How are they alike and how are they different?

Teach your classmates some dances or songs that have insects' names in their titles or lyrics, or write your own rap to help us remember the characteristics of two insects.

Create dioramas of the habitats of two insects. Label the parts of the habitats.

Use Kidspiration or Kid Pix to create a life cycle of two insects.

Write a story or poetry about two insects and illustrate it.

FIGURE **6.11** ◼
Sample doorknob
hanger created by
authors

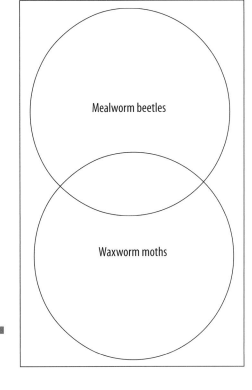

FIGURE **6.12** ◼
Sample Venn
diagram

## Resources for Chapter 6

| Cubing | The Ball State University Teachers College instructional link on Cubing | www.bsu.edu/gate/instruction/cubing.htm |
|---|---|---|
| | Blank Cubing Template in Word | http://jeffcoWeb.jeffco.k12.co.us/isu/gifted/Cubing pattern.doc |
| | Character Cube | www.babinlearn.com/pdf files/Cultivating Kids/ Character Cube.pdf |
| | The Cubing Anchor Activity link used in conjunction with Everyday Math in the Montgomery County Public Schools | www.mcps.k12.md.us/curriculum/enriched/giftedprograms/docs/ gradefive/unittwo/efivetwo.pdf |
| | Cubing on the Great Lakes | www.learningtogive.org/lessons/unit54/lesson3.html |
| | Teaching All Our Students and Differentiated Instruction: What Is the Fit? (Marcia B. Imbeau, PhD, is the author of the PowerPoint document, but she incorporates another PowerPoint document titled "ThinkDots: An Instructional Strategy for Differentiation by Readiness, Interest or Learning Style," by Kay Brimijoin. See slides 143–154 and 175–183.) | www.fssd.org/curriculum_profdev/Prof_Dev/DI_Day4(6–8)Imbeau.ppt |
| | Walking Students through the Cubing Process | www.glencoe.com/sec/teachingtoday/downloads/pdf/cubing2.pdf |
| Decision Making/ Consensus Building | Ground Rules Lesson | www.readwritethink.org/lessons/lesson_view.asp?id=218 |
| | Making Decisions: Grades 4–6 | www.acde.org/educate/46plan2.htm |

*continued*

## Resources for Chapter 6 *(continued)*

| | | |
|---|---|---|
| **Flexible Grouping/ Collaborative Learning** | **The Cooperative Learning Center at the University of Minnesota** | www.co-operation.org |
| | **Differentiated Grouping Plan** | www5.esc13.net/gt/docs/Lesson_Grouping_Plan1.pdf |
| | **ePals Global Network and Gaggle Net** (free and subscription-based "safe" e-mail accounts for students to use for collaborative projects) | www.epals.com<br>http://gaggle.net |
| | **Flexible Grouping** | www.eduplace.com/science/profdev/articles/valentino.html |
| | **The Global Schoolhouse and Houghton Mifflin's Project Place** (online collaborative projects) | www.globalschoolnet.org/GSH/pr/index.cfm<br>www.eduplace.com/projects/ |
| | **Grouping Strategies** | http://wblrd.sk.ca/~bestpractice/coop/process3.html<br>http://wblrd.sk.ca/~bestpractice/coop/examples.html<br>http://wblrd.sk.ca/~bestpractice/coop/process.html |
| | **How to Thrive—Not Just Survive— in a One-Computer Classroom** | www.educationworld.com/a_tech/tech/tech092.shtml |
| | **Inspirer software** (software that features computer-generated scavenger hunt assignments that call for work in collaborative teams) | www.tomsnyder.com/products/product.asp?SKU=INSINS |
| | **Manteno Community Unit's Literature Circles Page** | www.manteno.k12.il.us/curriculumdiff/literature_circles.htm |
| | **Monster Exchange** (online collaborative project that pairs classrooms together and requires group work in each classroom) | www.monsterexchange.org |
| | **Printable Cooperative Group Worksheets** | www.teachnology.com/worksheets/time_savers/grouping/ |
| | **Rotation Chart** | http://artsedge.kennedy-center.org/content/3801/3801_canUmeasureUp_rotate.pdf |
| | **Strategies to Enable More Independent Work at the Computer** | www.cdli.ca/%7Ejscaplen/integration/english/independent.html |
| | **Team Job Rubric/Assessment** | www.readwritethink.org/lesson_images/lesson218/rubric.pdf |
| | **Team Member Job Cards** | www.readwritethink.org/lesson_images/lesson218/jobcards.pdf |
| | **Think-Pair-Share Printable Template** | www.educationoasis.com/curriculum/GO_pdf/think_pair_share.pdf |
| **Software** | **2Simple's 2Create a Story** | www.2simpleusa.com |

## CHAPTER 7

# Using Technology *to* Differentiate *by* Product

You've probably heard about the USDA food pyramid and guidelines for healthy eating. Each category in the pyramid contains examples of foods that are good for you, along with specific amounts you should consume each day.

Dairy products (or the milk group), one of the categories in the food pyramid, consist of milk, cheese, and yogurt products. To consume your daily quota of milk products, you can choose from skim milk, low fat milk, flavored milk, cheddar cheese, cottage cheese, and any flavor of yogurt. The fruit group is another category in the food pyramid. To consume your daily quota of fruit products, you can choose from a wide variety of fruit, such as berries, bananas, melons, and apples.

You might begin to think about product differentiation as the "milk group" or the "fruit group" in your classroom. Similar to choosing various products within a food category to build a healthy body, students can be given product options to build healthier learning. In other words, students can choose how to express what they've learned in ways that appeal to their "taste buds" via interests, learning profiles, or readiness.

These options can work in several ways:

1. choices for forms of expression (written report versus diorama)
2. choices for individual versus small-group work
3. choices for self-created assignments versus teacher assignments

Why would you want to offer differentiated product choices to your students? Quite simply, today's classroom, with its diversity of students, just about requires you to do so. If you want your students to truly take ownership of their learning and their work, they'll respond more enthusiastically when given choices and particularly when given product activities that they've had a part in designing.

Creating powerful product assignments is a seven-step process for the teacher. Your goal is to provoke students to think about what they've learned over a period of time and apply and extend their new knowledge and skills in the creation of a self-selected product. Here are the seven steps, along with suggestions for building your product assignments:

1. **Identify the essentials of the unit that will determine what students learn, make sense of, and apply**. These fundamental understandings include which facts students need to know, which concepts must be comprehended, and which skills must be mastered. Product assignments can be created based on these key facts, concepts, and skills.

2. **Identify some possible formats or ways of expressing the product**. Can the products be based on the multiple intelligences of the learners? Can students create options? Can students choose from a set of options?

3. **Identify your expectations for quality**. These expectations revolve around quality of content, process, and product. Your expectations can be expressed in the rubrics you create and what you spell out for students to do.

4. **Identify the scaffolding needed for students' success**. Strategies might include rubrics, peer editing, timelines, and learning contracts.

5. **Identify modified versions of the assignment by readiness, interest, or learning profile**. These modified versions of product assignments allow for and honor various learning styles, interests, and abilities.

6. **Identify the product assignments to students, providing explanations, guidelines, and expectations**. This is the time to show sample products other students have made and distribute guideline sheets, rubrics, and other help sheets.

7. **Identify coaching, consulting, and public relations strategies to use with students**. We want our students to succeed with their products as they become engaged and excited about learning.

# Differentiating Products by Readiness, Interest, and Learning Profile

In the following examples, we use the States of the U.S. theme that's commonly included within Grades 3–5 units about U.S. regions. We'll show you how to set up a culminating product that's differentiated by readiness, interest, and learning profile. To help you, we provide a simple lesson plan for each strategy.

Prior to the culminating product, students will have

- identified states within regions of the United States;
- described major landforms, bodies of water, and climate of each region;
- located information about, and identified, major cities and landmarks of each region;
- identified the natural resources of each region;
- distinguished between goods and services of each region;
- identified major figures past and present of each region;
- distinguished between human resources and natural resources.

Prior to the culminating product, students will have selected, or been assigned to, a state they would like to research.

## Lesson Plan

### States of the U.S. Report Based on Readiness and Using Technology

| Grade | 3 | | |
|---|---|---|---|
| | **Teacher Assumptions and Observations** | | |
| | Struggling learners generally know… | Grade level learners generally know… | Advanced learners generally know… |
| **Readiness Characteristics** | **Social Studies**<br><br>States are divided into geographic regions<br><br>Names and locations of two to three major rivers<br><br>Names and locations of two mountain ranges<br><br>Some natural resources of some regions<br><br>Some characteristics of the climate of some regions | **Social Studies**<br><br>Geographic region to which each state belongs<br><br>Names and locations of top 10 populated cities<br><br>Names and locations and reason for settlement of early cities<br><br>Most natural resources of most regions<br><br>Most characteristics of the climate of most regions | **Social Studies**<br><br>Name, location, and capitals of all 50 states<br><br>Location and reason for settlement of four to five major U.S. cities<br><br>Nearly all natural resources of all regions<br><br>Nearly all characteristics of the climate of all regions |
| | **Language Arts/ Technology**<br><br>May need help with spelling checker<br><br>May need help with formatting text<br><br>May need help with inserting images<br><br>May need help with reformatting design if it's accidentally removed | **Language Arts/ Technology**<br><br>May know how to use thesaurus and spelling checker<br><br>May know how to format text<br><br>May know how to insert images | **Language Arts/ Technology**<br><br>Knows how to use thesaurus and spelling checker<br><br>Knows how to format text<br><br>Knows how to insert images |

| **Steps for Planning a States of the U.S. Unit or Lesson Tiered by Readiness and Technology** | **1. Grade Level Content Expectations:**<br><br>*Geography National Standards addressed:*<br><br>    Standard 4: The Physical and Human Characteristics of Places<br><br>    Standard 5: That People Create Regions to Interpret Earth's Complexity<br><br>    Standard 6: How Culture and Experience Influence People's Perceptions of Places and Regions<br><br>*National Educational Technology Standards for Students (NETS•S) addressed: (see appendix for full list)*<br><br>  **1.** Creativity and Innovation: 1.a., 1.b.<br><br>  **2.** Communication and Collaboration: 2.a., 2.b.<br><br>  **3.** Research and Information Fluency: 3.a., 3.b., 3.c., 3.d.<br><br>  **4.** Critical Thinking, Problem Solving, and Decision Making: 4.a., 4.b., 4.c.<br><br>  **6.** Technology Operations and Concepts: 6.b.<br><br>**2. Outcomes:** Decide what students should be able to do, know, or understand.<br><br>Students should be able to research a state of choice and produce a report about it according to teacher-created criteria. |

*continued*

## States of the U.S. Report Based on Readiness and Using Technology *(continued)*

**Steps for Planning a States of the U.S. Unit or Lesson Tiered by Readiness and Technology** *(continued)*

3. **Pre-Assess** your students on content and technology readiness. You may use a checklist, quiz, or teacher observation. What else do you know about your students based on observation and performance?

|  | **Struggling learners** | **Grade level learners** | **Advanced learners** |
|---|---|---|---|
| **Examples from work on regions** | Know absolute location, place | Know absolute and relative location, place, region, and human and environmental interaction | Can apply all five geography themes and emphasize movement themes |

4. **Select or create activities.** Use a common experience for the entire class that requires high-level thinking to understand a big idea.
   - Kickoff Activity: Ask students to make a list of what they know about their home state.
   - Create a two-column table with multiple rows. In the left column, write the category. In the right column, have students record facts they already know about the state. After you read the categories and give students time to respond in writing, check answers as a class and discuss the answers. [Note: Some facts will be impossible to know without research.] Here's an example of the table:

| What do I REALLY know about my home state: MICHIGAN | |
|---|---|
| Subject | What I know |
| 1. State stone | |
| 2. State bird | |
| 3. State flower | |
| 4. State reptile | |
| 5. State nickname | |
| 6. Year Michigan became a state | |

   - Following quiz-checking, display a map of the United States and ask students to write on a slip of paper the state they would most like to investigate and why. Perhaps they remember a state from the regional studies that interested them, or perhaps they've traveled to, or would like to travel to, a particular state.
   - Once their state of choice is selected, explain that students will learn facts about their selected state and that they'll be doing research to provide information to classmates. At this point, students could do a KWL (What I Know–What I Want to Know–What I Learned) chart to use with their state. Set up a system in which below-level learners will be assigned to or select option A, grade level learners will select option B, and advanced learners will select option C.

*continued*

## States of the U.S. Report Based on Readiness and Using Technology *(continued)*

**Steps for Planning a States of the U.S. Unit or Lesson Tiered by Readiness and Technology**
*(continued)*

5. **Think about** the range of possible activities students could do to explore and understand their state of choice. What types of activities will challenge learners, yet be successful?

| Suggested Products and Strategies for State Report | A. Struggling learners | B. Grade level learners | C. Advanced learners |
|---|---|---|---|
| | **Product** Teacher-created brochure template in Publisher or similar software application in which each panel is designed and categorized for the content to be included. (see sample at www.everythingdi.net) | **Product** Teacher-designed template for a state report in the form of a PowerPoint slide show | **Product** Student-designed state report in the form of a PowerPoint slide show (alternate: Flip Book of 8–10 pages; see resources section) |
| | **Strategies** Specific scaffolding in the form of written or direct instruction with respect to technology, panel content, and organization  Students may be paired to work on the same state but do their own separate brochures  Provide a rubric | **Strategies** Scaffolding as needed  Students may be paired to work on the same state but do their own slide shows  Provide one to two open-ended slides to offer students the opportunity to choose additional topics if desired or as time allows  Provide a rubric | **Strategies** Minimal scaffolding, especially if student pairs create the slide show  Provide some open-ended content categories to offer students the opportunity to choose additional topics  Provide a rubric |

6. **Assessment.** Determine how you'll assess students' performance. The rubric you provide can help assess both the final product and the working conditions. However, additional assessment tools might include self-reflection, a paper and pencil assessment, or another tool of your choice.

## Lesson Plan

### *States of the U.S. Report Based on Interest and Using Technology*

| Grade | 3 | | |
|---|---|---|---|
| | **Teacher Assumptions and Observations** | | |
| | **Struggling learners** | **Grade level learners** | **Advanced learners** |
| **Interest** | **Social Studies**<br>A state of choice | **Social Studies**<br>A state of choice | **Social Studies**<br>A state of choice |

| **Steps for Planning a States of the U.S. Unit or Lesson Tiered by Interest and Technology** | 1. **Grade Level Content Expectations:**<br><br>*Geography National Standards addressed:*<br><br>    Standard 4: The Physical and Human Characteristics of Places<br><br>    Standard 5: That People Create Regions to Interpret Earth's Complexity<br><br>    Standard 6: How Culture and Experience Influence People's Perceptions of Places and Regions<br><br>*National Educational Technology Standards for Students (NETS•S) addressed: (see appendix for full list)*<br><br>    1. Creativity and Innovation: 1.a., 1.b.<br><br>    2. Communication and Collaboration: 2.a., 2.b.<br><br>    3. Research and Information Fluency: 3.a., 3.b., 3.c., 3.d.<br><br>    4. Critical Thinking, Problem Solving, and Decision Making: 4.a., 4.b., 4.c.<br><br>    6. Technology Operations and Concepts: 6.b.<br><br>2. **Outcomes:** Decide what students should be able to do, know, or understand.<br><br>Students should be able to research a state of choice and produce a report about the state according to teacher-created criteria.<br><br>3. **Pre-Assess** your students on content and technology readiness or use teacher observation.<br><br>What else do you know about your students based on observation and performance?<br><br>4. **Select or create activities**. Use a common experience for the entire class that requires high-level thinking to understand a big idea.<br><br>    ■ Read aloud the book *Celebrate the 50 States*, by Loreen Leedy (1999) (or choose a similar book). This book features tasty morsels, colorful images, and a question about each state that will intrigue students. You might ask students to number their papers from 1 to 50 and write answers to each state question as you go along, then check them afterward. [Sample questions: How much did Alaska cost? What ferocious dinosaurs used to live in Colorado? What is the nickname for Michigan's Lower Peninsula?]<br><br>    ■ Following reading and quiz-checking, ask students to write on a slip of paper the state they would most like to investigate and why. Or pair students and ask them to choose a state for investigation and their reasons for choosing the state. |

*continued*

## States of the U.S. Report Based on Interest and Using Technology  *(continued)*

**Steps for Planning a States of the U.S. Unit or Lesson Tiered by Interest and Technology** *(continued)*

5.  **Think about** the range of possible activities students could do to explore and understand their state of choice. What types of activities will challenge learners yet be successful? Use a R.A.F.T. to guide students. (See chapter 2 for details on using a R.A.F.T.)

| Role | Audience | Format (choose 2) | Topic |
|------|----------|-------------------|-------|
| **Explorer or Settler** | Relatives and people back home | Early physical map of the terrain<br><br>Diary or letter (Word)<br><br>Sketches (Paint) | Describe the state in its early days and tell people back home what it's like |
| **Tour Director** (see Tour Director Examples that follow) | Modern-day students | Modern map with tourist attractions<br><br>Brochure (Publisher)<br><br>Facts Sheet (Word or Publisher) | Get people to come to the state to enjoy it |
| **Author/ Historian** | Newspaper reporters, librarians, and citizens | Timeline to the present (TimeLiner)<br><br>Famous people snippets (Word or Publisher)<br><br>Historic events snippets (Word or Publisher) | Leave information in a time capsule that will be opened in 2100 |

6.  **Assessment.** Determine how you'll assess students' performance. The rubric you provide can help assess both the final product and the working conditions. However, additional assessment tools might include self-reflection, a paper and pencil assessment, or another tool of your choice.

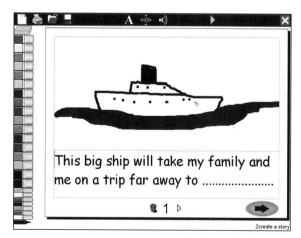

FIGURE **7.1** ■
**Example created in 2Create A Story software**

This big ship will take my family and me on a trip far away to .....................

Image created by Russell T. Smith.
Reprinted with permission of
2Simple Sofware, UK/2Simple USA Inc., USA.

## Tour Director Examples

| | |
|---|---|
| **Tour Director Example 1** | Students who choose the role of tour director will<br><br>1.  conduct research regarding their state's major tourist attractions, as well as such facts as size, population, capital city, major cities, industries, and other information you define;<br><br>2.  conduct their research from a variety of technology and print resources, such as online encyclopedias, state government and tourism pages, and a variety of student-friendly sites;<br><br>3.  record their information according to teacher-defined note-taking methods;<br><br>4.  use their information to create a modern map, brochure, or fact sheet. |
| **Tour Director Example 2** | Students who choose the role of tour director will<br><br>1.  conduct research regarding their state's major tourist attractions, as well as such facts as size, population, capital city, major cities, industries, and other information you define;<br><br>2.  conduct their research from a variety of technology and print resources such as online encyclopedias, state government and tourism pages, and a variety of student-friendly sites;<br><br>3.  record their information according to teacher-defined note-taking methods;<br><br>4.  use their information to create a story in which non-USA visitors take a trip to their state (see Fig. 7.1). |
| **Research sites** | **50States** — www.50states.com<br>**ABC Teach** — www.abcteach.com/States/StateTOC.htm<br>**ClassBrain** — www.classbrain.com/artstate/publish/<br>**Enchanted Learning** — www.enchantedlearning.com/usa/states/<br>**Explore the States** — http://americaslibrary.gov/cgi-bin/page.cgi/es/<br>**The Fifty States** — www.infoplease.com/states.html<br>**United States Fast Facts** — www.kidskonnect.com/States/StatesHome.html<br>**The US50** — www.theus50.com |
| **Information-Taking Forms** | **State Facts Report Form** — www.abcteach.com/free/s/statereport_upper_standard.pdf |
| **Brochure Construction Tools** | **Brochure Maker** — www.mybrochuremaker.com<br>Follow the directions to create a brochure online and print it.<br><br>**Word directions** — www.msad54.org/sahs/TechInteg/RefSheetsWeb/trifold.htm<br><br>**Appleworks directions** — http://hms.yarmouth.k12.me.us/Pages/YSD_HMSTechnology/Three-Fold Brochure.pdf<br><br>**Publisher directions** — www.microsoft.com/education/persuasionbrochure.mspx<br><br>**Brochure Template** — www.everythingdi.net |
| **Story Construction Tools** | 2Create A Story software from 2Simple Software |

# Lesson Plan

## *States of the U.S. Report Based on Learning Profile and Using Technology*

| Grade | 3 | | |
|---|---|---|---|

| | **Teacher Assumptions and Observations** | | |
|---|---|---|---|
| | **Struggling learners** | **Grade level learners** | **Advanced learners** |
| **Learning Profile** (based on previously determined multiple intelligences) | A variety of multiple intelligences can be honored in this assignment | A variety of multiple intelligences can be honored in this assignment | A variety of multiple intelligences can be honored in this assignment |
| **Steps for Planning a States of the U.S. Unit or Lesson Tiered by Learning Profile and Technology** | 1. **Grade Level Content Expectations:**<br><br>*Geography National Standards addressed:*<br><br>　　Standard 4: The Physical and Human Characteristics of Places<br><br>　　Standard 5: That People Create Regions to Interpret Earth's Complexity<br><br>　　Standard 6: How Culture and Experience Influence People's Perceptions of Places and Regions<br><br>*National Educational Technology Standards for Students (NETS•S) addressed: (see appendix for full list)*<br><br>　1. Creativity and Innovation: 1.a., 1.b.<br>　2. Communication and Collaboration: 2.a., 2.b.<br>　3. Research and Information Fluency: 3.a., 3.b., 3.c., 3.d.<br>　4. Critical Thinking, Problem Solving, and Decision Making: 4.a., 4.b., 4.c.<br>　6. Technology Operations and Concepts: 6.b.<br><br>2. **Outcomes:** Decide what students should be able to do, know, or understand.<br><br>Students should be able to research a state of choice and produce a report about the state according to teacher-created criteria.<br><br>3. **Pre-Assess** your students on content and technology readiness or use teacher observation.<br><br>What else do you know about your students based on observation and performance?<br><br>4. **Select or create activities.** Use a common experience for the entire class that requires high-level thinking to understand a big idea.<br><br>　■ Read aloud to students a section of the book *The Kids' Book of the 50 Great States,* by Scholastic Professional Books (1998) (or choose a similar book). Choose your home state. This book features information written by kids, so you might ask students to brainstorm what they would create about their selected state in terms of facts, maps, puzzles, pictures, poetry, and quizzes.<br><br>　■ Following reading and quiz-checking, ask students to write on a slip of paper the state they would most like to investigate and why. Or pair students and ask them to choose a state for investigation and their reasons for choosing the state. | | |

*continued*

## *States of the U.S. Report Based on Learning Profile and Using Technology* *(continued)*

**Steps for Planning a States of the U.S. Unit or Lesson Tiered by Learning Profile and Technology** *(continued)*

5. **Think about** the range of possible activities students could do to explore and understand their state of choice. What types of activities will challenge learners yet be successful? Use a Tic-Tac-Toe Board based on the multiple intelligences and technology. Ask students to complete three activities about their state to make a Tic-Tac-Toe.

| | | |
|---|---|---|
| Write a rap or song about your state and perform it.<br><br>(Musical Intelligence + Music Ace software) | Create a set of graphs using statistics about your state and label the parts.<br><br>(Mathematic Intelligence + Graph Club or Excel) | Have your state speak for itself. Pen a monologue in which your state reflects on its beginnings and acceptance into the Union. Tape your presentation.<br><br>(Intrapersonal Intelligence + recorder) |
| Write a newspaper or brochure about your state and distribute it.<br><br>(Linguistic Intelligence + Publisher) | Create a dance about your state, list the steps, and perform it.<br><br>(Bodily Intelligence + Word) | Create trading cards about plants and animals that are native to your state (see Fig. 7.2).<br><br>(Naturalist Intelligence + Publisher) |
| Draw a mural about your state and present it.<br><br>(Spatial Intelligence + Paint) | Interview students about your state and present results in a press conference.<br><br>(Interpersonal Intelligence + Word) | Why did early settlers come to your state? Make an advertising flier that could have been used to attract settlers.<br><br>(Existentialist Intelligence + Publisher) |

6. **Assessment.** Determine how you'll assess students' performance. The rubric you provide can help assess both the final product and the working conditions. However, additional assessment tools might include self-reflection, a paper and pencil assessment, or another tool of your choice.

**State Trading Card**

| | |
|---|---|
| **Helpful Sites** | www.50states.com |
| | www.pics4learning.com |
| | www.enchantedlearning.com/usa/states/ |
| | www.everythingdi.net |

### Indiana State Flower

The peony became Indiana's state flower in 1957. The peony blooms in May and June. Peonies can have white, red, or pink flowers.

The zinnia was Indiana's state flower from 1931-1957.

FIGURE **7.2** ■ Trading card example created by authors

As you can see, students can demonstrate understanding of concepts in many ways through a wide range of product choices. Unlike short-term process activities, products typically are longer term and help students apply and even increase what they've learned during the unit being studied. In the resources section that follows, you can take advantage of ready-made templates and Web sites that connect students to information about their state.

## Resources for Chapter 7

| | | |
|---|---|---|
| **Books for the Classroom** | *The Kids' Book of the 50 Great States,* by Scholastic Professional Books (1998) | |
| | *Celebrate the 50 States,* by Loreen Leedy (1999) | |
| **Brochure Templates** | My Brochure Maker | www.mybrochuremaker.com |
| | Read•Write•Think Printing Press | http://interactives.mped.org/view_interactive.aspx?id=110&title |
| | Create a Brochure in Publisher (teacher tutorial) | www.microsoft.com/education/PersuasionBrochure.mspx |
| | Student Sample (open document in Publisher) | www.edina.k12.mn.us/support/technology/tech05/florida.pub |
| **Flip Book** | Read•Write•Think flipbook creator | www.readwritethink.org/materials/flipbook/ |
| **PowerPoint Templates for State Reports** | Our 50 States presentation | www.paducah.k12.ky.us/curriculum/PPoint/Templates/State report.ppt |
| | Our 50 States presentation | www.cbisd.com/powerpoints/Our 50 States template.ppt |
| | States and Capitals Interactive Game | http://it.coe.uga.edu/~lrieber/pptgames/states.ppt |
| **Research Form** | State Research worksheet | www.teachersnetwork.org/readysettech/forsberg/researchwksht.pdf |
| **Sample Rubrics** | Rubistar: Interactive Online Rubrics for presentations, project-based learning | http://rubistar.4teachers.org/index.php?ts=1147145447 |
| **State in A Box Ideas** | State in a Box: State Reports with Chosen, Representative Objects | www.raft.net/ideas/State in a Box.pdf |
| **State Fact Report Forms, Printouts, and Maps** | ABC Teach Directory for United States | www.abcteach.com/directory/theme_units/social_studies/state_reports/ |
| | US States: Facts, Maps, and State Symbols | www.enchantedlearning.com/usa/states/ |
| | USA Label Map Printouts | www.enchantedlearning.com/label/usa.shtml |
| **Student Research Sites** | States and Capitals | www.50states.com |
| | America's Library: Interactive Information | www.americaslibrary.gov/cgi-bin/page.cgi/es/ |
| | Ben's Guide to U.S. Government for Kids | http://bensguide.gpo.gov/3-5/state/ |
| | Fact Monster: The Fifty States | www.factmonster.com/states.html |
| | Kids Konnect: State information | www.kidskonnect.com/content/category/4/33/27/ |
| | Color Landform Atlas of the United States | http://fermi.jhuapl.edu/states/states.html |
| | Class Brain: State information | www.classbrain.com/artstate/publish/ |
| | NetState: Learn About the 50 States | www.netstate.com/states/ |
| | Around the World—U.S. States | http://kids.yahoo.com/directory/Around-the-World/U.S.-States |

*continued*

## Resources for Chapter 7 *(continued)*

| | | |
|---|---|---|
| **Student Learning Games** | US State Capitals | www.quia.com/custom/4main.html |
| | 50 States Toolbox | www.50states.com/tools/ |
| | All About the United States | www.sheppardsoftware.com/web_games.htm |
| | Puzzled States! | www.scholastic.com/play/prestates.htm |
| **Teacher Tools** | Spectacular State Studies | http://teacher.scholastic.com/products/instructor/oct03_state_studies.htm |
| | Taking in the States (field trip) | http://teacher.scholastic.com/fieldtrp/socstu/states.htm |
| | Make State Maps with MapMachine | www.nationalgeographic.com/xpeditions/lessons/03/g35/exploremaps.html |

## CHAPTER 8

# Using Technology *in* Encore Subjects: Art, Foreign Languages, Music, *and* PE

Most teachers know very well that some of the greatest challenges facing education today are the budget cuts and lack of sufficient revenue (from property taxes, sales taxes, and so forth) that help us support schools. This drop in financial resources has caused a dramatic reduction of staff teaching encore subjects, such as art, foreign languages, music, and physical education. More frequently, "regular" K–5 classroom instructors must take on the additional responsibility of teaching some of these encore subjects within their classrooms.

We've also found that teachers of encore subjects aren't always given the recognition or legitimacy they merit as full-time instructors. They may not have their own classrooms, and professional development and training often focus on core curricular areas rather than "extra," "nonessential" subjects. An additional difficulty is the fact that encore teachers meet with the same students only one to two times per week for approximately 20–60 minutes per session. Therefore, it takes longer for them to assess each student's skills and knowledge and to develop a cohesive learning community.

Over the last few decades, a significant shift has occurred in the core content of encore classes. This change isn't a surprising phenomenon because curricular changes happen rather frequently in all grades and all subjects. However, a closer look is warranted.

In the past, the core content of most encore classes was skills based. That is, teachers focused on teaching students how to develop a particular skill or talent, such as painting with watercolors, playing the recorder, and so forth. At present, they still train students to cultivate similar skills, but they also impart considerably more cultural, historical, health-related, and social knowledge about the artists and their works. By the word *artists*, here, we mean those who create visual arts, music, drama, and literature, as well as the athletes who create "physical" art.

Stephanie can remember making the standard clay pot (with coiled links) some 30 years ago without learning about María Montoya Martínez or Native American pottery. The same could be said for even more familiar artists, such as Henry Matisse, whom we never studied when we created collages. Without a doubt, encore teachers teach across curricular areas in their classrooms, although we tend to label their courses as more "specialized."

Many of the aforementioned factors seem like great obstacles that would work to impede effective use of differentiated instruction. In our experience, however, we've discovered just the opposite. Differentiated instruction strategies can be incorporated successfully into encore classes and can bring about positive results.

Before adding our powerful ally, technology, to the mix, we begin with a brief overview of a variety of content- and skills-based areas in which we might differentiate in the encore classroom. We've selected three differentiation strategies to investigate in more depth in this chapter because they lend themselves well to *all* classroom subjects, including encore. We then provide tech-enhanced sample activities for the art, foreign language, music, and physical education classrooms using learning centers and R.A.F.T.s. We also walk you through the creation of a WebQuest for the elementary Spanish classroom. Finally, we take a closer look at some tech resources and tools that are more specific to each encore subject area.

## Differentiating in the Encore Classroom

As is the case with the majority of core subjects, there are many areas in which we might differentiate to better serve our encore students. As we've mentioned, today's encore teachers face a heavier load in terms of the amount of content-based knowledge and skills they must cover in the classroom. While many of you may have already experimented with one or more of the variations below, see if there are any suggestions you haven't tried.

The lists that follow aren't comprehensive by any means; they're points of departure to get you started. They offer alternatives you might draw on in your attempt to reach all students through differentiation. Think about additional options you might add to the lists and put to the test in your classroom.

If you teach art, in addition to your students' level of readiness consider the final product you might ask them to produce and how you might think about either simplifying or making the creative process more complex or detailed. Your students' interests might factor into the equation, particularly in the choice of media used or genre. Here is a list of possible ways you might differentiate by product:

- Restrict creation to pure imitation of another's technique or extend the liberty to create freely.

- Heighten or diminish the level of abstraction.

- Vary the type of media used.

- Expand or reduce the levels of dimension, such as three dimensional versus one dimensional.

- Minimize or maximize the complexity or intricacy of shape.

- Intensify or lessen the complexity or intricacy of pattern.

- Minimize or maximize the complexity or intricacy of shading.

- Reduce or expand the number of colors used.

- Add or eliminate the number or types of textures employed.

- Include options for different schools or genres of art.

If you teach a foreign language, you're probably familiar with the traditional four language-skill areas: reading, writing, listening, and speaking. A more current trend in foreign language instruction is attention to the three "communicative modes"—interpersonal, interpretive, and presentational—that form the basis of the communication goal area included in the standards of the American Council on the Teaching of Foreign Languages (ACTFL). The standards center on five goal areas, called the "5 Cs": communication, cultures, connections, comparisons, and communities.

The traditional four-skills approach treats reading, writing, listening, and speaking in the target language in a more isolated manner, whereas the communicative modes stress the purpose and the context of communication. The latter approach seems to strengthen and deepen the connection between real life and the activities inside the language classroom.

The incorporation of the remaining four Cs also encourages a well-rounded approach that enables us to better prepare our students for the global society in which they live. This approach embraces awareness and instruction on cultural topics, comparison and contrast of language patterns, multicultural and multilingual community experiences in the field, use of the Internet, and so forth. Glance at the performance indicators for the communication standard (the full standards can be viewed at www.actfl.org/files/public/execsumm.pdf).

**Standard 1.1: Interpersonal Communication**
Students engage in conversations, provide and obtain information, express feelings and emotions, and exchange opinions.

**Standard 1.2: Interpretive Communication**
Students understand and interpret written and spoken language on a variety of topics.

**Standard 1.3: Presentational Communication**
Students present information, concepts, and ideas to an audience of listeners or readers on a variety of topics.

Although foreign language is taught as an encore subject in the K–5 arena, its core content is similar to that of other primary subjects, such as English language arts (ELA), in which K–5 teachers work on virtually identical skills in English. It would seem to be easy to accommodate differentiation within the foreign language classroom because it parallels academic instruction in English. However, due to the fact that foreign language instruction occurs less frequently than that of core curricular subjects, K–5 teachers cannot follow a comprehensive curriculum. Teachers of other encore subjects also face similar time constraints that impact instruction.

Foreign language teachers consider the readiness levels of their students, as well as the content to be communicated, in order to impart specific knowledge. Interests and learning profile play a big part in terms of the students' receptivity and apprehension of the material. Differentiation of process-based activities and diverse product formats are essential to accommodate all levels and types of learners. Teachers have multiple options in each of the traits and elements. Here are a few basic ideas to begin to think about differentiation in a foreign language:

- Isolate or focus on a particular skill (such as writing), or require the use of two to four skills.

- Increase or decrease the number of tenses used.

- Intensify or lessen the level of vocabulary.

- Teach culture in students' native language or in the target language.

- Communicate facts only or incorporate feelings and emotions.

- Comprehend by listening, or comprehend by listening and then respond orally or in writing.

- Vary the length or complexity of an exercise, document, or text.

- Request structured responses or free responses.

- Incorporate simple or advanced realia and authentic documents.

- Invite recorded responses or spontaneous ones.

- Use group or individual presentations or assignments

If you're a music teacher, ponder the readiness levels of your students as well as the final product they'll generate. Your students' interests might play a role here, too, particularly in terms of the genres of music and the kinds of instruments they prefer. You might also challenge them in the process phase by asking them to play or sing at various tempos, different dynamics, and so forth, which in turn will affect their final products. Here are some suggestions:

- Lengthen or shorten the composition or piece.
- Vary the type of instruments used.
- Increase or decrease the number of instruments played.
- Play the treble clef or both the treble and bass clefs.
- Increase or decrease the range of the piece.
- Modify the rhythm.
- Speed up or slow down the tempo.
- Heighten or lessen the dynamics.
- Simplify or intensify the complexity or difficulty of the piece.
- Allow for various types of parts or harmony: solo, duet, trio, quartet, whole ensemble or choir, and so forth.
- Include pieces of various classifications of music.

If you're a physical education teacher, reflect on the readiness levels of your students and the skill levels you wish them to attain. Contemplate how you might alter the level of difficulty of each task as a part of the learning process. Some of the ways you might challenge your students beyond their comfort zones are:

- Intensify or lessen the level of competition.
- Maximize or minimize the speed of the task.
- Increase or decrease the distance between performers.
- Reduce or expand the size of the playing area.
- Require the use of the weaker limb, or permit the use of both limbs or the stronger limb.
- Change the levels of movement: stationary skills, tasks, or targets; moving tasks, skills, or targets. Add or eliminate defenders.
- Place or remove restrictions upon game play or technique.
- Break skills-development practice or tasks into parts, or perform skills or tasks outright.

Take a second look at the subject area you teach, and pinpoint one or two areas of differentiation you haven't yet experimented with. Make a commitment to try one out in the next few weeks or months to see if it's effective for you and your students.

# Differentiating Encore Subjects with Technology

Before we move on to our strategies of focus for this chapter, we'd like you to quickly examine a table of resources. In this table we've listed hardware, software or computer-assisted instruction resources, lesson plan resources, and virtual environments that you could use in *any* of the encore subject areas. This isn't a comprehensive list, but we wanted to get you thinking about technology right away. You'll see some of these tools and resources in our sample plans. What additional resources could you add to this table from your classroom experience?

TABLE **8.1** ■ Resources for encore subject areas

| | | |
|---|---|---|
| **Hardware** | Digital cameras | Smartboards |
| | Elmo projectors | Tape recorders or DVD players |
| | Hand-held devices or PDAs | Video cameras |
| | Laptops and desktop computers | |
| **Software or Computer-Assisted Instruction** | Audio CDs or DVDs | Online flashcards |
| | Clip art | Online games and drills |
| | Drawing software (Paint) | Online podcasts, videos, or clips |
| | E-mail | Photoshop |
| | Graph Club or Graph Master | Presentation software (PowerPoint) |
| | Kid Pix | Publishing software (Publisher) |
| | Kidspiration or Inspiration | Spreadsheet software (Excel) |
| | Online audio files | TimeLiner |
| | Online dictionaries or glossaries | Word Processing software (Word) |
| **Lesson Plan Resources** | Graphic organizers, note-taking forms, or other templates | Surveys, questionnaires, or other pre-assessment tools |
| | Internet scavenger hunts | ThinkQuests |
| | Lesson plan links | Video streaming |
| | | WebQuests |
| **Virtual Environments** | Kids' chats and Keypals | Virtual museums and other cultural institutions |
| | MUSHes, MOOs, CU See ME | Webcams |
| | Online collaborative projects | |
| | Virtual field trips | |

How and why might you use some of these wonderful resources in your encore classroom? Let's look at two examples: Internet scavenger hunts and virtual field trips.

### Internet Scavenger Hunts

Internet scavenger hunts are a magnificent way to encourage your encore students to search out and sift through information about a classroom theme or an individualized research topic. The Internet offers numerous free scavenger or treasure hunts for all sorts of subjects. An example is the Dental Health Scavenger Hunt shown below. Most students are eager to hunt for treasure via the Internet, and they find it even more enjoyable when they're paired up with a partner or find that puzzles or games play a part in the quest. You may choose to pair a student with advanced browsing skills with one who has less experience in this area.

Internet scavenger hunts are not difficult to create because you can use a template. The most time-consuming portion of the task is to find a relevant, yet varied, group of Web sites that you plan to have the students visit. As you prepare your scavenger hunt template in Word or another word processing program (or, perhaps, even a special Web site), make sure your instructions are very straightforward. Ask students to find answers to specific questions at each site. If possible, provide hyperlinks so that students may click on your links and go directly to the sites (to avoid having to type in all the URLs). Treasure hunts offer students the chance to use the computer, which engages them and provides a break from the daily routine.

---

**Dental Health Scavenger Hunt**

This scavenger hunt is available at:
www.vickiblackwell.com/scavenger hunt/Dental Health Scavenger Hunt.doc.

1. Click on Seal Out Decay. Read the story and answer the following questions.

   What are sealants? _____

   What color is the sealant material? _____

   www.ms-flossy.com/SmileysPlace/

2. Click on After School Treats. Play the game Let's Raid the Kitchen!

   Name four healthy snacks you found. _____

   Name two not so healthy snacks you found. _____

   www.adha.org/kidstuff/games.htm

3. Take the Dental Health Quiz. Answer the 10 questions about plaque by selecting True or False. Check your answers. How many did you get right? _____ How many did you get wrong?_____

   www.crest.com/dental_health/toothOrFalse.jsp

4. Click on "How many words can you find in our word search puzzle?" Find and circle as many of the toothy words as you can. Write the words you found.

   _____

   _____

*continued*

---

> **Dental Health Scavenger Hunt**   *(continued)*
>
> 5. Click on Attack of the Plaque Monsters game and play "What was your score?"_____
>    www.colgate.com/app/Kids-World/US/HomePage.cvsp
>
> 6. Read the page about Do You Know Your Teeth? Answer the following questions.
>    What are four kinds of teeth? _____
>    How many teeth do adults have? _____
>    What are two things teeth help you do? _____
>    www.adha.org/kidstuff/
>
> 7. Click on "Take our quiz and find out." Answer the five questions. Check your answers. How many did you
>    get right? _____ How many did you get wrong? _____
>    http://smilekids.deltadentalca.org/games.html
>
> 8. Read Fun Facts. Fill in the blanks.
>    Teeth are made of _____.
>    Dogs have _____ teeth.
>    _____ have 44 teeth.
>    _____ have 30 teeth.
>    When you grow up you will have _____ teeth.
>    http://smilekids.deltadentalca.org/healthyTeeth.html

Reprinted with permission of Debra S. Schanzbach.

## Virtual Field Trips

Virtual field trips bring the world to your classroom with just the touch of a few keys. They allow your students to "travel" to places they may never actually visit in their lifetimes. On top of that, they're less costly! Students will appreciate the opportunity to travel in cyberspace and explore.

Keep in mind that you need to prepare yourself by previewing the site and the links that make up the virtual tour. Prime your students by teaching at least one lesson about the topic or place prior to their "departure." As the day of the trip arrives, think about whether you wish to take the trip as a whole class (with the help of a projector), pair students together, or have them travel individually.

In addition to all of the images and facts made available to us on the Internet, there are some neat activities you could use with your students as a follow-up to their online visits. Completing a travel log or journal, writing a virtual postcard, or creating a digital scrapbook or collage in Word, Publisher, or PowerPoint (perhaps about their favorite stops on the tour or new facts they learned that surprised them) will help cement connections between curricular content and the online experience.

Following is the home page of a very cool virtual field trip to Paris.

## *Virtual Trip to Paris*

Paris

Home    Map    France    Fun Facts    Monuments

Resources

Boys and girls, buckle your seat belts. We are about to take a trip across the Atlantic Ocean to Paris, France. We're going to a different country, so I hope you have your passports!

Now, do you have your plane ticket?

OK, boys and girls, this is going to be a long ride. Here we go, up into the sky, soaring like birds. There's Smethport, Pennsylvania.

There's the Atlantic Ocean.

Finally, we're in Paris, France. I hope everyone is ready to do some sightseeing. There are so many places I want to take you. Let's get started so that we don't run out of time.

(This virtual trip is available at http://pt3.sbu.edu/vfts/Paris/)

Reprinted with permission of Paris Virtual Field Trip creator, Tonya R. Beardsley.

In addition to the technology resources we can integrate into our plans for learning centers, R.A.F.T.s, and WebQuests, each encore subject has a wealth of hardware, software, lesson plan resources, or Web sites. Virtual environments specific to particular curricular areas are also available.

While it's impossible to provide an exhaustive listing of such resources in this chapter, we would like to help you get started. You'll recognize some of the resources we've incorporated into other activities in this book as well as those you rely on yourself. While we recognize the wealth of some large-scale resources such as labs, we've refrained from creating tasks dependent on them because some schools don't have a keyboarding lab for music or a language lab for foreign languages. Furthermore, the labs themselves vary greatly in terms of layout, size, availability, and software and hardware used, so it would be very difficult and unwise to make generalizations.

Check the lengthy resources section at the end of this chapter for some magnificent links that will help you differentiate by content, process, product, readiness, interest, and learning profile. On top of all that, we've listed a number of technology-specific resources to match those you noticed in Table 8.1, such as Webcams, virtual field trips, and so forth.

## Learning Centers or Stations

Learning centers or stations are old friends to most elementary teachers. Most K–5 teachers have tried learning centers as a DI strategy in their classrooms, and many use them on a regular basis. Some DI practitioners differentiate between learning centers and stations, as explained on the Montgomery County Public Schools' Web site: "Centers are areas in the classroom where students refine a skill or extend a concept. Stations are different places in the classroom where students work on tasks simultaneously, and whose activities are linked" (Montgomery County Public Schools, 2005, para. 1).

Although this strategy might not be new to you, we'd like to take a moment to review the basics. If you're comfortable with the nuts and bolts of learning centers, such as types, organization, movement between them, and so forth, please feel free to move on to the illustrations for each encore subject.

You'll notice that we've chosen a more traditional (purely physical) set of activities for the physical education learning center. We elected to include this traditional set to illustrate that learning centers can accommodate all types of activities.

In the previous section, we offered some recommendations about how you might differentiate even the purely physical tasks, as well as some of the basic skills in the other encore subjects. If you're a product of a private, parochial, or public school of that past that didn't embrace differentiation, we think you'll be surprised to discover that you truly can differentiate in many of the skill areas that are more physically based, such as tempo, speed of task, intricacy of pattern, and so forth. If your educational experience was anything like ours, your encore teachers picked an activity, and everyone completed the *same* task.

You'll also find that many of our learning center tasks are designed for upper elementary students. We realize that learning centers are quite popular with the lower grades, and we wanted to demonstrate that they can be used effectively in upper level classrooms as well.

## Profile: *Learning Centers*

### Function

To engage students in active learning tasks at various stations in order to apply and extend specific skills, content-based knowledge, exploration, or enrichment.

### Advantages

- Accommodates differentiation by the three curricular elements and student traits.
- Provides for active hands-on learning and student choice.
- Permits use of multiple technologies and a variety of tasks.
- Encourages peer collaboration *and* independent learning.
- Allows for flexible grouping (teacher-determined) or student placement.
- Grants teacher time to work with a specific group or individual (conferencing, guided reading, and so forth).
- Assists in the advancement of creative- and critical-thinking skills.
- Reduces boredom through movement, exploration, and enrichment.

### Components

- **A.** Establish ground rules and develop consensus-building or decision-making skills.
- **B.** Choose center type.
- **C.** Prepare physical components or setup.
- **D.** Introduce centers and tasks.
- **E.** Set up center rotations.
- **F.** Plan closing.

### *Steps to Create Learning Centers*

1.  For component A (ground rules and consensus building):

    - develop a broad or general theme and determine the core concepts that students must comprehend.

2.  For component B (selection of center type), choose from the following center types (dependent on your end goals):

    - exploratory or interest driven
    - literacy
    - publishing or technology driven
    - research
    - subject areas
    - thematic

3.  For component C (physical components or setup):

    - decide upon a large group meeting area
    - determine whether you need to separate noisy stations from quiet stations
    - plan for stations requiring technology (near outlets)
    - think about possible physical designs—grouped desks; sides of filing cabinets; counters; floor; portable stations that use file folders, cardboard boxes, or display boards as separators; bulletin boards
    - prepare means to store center manipulatives, student records, and displays

4.  For component D (introduction of centers and tasks):

    - present a mini-lesson or a brief overview of the learning goals and how they're related to current content
    - remind students of ground rules and consensus-building skills
    - review specific directions
    - walk through the various centers, showing students the tools they'll use and the activities they must complete
    - go over instructions about how to move from one center to another as well as a signal you'll use when the noise level is too high

- talk about what students should do if they don't complete a task at one of the centers

- relay any specific directions for setting up and cleaning up

- describe how students may choose centers and how many students may work at each center, or assign them to a particular rotation or group using a wheel with names, a board with pockets or hooks, grouping by numbers out loud, and so forth

**5.** For component E (center rotations):

- circulate around the classroom to monitor activities

- have classroom assistants such as parents or aides work at each station if possible

- if you desire, conference with individual students or a small group of students at one station or at your desk, or lead a station on guided reading

**6.** For component F (closing):

- return to large meeting area to share positive results and difficulties

- have students share their own self-assessments, if desired

## Learning Centers: *Art*

This group of centers revolves around paintings that students have created using a particular artist's style or technique, such as that of Picasso, Monet, Matisse, and so forth. Students will mount their paintings digitally, pose as the artists themselves to explain their techniques, participate in an interview, and produce a photo essay about their artists. If you choose, other forms of art such as ceramics or drawing could be used. You could also allow students to write using first person, as if they're the artists themselves (Center D task).

**Center A**
"Mount" the digital photo of your artwork into a new PowerPoint file. Design the background and label your painting. (PowerPoint tutorial resources were suggested in chapter 2.)

**Center B**
Record a how-to video of your painting technique. You may use a traditional video camera or Movie Maker software along with a miniDV camera. For more details, see the How to Create a Video with Movie Maker sidebar.

**Center D**
Create a short photo essay (using Word or PowerPoint) that describes your artist's contribution to the world of art. Use the photo resources from WebMuseum, Online Picasso Project, Monet & the Impressionists for Kids, and Matisse Images on the Web (see Resources section for links).

**Center C**
Record an oral interview between the artist and a radio talk show host using microphones and an audio recorder. You pose as the artist and your partner as the host. Then switch so that you play the role of host and your partner can pretend to be the artist. (You could use Audacity software for this. See the Music R.A.F.T. example for directions.)

### How to Create a Video with Movie Maker

1. Record interview video with your mini-DV camera or another video source.

2. Connect your camera to an IEEE 1394 port, and then set the camera mode to play recorded video.

3. Click Capture Video on the File menu.

4. Select DV Camera or the appropriate video source under Available Devices on the Video Capture Device page.

5. Enter a name for your captured video file and choose where to save it.

6. Choose the setting you wish to use on the Video Setting page (for both audio and video).

7. On the Capture Method Page, select whether you wish to Capture the entire tape automatically or Capture the tape manually.

8. You will then have the option of choosing other commands, such as separating the video into smaller clips or stop capturing before the end of the tape.

9. Click Finish to close the Video Capture Wizard.

# Related Technologies: *Art Learning Centers*

## *Video Creation/Editing Software*

**How video creation/editing software will be used in the activity:**
In Center B, students record a how-to video to explain an art technique. To complete this activity, students must be familiar with how to use Movie Maker (or may choose to use a traditional video recorder), and ideally, you will have spent time teaching them how to use it prior to this lesson.

**Implementation challenges:** Movie Maker is a user-friendly tool because it allows you to build your creation via drag-and-drops. However, there are many options and formats from which to choose, which can be somewhat overwhelming at first. Students usually become comfortable with it after a little practice, but at the same time, there does not seem to be a great amount of help within the program when it comes to trying out some of the advanced options.

| Resources for Video Creation/Editing Software | |
|---|---|
| **Description** | Movie Maker is video creating/editing software that allows you to build, edit and share your videos. |
| **Where to find the tools** | Today, video creation/editing software such as Movie Maker may come with your computer if you purchase a recent version of Windows. You may also download it for free online. |
| **Where to get help** | Movie Maker has a built-in help feature with searchable contents. If you can't find the answer to your question, it will ask you if you wish to search for the answer via Microsoft's Answer Wizard on the Web. In addition, the additional resources below may be helpful to you. |
| | **Mighty Coach Online Video Training (tutorials and tips)** |
| | www.mightycoach.com/articles/mm2/ |
| | **Atomic Learning's tutorial series** |
| | www.atomiclearning.com/moviemaker2/ |
| | **Windows Movie Maker 2.1 Download** |
| | http://www.microsoft.com/windowsxp/down 0loads/updates/moviemaker2.mspx |
| | **Getting Started with Windows Movie Maker** |
| | http://windowshelp.microsoft.com/Windows/en-US/Help/ ec3fff68-e53c-4168-ae74-8557325e57e21033.mspx |
| | **Windows Movie Maker Community** |
| | http://www.microsoft.com/windowsxp/expertzone/communities/movie.mspx |

## Learning Centers: *Foreign Language*

This set of activities focuses on dessert vocabulary, menus, and ordering in a restaurant. Spanish is used as the target language, but you could substitute any world language. Students will add a dessert section to a menu they've created previously, participate in a role-play that requires ordering from their menus, pen riddles or clues to practice dessert vocabulary, and conduct a survey to determine their classmates' favorite desserts.

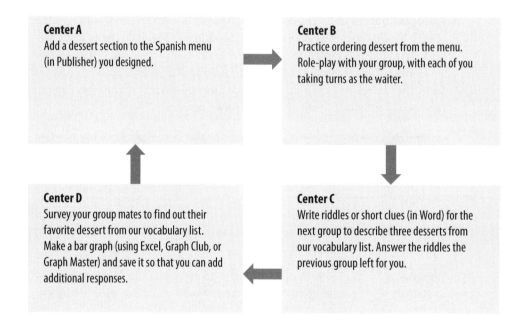

**Center A**
Add a dessert section to the Spanish menu (in Publisher) you designed.

**Center B**
Practice ordering dessert from the menu. Role-play with your group, with each of you taking turns as the waiter.

**Center D**
Survey your group mates to find out their favorite dessert from our vocabulary list. Make a bar graph (using Excel, Graph Club, or Graph Master) and save it so that you can add additional responses.

**Center C**
Write riddles or short clues (in Word) for the next group to describe three desserts from our vocabulary list. Answer the riddles the previous group left for you.

# Learning Centers: *Music*

The following music centers enable students to learn more about a musician's life and work. After listening to a musician's biography, they follow a listening map or storyline of a major work while they hear the piece. As they listen a second time, they assign specific instruments to major characters in the storyline and compare and contrast the first piece with another piece by the same musician.

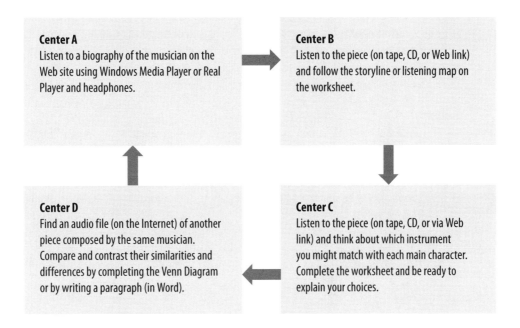

**Center A**
Listen to a biography of the musician on the Web site using Windows Media Player or Real Player and headphones.

**Center B**
Listen to the piece (on tape, CD, or Web link) and follow the storyline or listening map on the worksheet.

**Center D**
Find an audio file (on the Internet) of another piece composed by the same musician. Compare and contrast their similarities and differences by completing the Venn Diagram or by writing a paragraph (in Word).

**Center C**
Listen to the piece (on tape, CD, or via Web link) and think about which instrument you might match with each main character. Complete the worksheet and be ready to explain your choices.

Examples of online resources for music centers include Classics for Kids (www.classicsforkids.com/shows/past.asp), which offers free downloads of their radio shows about composers and their music. In most cases, you'll find three shows about each composer. This site also offers corresponding activity sheets (www.classicsforkids.com/shows/activity.asp).

Classical Archives (www.classicalarchives.com) is a magnificent resource, with biographical information, timelines, music appreciation and history, and tons of audio files. K–12 Resources for Music Educators (www.isd77.k12.mn.us/music/ k-12music/) has a wealth of information, including midi files; biographies; links for band, choral, and classroom teachers; music newsgroups; and commercial resources.

## Learning Centers: *Physical Education*

The focal theme of this set of centers is cardio-respiratory fitness. We designed it in conjunction with a video from Discovery Education *unitedstreaming* entitled "Inside Story with Slim Goodbody, The: Lubba Dubba: The Inside Story of Your Heart and Blood." The video can be found at their Web site, either by searching on the title or though the following link: http://www.unitedstreaming.com/search/assetDetail. cfm?guidAssetID=A6903E83-D941-43CF-84F9-7DDAB3B31363/. Students watch a short video (15 minutes) prior to engaging in the various centers. Students measure and graph heart rates, produce word pictures of key vocabulary (using draw or paint software), and develop two aerobic exercises or moves to share with their classmates.

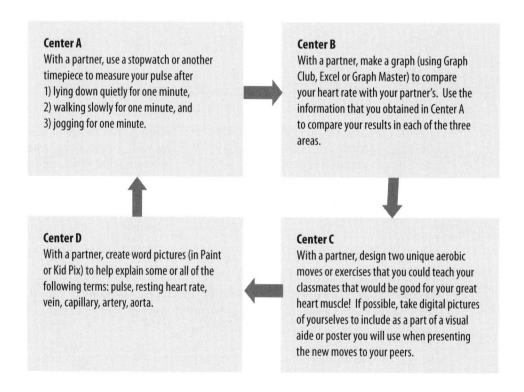

**Center A**
With a partner, use a stopwatch or another timepiece to measure your pulse after
1) lying down quietly for one minute,
2) walking slowly for one minute, and
3) jogging for one minute.

**Center B**
With a partner, make a graph (using Graph Club, Excel or Graph Master) to compare your heart rate with your partner's. Use the information that you obtained in Center A to compare your results in each of the three areas.

**Center D**
With a partner, create word pictures (in Paint or Kid Pix) to help explain some or all of the following terms: pulse, resting heart rate, vein, capillary, artery, aorta.

**Center C**
With a partner, design two unique aerobic moves or exercises that you could teach your classmates that would be good for your great heart muscle! If possible, take digital pictures of yourselves to include as a part of a visual aide or poster you will use when presenting the new moves to your peers.

We hope the examples we supplied for learning centers inspired you to try something fresh in your classroom, particularly with the aid of technology. Let's move on to our sample R.A.F.T.s so that you can take a glimpse at how we might use another differentiation strategy in the four encore areas.

# R.A.F.T. Strategy

We investigated the R.A.F.T. strategy in chapter 2, "Using Technology to Differentiate by Interest." R.A.F.T. is another higher adaptable strategy that we may use across curricular areas. If you need to review the essential components of a R.A.F.T., turn to the R.A.F.T. profile in chapter 2.

Perhaps you might question the use of written documents or assignments in encore classes. We hope the following samples will show you some of the ways teachers can encourage students to use the historical and social knowledge they've learned as a part of the core content. The tasks we've listed suggest ways students may then apply that knowledge to an activity that mimics a possible real-life situation.

As our world grows smaller and competition for jobs in the global marketplace increases, we believe students who can demonstrate skills and knowledge in multiple areas (not solely in their areas of specialization) will have the upper hand. If we tie the content we're communicating to our students to real-life tasks, students might be more receptive, particularly when technology is involved.

## R.A.F.T.: *Art*

The tasks listed in the art R.A.F.T. encourage students to develop a product that distributes art-related information or publicizes art-centered events that might interest or involve children at their school.

TABLE **8.2** ■ R.A.F.T. art task chart

| Role | Audience | Format | Topic |
|---|---|---|---|
| Art Historian | School Webmaster | Slideshow | Design a slideshow (using PowerPoint) for a Web site that kids at your school can use to find biographical information about an artist. Include some sample artwork. |
| Landscape Artist | Maintenance Director or Groundskeeper | Watercolor landscape (or medium used by selected artist) | A brand new school in the area (yours) is having a contest to choose a landscaping design (plants, trees, flowers, and so forth). Paint a picture (using Microsoft Paint or actual paint) that you might enter in the competition. |
| Curator | Art Teachers | Brochure | Produce a brochure (using Publisher or Word). Provide appropriate information about the educational programs and tours that your museum offers to school groups. |
| Students | Parents and Community Members | Invitation | Create an invitation (using Publisher or Word) for the upcoming art exhibition at your school. |

# R.A.F.T.: *Foreign Language*

The following R.A.F.T. requires the use of clothing vocabulary in the target language to complete a written document or diagram giving or asking for advice or information.

TABLE **8.3** ■ R.A.F.T. foreign language task chart

| Role | Audience | Format | Topic |
|------|----------|--------|-------|
| Manager | Prospective Employees | Ad | Write a short classified ad (in Word) for an open sales position at a clothing store. |
| Fashion Designer | Client | Labeled Diagrams | Advise your client about what to wear to these events: the theater, a picnic in July, a football game in November in the Midwest, and a job interview. (Use Paint or your own colored pencil diagrams.) |
| You | Mom, Dad, or Other Relative | List or Table | Prepare a list of clothing (using Word or Excel) you'd like your relative to purchase for you for the new school year. Include approximate prices. |
| Potential Customer | Customer Service | E-mail | Write a short note to inquire about the availability of a certain piece of clothing you're searching for in a particular size and color. |

# R.A.F.T.: *Music*

The music R.A.F.T. invites students to design an announcement or inquiry about events at a local cultural facility.

TABLE **8.4** ■ R.A.F.T. music task chart

| Role | Audience | Format | Topic |
|------|----------|--------|-------|
| Music Teacher | Educational Director of Local Symphony Orchestra | E-mail | Write a note of inquiry to ask for details about arranging a class trip to the symphony. |
| Advertising Representative for Your Local Symphony Orchestra | Prospective Customers | Radio Ad with Sound Clip | Announce the two-for-one summer concert series. Record your ad, and use a sound link or CD for your clip. |
| Music Historian | Students and Teachers | Trading Cards | Create a set of trading cards that your local museum or symphony might pass out or sell to educational groups. Provide a portrait of each musician and key facts about them (Fig. 8.1). |
| Composer | General Public | Video Clip/Ad | Invite the public to the new wax museum of artists. In your clip, provide basic information, such as attractions, special events, hours, and location. |

**GEORGE GERSHWIN**

George Gershwin was born in New York in 1898. He taught himself how to play the piano. He wrote the musical *Porgy and Bess*, and one of his most popular works is "Rhapsody in Blue." He composed some music with his brother Ira. He died in 1937.

FIGURE **8.1** ■ Sample trading card created by authors

## Related Technologies: *Music R.A.F.T.*

### *Audio Creation/Editing Software*

**How audio creation/editing software will be used in the activity:** In the Advertising Representative role in the music R.A.F.T., students may choose to record a radio ad with a sound clip. To complete this activity, students must be familiar with how to use Audacity, and you will have to download it ahead of time. Ideally, students will have been able to practice with it prior to this lesson.

**Implementation challenges:** While Audacity does offer many features, this lesson does not require the use of complex ones.  Students should be able to complete a short recording without too many glitches.

| Resources for Audio Creation/Editing Software | |
| --- | --- |
| **Description** | Audacity is audio creating/editing software that allows you to build, edit and share your audio recordings. |
| **Where to find the software** | You may download it for free online. |
| **Where to get help** | **Audacity Home and Download**<br>    http://audacity.sourceforge.net<br>**Beginner's Tutorial for Audacity**<br>    http://podcasting.about.com/od/podcastingsoftware/qt/Beginaudacity.htm<br>**Audacity's Documentation and Support**<br>    http://audacity.sourceforge.net/help/<br>    *This page has FAQs, tutorials, a link to a forum, and other helpful resources.* |

| Using Audacity to Record a Radio Ad |
| --- |
| 1.  Download Audacity at http://audacity.sourceforge.net. |
| 2.  Check your Preferences under the File menu to make sure the correct output device is selected. |
| 3.  Click the Record button and speak into your microphone. Click Stop when you're finished. |
| 4.  Save your file. |

# R.A.F.T.: *Physical Education*

This R.A.F.T. asks students to produce an artifact that reflects on their health, assessments of their fitness, and how to improve their physical well-being.

TABLE **8.5** ■ R.A.F.T. for physical education task chart

| Role | Audience | Format | Topic |
|---|---|---|---|
| Student | Parents or Principal | Brochure | Develop a brochure (in Publisher) to explain or display what you've learned in class about becoming a healthier person. |
| Nutritionist | Director of Food Services | Menu | Revise your school's menu (using Word or Publisher) so that it offers healthier food choices. |
| Nutritionist or Personal Trainer | Client (Classmate) | Spreadsheet | Critique your client's daily exercise and diet logs. Place short comments and suggestions for improvement alongside the records in a different font color (Fig. 8.2). |
| Physical Education Teacher | President | Graph | Prepare a graph (using Excel, Graph Club, or Graph Master) of the average student performance (in your class) in each of the Physical Fitness Test events. |

| | A | B | C | D |
|---|---|---|---|---|
| 1 | **Breakfast** | **Lunch** | **Dinner** | **Exercise** |
| 2 | 2 scrambled eggs | cheeseburger | spaghetti | Ran 1 mile after school |
| 3 | 3 slices bacon | apple | salad | |
| 4 | 1 cup orange juice | chips | garlic bread | |
| 5 | | chocolate milk | Coke | |
| 6 | | | | |
| 7 | Try a piece of wheat toast with peanut butter and a piece of fruit or yogurt. Drink water. | Wow!! This is a lot of fatty stuff! The apple is good, but stick with skim milk, eat pretzels instead of chips. | Good job on the salad, but you have a lot of carbs and sugar here. Drink water and try to give up the bread. | Good job! |

FIGURE **8.2** ■ Sample food log with comments created in Excel

## WebQuest Strategy

A final strategy we wish to examine in more detail is the WebQuest. In this case, we'll focus on one encore subject area (foreign language), and we'll walk you through the steps to create a WebQuest for a Spanish class.

We've already looked at the structure of WebQuests in chapter 2, "Using Technology to Differentiate by Interest." If you need to brush up on the other features of this strategy, such as its benefits, its components, and so forth, return to the WebQuest profile section.

We used the steps from the WebQuest profile, then added commentary on our experience as we endeavored to create a WebQuest from scratch. Remember that while these steps are fairly standard, you might encounter some variation.

### Spanish WebQuest Step 1

**Brainstorm ideas:** If at all possible, involve your students in the selection of subtopics associated with the broad theme of the WebQuest they're intrigued with or passionate about. As a substitute for brainstorming or a supplemental activity, you might choose to use a checklist, questionnaire, survey, written list, KWL chart, or interest map to help with the identification of promising topics of interest.

The sample topic we've chosen is Hispanic Celebrations or Holidays (celebraciones/días festivos/días feriados hispánicos). (See Table 8.6.) If you need a little help with brainstorming possible subtopics, a search engine such as Google can really be an asset. One of our favorite search engines for students is KidsClick! (www.kidsclick.org), but when a foreign language theme is our central topic of investigation, we sometimes have to search a little deeper or longer to find what we need.

TABLE **8.6** ■ Hispanic celebrations or holidays

| La Quinceañera | La Navidad | El Día de los Muertos |
|---|---|---|
| El Día de Independencia (of a particular country) | Cinco de Mayo | Los Sanfermines/El Encierro |
| El Día de los Reyes Magos/de los Santos Reyes | La Semana Santa | El Día de las Madres |
| El Primero de Mayo/Día del Trabajo/Día del Trabajador | Las Posadas | El Día de la Virgen de Guadalupe |
| El Día de la Raza | El Año Nuevo | El Cumpleaños |

### Spanish WebQuest Step 2

**Search for Web links and other resources to support the big idea of the WebQuest:**

- Determine the task the students will complete after your brainstorming session or interest inventory. As mentioned in the components section, the task will require that they solve a problem or answer a question, or something similar.

- Begin to investigate the Internet for suitable links. Consider other useful resources that aren't Web-based.

We've chosen a simple task for our students because the details about this cultural event are unfamiliar to most Americans and we're working with elementary-aged children. For our WebQuest, our students must imagine that they've traveled to Pamplona to witness and take part in Los Sanfermines. This celebrated event in Spain is more commonly known as the Running of the Bulls. It occurs in Pamplona every July.

It's the students' responsibility to return home and describe several aspects of the festival and the place where it occurs so that other Americans can gain a better appreciation for what takes place and the motivation behind it. Each group will craft a product that offers a specific perspective on one of the key elements of Los Sanfermines, such as its history, its events, and so forth.

---

### KidsClick! A Super Search Engine

KidsClick! is a really wonderful Web site because it will generate a list of links for you based on the topic you've selected. At the bottom of the home page, you may click on a link that allows you to see the same page "through a librarian's eyes." This neat feature categorizes the topics for you according to their corresponding numbers in the Dewey decimal system. Of course, KidsClick! doesn't make any promises that the list of subtopics it creates for you will be completely free of any subtopics or accompanying links that you've already generated yourself.

Another benefit of relying on a search engine specifically directed toward children is that it often (but not always) locates other sites that might be more appropriate for kids. While the Internet is a fantastic resource, we have to make sure we review the sites and their content very carefully for our young students. At times, it can be very challenging to find suitable Web sites.

KidsClick! also has a link that takes you to a number of other search tools for students, some of which use specific filtering devices to protect students' best interests.

---

We wanted to choose a topic that was somewhat familiar but not either overly popular or too obscure. We didn't encounter many WebQuests or Web-based exercises on this particular theme, much less for our target group (Grades K–5), and some of the useful sites have questionable content that you might opt to filter out or just use as a resource for yourself. In fact, this WebQuest is most suited to upper elementary students, preferably those in Grade 5. You know your students best (what they can tolerate) and what is acceptable at your institution.

Some of the problematic issues might include both the consumption of alcoholic beverages that occurs as a part of many celebrations and the injuries to participants. At the same time, you'll discover some attention-grabbing links, such as the one with the Webcam that allows us to see the bulls and the runners (¡locos!) in action.

While we realize this topic might be more challenging, it also presents an opportunity to explore a cultural topic that's totally foreign to American children. It can lead to discussion and investigation of related topics, such as bullfighting and the celebration of rituals, arts, or sports that don't take place in the United States.

Below you'll find a list of some of the links we found. This isn't a comprehensive list, and some of them (or parts of them) are inappropriate for students (but useful for teachers). Maybe you could create your own child-friendly site!

TABLE **8.7** ■ Links for Spanish WebQuest

- **Información turística about los Sanfermines at El Reyno de Navarra** (www.turismo.navarra.es/esp/propuestas/san-fermines/) can be viewed in English, too. It offers FAQs, a program of events, history, suggested places to eat and stay, and detailed information about the bulls.

- **Education Guardian's Language Resources Site** (http://education.guardian.co.uk/languageresources/ spanish/story/0,,682814,00.html) provides an interview in Spanish with younger Spaniards that explains what attracts them to the events of the Sanfermines.

- **The Festival of San Fermín** (www.abc.net.au/civics/celebrations/pamp1.htm) describes the history and events that take place. It's written in simple, clear, clean language. There are no offensive images, and there's a "personal view" from a Spaniard who describes the first time he saw the running of the bulls.

- **Fiestas de España** at the BBC's Primary Spanish: Festivals site (http://www.bbc.co.uk/schools/ primaryspanish/festivals/fiestas/) doesn't exclusively deal with the running of the bulls, but it's a useful tool. Students read short descriptions of various festivals and see pictures. Then they're asked basic oral questions about the celebrations in Spain. In addition, there are games to practice the selected vocabulary associated with the theme. Students may hear audio clips of the vocabulary, too.

- **Fiestas de San Fermín** (http://www.fiestasdesanfermin.com/sf2003/index.asp) has some interactive features, such as videochats, e-postcards, forums, surveys, and so forth. Some of the images could bother students. On the Guía del Novato link, you're able to read a description of each part of the festivities, learn about its history, and look at old photos of each activity.

*continued*

TABLE **8.7**  ■  Links for Spanish WebQuest *(continued)*

- **Fiestas populares at El Ayuntamiento de Pamplona** (www.pamplona.es) is Pamplona's official "city council" site, and you can change the language to English. It supplies background, historical information, and a description of the various activities.

- **NIE: Newspapers in Education—The Cincinnati Enquirer** (www.cincinnati.com/nie/archive/07-09-02/) furnishes a short article about the first day of los Sanfermines, and then a number of links for a virtual journey. Unfortunately, many links are dead.

- **Pamplona Bull Run** (San Fermín) at Spanish-Fiestas.com (http://www.spanish-fiestas.com/ spanish-festivals/pamplona-bull-running-san-fermin.htm) offers a short history of the fiesta.

- **Running of the Bulls** (http://www.uen.org/utahlink/tours/tourElement.cgi?element_id=26281&tour_ id=14712&c) provides a short description of the Encierro, and it has links you may click to see photos. Some photos could be disturbing, but each link has a title that will clearly indicate to your students whether they wish to view it or not.

- **Running of the Bulls Google Image Search** (http://images.google.com/images?q=running+of+the+ bulls&hl=en/) has a large quantity of photos available, some of which you won't want students to view. However, you may pick and choose as you wish, and save those that are appropriate. The neat thing about this site is that many of the images come from newspaper articles, many of which appear when you click on the photo.

- **The Running of the Bulls Info.com** (http://members.aol.com/_ht_a/pamplonaWeb/pwindex.htm) describes the origin, the route, tips on and rules governing human participation, a visitor's guide (places to stay, eat, and so forth), maps, quick facts on Pamplona, a photo tour of Pamplona, a chat room, a Webcam, and a photo gallery.

- **Run the Planet: The Running of the Bulls** (www.runtheplanet.com/pages/refer/bullsrun.php) lists tips on and rules for running identical to those mentioned on the Web site above, as well as the origin of the fiesta.

- **San Fermín at Wikipedia,** the Free Encyclopedia (http://en.wikipedia.org/wiki/San_Fermin/) details the history of los Sanfermines, el Encierro, related activities, and suggested links.

- **San Fermín Guide** (www.sanfermin.com/guia/) has some of the same features and links as the Fiestas de San Fermín above, but it also lists suggested places to stay, eat, drink, and so forth, as well as what to avoid (alcohol-related and sexual terms mentioned here). It can be viewed in English.

- **San Fermín, la fiesta de los sanfermines en directo** (www.sanferminonline.net) supplies a Webcam, last year's program (detailing daily activities), a virtual tour of Pamplona, a photo gallery, videos of last year's Sanfermines, and online viewing or direct transmission of Sanfermines.

- **Sizzling Sanfermines at Spain and Portugal for Visitors** (http://spainforvisitors.com/sections/ sanfermin.htm) has a short description of the main elements of the celebration. Some alcohol-related information or commentary is included in the descriptions.

### *Spanish WebQuest Step 3*

**Identify student roles:** Upon completion of your search for resources, think about potential roles that students might take on during the WebQuest. Following are four possible methods to group students based on the roles they assume:

- Establish groups according to learning styles, multiple intelligences, or some other means. (Each group crafts a unique product such as a skit, a letter, a journal entry, and so forth.)

- Divide students into homogeneous groups that are solely made up of geographers, scientists, writers, artists, or some other profession.

- Form heterogeneous groups in which each student assumes a different role. The groups might consist of journalists, biographers, environmentalists, governors, and so forth.

- Build groups according to interest areas or subtopics of the broad theme.

For our particular WebQuest, we thought it would be engaging for students to craft a unique product so that they could share it with other students. You could easily modify this set of activities for heterogeneous or homogeneous groups and use such labels as historians, publishers, travel agents, and so forth. f you have ample time to spend on the project, we have provided more than one activity option under each group number. If you're looking for a less complicated assignment, feel free to simplify our suggestions or ask students to complete the easiest option. Take a peek at our plans for student groups, and you'll be able to follow our train of thought.

**Group 1**: Students prepare a skit with props that communicates some of the history of los Sanfermines. The skit could include brief "interviews" with people that speak to why they enjoy the festival.

**Group 2**: Students prepare an imaginative photo essay or two to three scrapbook pages with digital photos to describe their experience watching the running of the bulls in Pamplona. You might ask students to supply a short list of common terms (in Spanish and English) used in connection with the festival, such as el encierro, los mozos, and so forth.

**Group 3**: Students prepare an imaginative journal entry written by a mozo (runner) in los Sanfermines. The journal entry describes his experience and also includes colorful, labeled drawings of his outfit.

**Group 4**: Students prepare a mini travel kit for those who might be interested in traveling to Pamplona to see the running of the bulls. They should include a map and describe the major events that make up los Sanfermines. If desired, they could produce their own program or brochure about the festival.

**Group 5**: Students prepare a letter to the editor that discusses the pros and cons of this particular Spanish festival. If possible, have them include one or two pieces of evidence or statistics of past injuries to participants. Table 8.7 offers a sample rubric for this product.

**Group 6**: Students prepare a mural or another piece of artwork that illustrates some of the highlights of los Sanfermines. Another option would be to have them create a scaled-down version of cabezudo or gigante (giant heads that people wear as part of a parade or festival) that they didn't see in any pictures. This could be a delicate project (as it could be messy). If that doesn't appeal to you, students could generate two to three drawings in Paint or another medium for new cabezudos or gigantes.

### Spanish WebQuest Steps 4 and 5

**Determine if the WebQuest warrants your time and energy:** If you think your students would benefit from the task, and you find appropriate resources that support it, move to step five!

**Complete the WebQuest:** Create the Web page.

- Set up scaffolding.
- Formulate rubrics (see Table 8.8 for sample rubric).

As we mentioned in chapter 2, there are now many tools and helps that make the creation of a Web page much easier than ever before. QuestGarden (www.questgarden.com) generates a WebQuest with Web pages for you. You follow prompts for information, and it produces an attractive Web page with tasks, scaffolding, and rubrics designed to your specifications.

You could also construct your own WebQuest using FrontPage, Word, or Publisher. Completed Word and Publisher files can be easily converted into HTML documents, while FrontPage actually converts your characters into HTML as you type. When I (Stephanie) was using BlackBoard for an online class, my preferred method was to create my lesson in Word with clip art and save it as a Web archive (MHTML). It was very quick and simple.

San Diego City Schools' Anatomy of the New WebQuest page (http://projects.edtech.sandi.net/staffdev/tpss99/anatomy.htm) offers various templates and an explanation of each page in a WebQuest. We also describe the components of a WebQuest in chapter 2 of this book.

TABLE **8.8** ■ Sample rubric for letter to editor product

| Category | 4 | 3 | 2 | 1 |
|---|---|---|---|---|
| Format | Business letter format is 100% correct. | Business letter format is 80%–89% correct. | Business letter format is 70%–77% correct. | 69% or less of the business letter format is correct. |
| Content Accuracy and Evidence of Opinion | All pros and cons are backed by specific facts or evidence. At least four pros and four cons are included. | 80%–89% of the pros and cons are backed by specific facts or evidence. At least three pros and three cons are included. | 70%–79% of the pros and cons are backed by specific facts or evidence. Only two pros and two cons are included. | 69% or less of the pros and cons are backed by specific facts or evidence. Only one pro and one con are included. |
| Grammar and Mechanics | There are no errors in grammar or spelling. | There are one to two errors in grammar or spelling. | There are three to four errors in grammar or spelling. | There are more than four errors in grammar or spelling. |
| Envelope | 100% complete and accurate return address and recipient address. Addresses in correct positions. | Return and recipient addresses and positioning are 80%–89% correct. | Return and recipient addresses and positioning are 70%–79% correct. | 69% or less of return and recipient addresses and positioning are correct. |

We realize that not all of you are Spanish teachers, but we expect that this walk-through will spur you to create a WebQuest for your students in your own area of specialization. We anticipate that you, too, will get energized as you search for some neat resources and create some interesting tasks for your students.

After you complete the organizational work up front, sit back and enjoy the fruits of your labor as your students generate some intriguing products! The same is true for the other strategies we've examined in this chapter: learning centers or stations and R.A.F.T.s.

We believe your students will be eager to try out new formats that involve hands-on learning and real-life scenarios. Most of all, they'll be thrilled to work with the wide span of technology resources mentioned in this chapter. They'll be shouting, *"Encore! Encore!"* for a twofold reason: because they love their encore class activities, and because they're ready to test out yet another exciting technology tool. Don't keep them waiting—*¡Ándale!*

## Resources for Chapter 8

| | | |
|---|---|---|
| **Art** | Grosse Pointe Public Schools' Technology Integration Resources for K–5 Art | www.gpschools.org/ci/ce/elem/art/home.htm |
| | Hartland Technology Infusion Team's General Art Websites 2006 | www.aea11.k12.ia.us/tech/TIC/Art Gems.pdf |
| | Matisse Images on the Web | www.artchive.com/artchive/ftptoc/matisse_ext.html |
| | Monet & the Impressionists for Kids | http://members.aol.com/sabbeth/monetforkids.html |
| | Mrs. Donn's Performing Arts Lesson Plans & Activities for Kids & Teachers | http://lessonplans.mrdonn.org/arts.html |
| | MuseumStuff.com | www.museumstuff.com |
| | Online Picasso Project | www.picasso.com/gallery/ |
| | Painter Classic Software | |
| | Princeton Online Art Education | www.princetonol.com/groups/iad/lessons/middle/arted.htm |
| | TeAchnology: Arts & Humanities Lesson Plans | www.teach-nology.com/teachers/lesson_plans/arts/ |
| | Revelation Natural Art Software | www.logo.com/cat/view/revelation-natural-art.html |
| | WebMuseum | www.ibiblio.org/wm/paint/auth/ |
| **Foreign Languages** | **French, German, and Japanese** | |
| | German Internet Project | www.uncg.edu/~lixlpurc/GIP/ |
| | Japan @ UT-Martin's Globe-Gate | www.utm.edu/staff/globeg/japan.shtml |
| | TeAchnology: French Lesson Plans | www.teach-nology.com/teachers/lesson_plans/languages/french/ |
| | TeAchnology: German Lesson Plans | www.teach-nology.com/teachers/lesson_plans/languages/german/ |
| | Tennessee Bob's Famous French Links | www.utm.edu/departments/french/french.html |
| | WebGerman | http://Webgerman.com |
| | **Spanish** | |
| | Foreign Language in the Elementary Classroom: Tredyffrin/Easttown School District | www.tesd.k12.pa.us/fles/ |
| | GlobeGate Spanish Language and Culture Pages | http://globegate.utm.edu/spanish/ |
| | Helping Kids Learn Spanish (music, video, and software recommendations) | www.edutainingkids.com/articles/kidslearnspanish.html |
| | Hot Internet Sites ¡en Español! | www.kn.sbc.com/wired/fil/pages/listspanish.html |
| | Knowledge Network Explorer: ¡Epecially Español! | www.kn.sbc.com/wired/espanol/ |
| | Musical Spanish | www.musicalspanish.com/ |
| | Pratt's Educational Spanish Resources | www.fastq.com/~jbpratt/education/spanish/links.html |
| | Quia's Free Online Games/Exercises | www.quia.com/dir/spanish/index_by_title.html |
| | Songs for Teaching: Spanish Songs | www.songsforteaching.com/spanishsongs.htm |

*continued*

## Resources for Chapter 8 *(continued)*

| | Spanish *(continued)* | |
|---|---|---|
| **Foreign Languages** *(continued)* | Spanish Class Online | www.spanishclassonline.com/games/<br>www.spanishclassonline.com/vocabulary/ |
| | Spanish Flashcards | http://members.tripod.com/spanishflashcards/ |
| | Spanish Learning Activities at Enchanted Learning | www.enchantedlearning.com/themes/spanish.shtml |
| | Sr. Hauck Spanish: Recursos para estudiantes y profesores | http://spider.nlsd.org/nlhs/thauck/srhauck Web/<br>     recursos.html#paraprofesores |
| | Super Links to Spanish Websites (Jim Becker's site) | www.uni.edu/becker/Spanish3.html |
| | Support for Elementary Educators Through Distance Education in Spanish | www.outreach.usf.edu/seeds/spanishEnhance/main2.html |
| | Tom's Spanish Web Page | http://tpduggan.tripod.com/spanish.html |
| | World Language Resources for Elementary School Spanish Teachers | www.geocities.com/sra_rk/worldlang_resources0.htm |
| **Foreign Languages— Multiple World Languages** | Activities for ESL Students | http://a4esl.org |
| | BBC Languages | www.bbc.co.uk/languages/ |
| | CASLT Digital Newsletter | www.caslt.org/Info/sites_en.htm |
| | Dr. Tony Erben's Home Page | www.coedu.usf.edu/terben/ |
| | Foreign Language Lesson Plans and Resources for Teachers (Marty Levine's) | www.csun.edu/~hcedu013/eslsp.html<br>www.csun.edu/~hcedu013/eslindex.html |
| | Foreign Languages @ Elementary Schools | www.public.iastate.edu/~egarcia/fles.html |
| | Foreign Language Teaching Forum: WWW Resources for Language Teachers | www.cortland.edu/flteach/flteach-res.html |
| | iLoveLanguages: Your Guide to Foreign Language Resources on the Web | www.ilovelanguages.com |
| | Internet Activities for Foreign Language Classes | www.clta.net/lessons/ |
| | Kathy Shrock's Guide for Educators: Regions of the World & World Languages | http://school.discovery.com/schrockguide/world/worldrw.html |
| | Mount Hebron High School Library: Media Center Curriculum Links: Foreign Language | www.howard.k12.md.us/mhmedia/media_links_for-lang.html |
| | Mrs. Donn's World Languages: Lesson Plans & Activities for Kids & Teachers | http://lessonplans.mrdonn.org/worldlanguages.html |
| | (Dr. Sass') Resources and Lesson Plans for World Languages | www.cloudnet.com/~edrbsass/edwor.htm |
| | Multilingual Books (courses, tapes, video, and software for numerous languages) | www.multilingualbooks.com |

*continued*

## Resources for Chapter 8   *(continued)*

| | | |
|---|---|---|
| **Foreign Languages— Multiple World Languages** *(continued)* | Teaching Foreign Languages K–12 Workshop | www.learner.org/channel/workshops/tfl/ |
| | Teaching with the Web: Language Links | http://polyglot.lss.wisc.edu/lss/lang/teach.html |
| | TeAchnology: Spanish Lesson Plans | www.teach-nology.com/teachers/lesson_plans/languages/spanish/ |
| | Tennessee Bob's International Search | www.utm.edu/vlibrary/search.shtml |
| | Thiesen, Tony. (2002). Differentiated Instruction in the Foreign Language Classroom: Meeting the Diverse Needs of All Learners [Electronic version]. *LOTE CED Communiqué Newsletter 6,* 1–8 | www.sedl.org/loteced/communique/n06.html |
| | University of Texas at Austin: Foreign Language Lesson Plans for K–12 Educators | http://utopia.utexas.edu/educators/foreign.html |
| | Rosetta Stone Software | www.rosettastone.com |
| | Jump Start Software | www.jumpstart.com |
| | KidSpeak Software | www.transparent.com/products/kidspeak.htm |
| | Power-Glide Software | www.power-glide.com |
| **Handheld Devices** | Handhelds in the Classroom | www.education-world.com/a_tech/tech083.shtml |
| | Handhelds Go to Class | www.edutopia.org/php/article.php?id=art_955 |
| **Learning Centers/ Stations** | Best Practices: Instructional Strategies & Techniques: Learning Centers | http://wblrd.sk.ca/~bestpractice/centres/ |
| | Kathy Schrock's Guide for Educators/Learning Centers | http://school.discovery.com/schrockguide/edlearn.html |
| | Math Stations | www.mcps.k12.md.us/curriculum/enriched/giftedprograms/ mathstations.shtm |
| **Lesson Plans or Multiple Resources** | 4 Teachers (great teaching tools for rubrics, notes, activities with Web links, and so forth) | www.4teachers.org/tools/ |
| | Cool Teaching Lessons and Units (plus student and teacher resources) | www.coollessons.org/coolunits.htm |
| | Education World's Tech in the Classroom: Online Projects | http://db.educationworld.com/perl/browse?cat_id=6598 |
| | Hazel's Homepage Site Index | www.marshall-es.marshall.k12.tn.us/jobe/siteindex.html |
| | Interactive Classroom | www.ga.k12.pa.us/curtech/interactive/interactive.htm |
| | Internet 4 Classrooms: Lesson Plans and Templates | www.Internet4classrooms.com/lesson.htm |
| | Laptops in the Classroom | http://moore.portlandschools.org/ibook/science.html |
| | Squeakland | www.squeakland.org |
| | Teaching with Podcasts | http://teachingwithpodcasts.blogspot.com |

*continued*

## Resources for Chapter 8  *(continued)*

| | | |
|---|---|---|
| **MOOs, MUSHes, Chats, CU See Me, KeyPals, and so forth** | DU Rainbow Moo | http://it.uwp.edu/rainbow/ |
| | CU-SeMe for Elementary Education | http://pixel.cs.vt.edu/~rmohn/k12/edcusm.html |
| | Global SchoolNet Foundation | www.globalschoolnet.org |
| | Kidlink Global Networking for Youth through Secondary School Age | www.kidlink.org |
| | Knowledge Network Explorer: Video Conferencing Directory | www.kn.pacbell.com/wired/vidconf/directory.cfm |
| | Mundo Hispano (MOO) | www.umsl.edu/~moosproj/mundo.html |
| **Music** | Grosse Pointe Public Schools' Technology Integration Resources for Music | www.gpschools.org/ci/ce/elem/music/music.htm |
| | Heartland Technology Infusion Team's Music Gems | www.aea11.k12.ia.us/tech/TIC/Music Gems.pdf |
| | New Hampshire Public Television Network's Classroom Internet Library: Music Lesson Plans & WebQuests | www.nhptv.org/kn/vs/musla2.htm |
| | TeachersFirst Resource Listings | www.teachersfirst.com/20/tchr-subj-date.cfm?subject=27&lower= 1&upper=5 |
| | Vermont Midi Project | www.vtmidi.org |
| | Midi Software | |
| | Music Ace and Music Ace 2 Software | |
| | Making Music and Making More Music Software | http://www.viva-media.com/product_info.php?products_id= 36&osCsid=884b1e946fc726204b75f3d6647e |
| | Band in a Box Software | http://www.viva-media.com/product_info.php?products_id= 46&osCsid=884b1e946fc726204b75f3d6647e |
| **Physical Education** | Grosse Pointe Public Schools' Physical Education Resources | www.gpschools.org/ci/depts/pe/home.htm |
| | Hartland Technology Infusion Team's Physical Education Gems | www.aea11.k12.ia.us/tech/TIC/Physical Education Gems.pdf |
| | Mrs. Donn's Lesson Plans & Activities for Kids & Teachers: Physical Education, Health & Nutrition | http://lessonplans.mrdonn.org/health.html |
| | Teacher Tap: Internet Resources for Health, Fitness, and Physical Education | http://eduscapes.com/tap/taphealth.html |
| | Health-Related Fitness Tutorial Software | Product description: www.pesoftware.com/Technews/news0506.html<br><br>Product: http://shop.pesoftware.com/ViewProductasp?misc= 18&prod=143 |
| | Hardware appropriate for physical education: GPS devices, heart monitors, pedometers | |

*continued*

## Resources for Chapter 8 *(continued)*

| | | |
|---|---|---|
| **Virtual Field Trips** | Internet 4 Classrooms: Virtual Field Trips | www.Internet4classrooms.com/vft.htm |
| | Saskatoon (East) School Division | http://sesd.sk.ca/teacherresource/virtualtour/virtualtours.htm |
| | No. 41: Virtual Tours and Field Trips The Teacher's Guide: Virtual Fieldtrips | www.theteachersguide.com/virtualtours.html |
| | The WWW Virtual Library | http://vlib.org |
| | Tramline (trial software, discussion boards, trips) | www.field-guides.com |
| | Two Way Interactive Connections in Education: Videoconference Field Trips | www.twice.cc/fieldtrips.html |
| | Virtual Field Trips | www.uen.org/utahlink/tours/ |
| | Virtual Field Trips | www.virtual-field-trips.com |
| | Virtual Schoolhouse | www.ibiblio.org/cisco/schoolhouse/ |
| **Webcams** | CamVista | www.camvista.com/worldcams/ |
| | EarthCam | www.earthcam.com |
| | Surfing the Net with Kids: Animal Cams | www.surfnetkids.com/animalcams.htm |
| | WebCam Central | www.camcentral.com |
| **WebQuests** | (Dr. Sass') WebQuests Across the Curriculum | www.cloudnet.com/~edrbsass/Webquest.html |
| | A Virtual Library of Useful URLs: 371.3 WebQuests (arranged by Dewey decimal system) | www.aresearchguide.com/Webquests.html |
| | Foreign Language WebQuests | www.serve.com/shea/fl_Webquest.htm |
| | Pre-Writing Your WebQuest | http://tommarch.com/learning/prewrite.php |
| | Waukegan Community District Unit 60: WebQuests | www.waukeganschools.org/teachers/stories/storyReader$24 |
| | WebQuest Templates | http://Webquest.sdsu.edu/LessonTemplate.html |

## CHAPTER 9

# Using Technology *to* Assess Learning

When educators think of the term assessment, the image of paper and pencil usually comes to mind. The thought of paper and pencil tests may be buried deep in teachers' brains, because for many years, this type of test was about all that many teachers used to assess learning. Today, however, teachers can use many types of assessment strategies to measure learning and discover information needed for differentiating instruction.

Just to clarify terms, assessment means the collecting of data to more completely understand students' current knowledge and skills as well as their readiness, interests, and learning profiles. Evaluation, on the other hand, concerns the summative analysis of learners' skills, abilities, and performances at a particular time in order to make judgments and compute letter grades. Evaluations are usually made at the end of a card marking, semester, or school year.

In this chapter, we'll focus on three categories of assessment:

1. *Pre-assessment*: assessment that occurs prior to an instructional segment

2. *Formative Assessment*: assessment that takes place simultaneously with instruction and learning

3. *Summative Assessment:* assessment that follows instruction and is used for evaluation purposes

We'll also review some common assessment strategies and, along the way, how technology can help you move beyond these conventional strategies. If you'd like more information and resources regarding assessment of student technology skills, get hold of *Resources for Student Assessment* (Kelly & Haber, 2006).

# Curriculum–Instruction–Assessment + Technology

The three components of any course are

1. curriculum or content,

2. instructional strategies teachers use to deliver that content, and

3. assessment that measures how well content learning goals have been accomplished.

Assessment plays an important role because it measures student learning, provides feedback on instruction, and provides data and direction for modifying and differentiating curriculum.

We like the diagrams portrayed on the Manatee County School District (Florida) Web page; the USD 204 Bonner Springs/Edwardsville, Kansas, site; and the FLAG site (see chapter 8's resources section for links to these sites). All three illustrations show the traditional interrelationship between curriculum, instruction, and assessment, with the three parts making up the whole.

However, we propose an updated model that includes the technologies both students and educators use in instruction, curriculum, and assessment. Instructional technologies have such a powerful impact on teaching, learning, and assessment, as well as on 21st-century skills, that the technology component can stand on its own. That said, our model consists of the four components fitting tightly together as pieces of the learning and teaching puzzle.

Technology is changing the ways curriculum is provided, delivered, and assessed. Most of the newer K–5 software products, for example, have built-in assessment tools so that pre-, formative, and summative assessments can be made.

FIGURE **9.1** ◼
Model depicting the interrelationships among curriculum, instruction, assessment, and technology

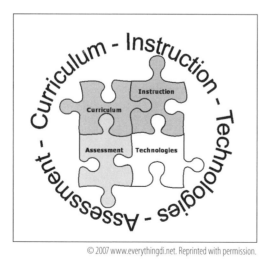

© 2007 www.everythingdi.net. Reprinted with permission.

StudyDog (www.studydog.com) is a good example of newer software in which the content is provided, delivered, and assessed electronically. StudyDog is available free to low-income families. A school version with enhanced features is also available for purchase. Notice in the chart below the content StudyDog delivers per grade level. Each level also uses a tracking system of points to show progress and achievement. The school version employs a diagnostic reading test and weekly e-mail reports to parents.

| Level 1 | Level 2 | Level 3 |
|---|---|---|
| Pre–K | Grades K–1 | Grades 1–2 |
| Features 21 lessons covering areas of the alphabet, consonant sounds, rhyming words, sight words, and more | Features 21 lessons covering topics such as rhyming words, sight words, vowels, contractions, and consonant blends | Features 25 lessons covering vowels, contractions, consonant blends, complex words, spelling, word families, and more |

FASTT Math (www.tomsnyder.com/products/product.asp?SKU=FASFAS) is another software program that delivers content based on three types of assessment. The Placement Quiz (Fig. 9.2) assesses students' fluent and non-fluent facts. Based on this assessment, the program creates a customized course of study for individual students.

During instruction, the program generates frequent, automatic assessments to ensure that students are receiving the correct amount of practice exactly where they need it. Finally, the Fact Fluency Foundations guide provides assessments for teachers to determine where students need additional help.

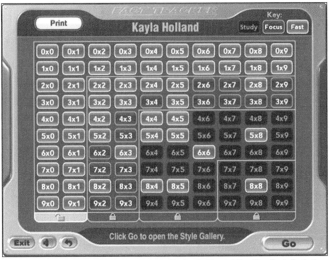

FIGURE **9.2** ▥ FASTT Math's placement assessment

Reprinted with permission of Tom Snyder Productions.

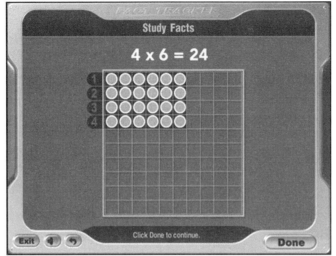

FIGURE **9.3** ■ FASTT Math features adaptive instruction, customizing instruction to target fluency gaps.

Figure 9.2 shows sample results of a placement assessment in FASTT Math. Color shading indicates the facts the student is already fluent in, the facts the student will currently focus on, and facts to be learned. Figure 9.3 illustrates customized instruction to help the student visualize and learn the facts. In FASTT Math software, the computer assesses students' progress and specifies individual instruction based on students' responses.

Destination Math and Destination Reading (www.riverdeep.net) are two online, content-delivered programs with built-in assessments and tracking. You can get a free trial of several products to use with your students.

From these programs alone, you can see how technology is making assessment quite easy to manage. Even if your district can't afford commercial programs, you can let technology help you assess learning in many ways. So let's get started!

## Pre-Assessment

The purpose of pre-assessment is to gather information and diagnose learners' entry levels. Pre-assessments determine students' current level of readiness, interest, or learning profile and allow teachers to meet students *wherever they currently are*. In other words, the intention of any pre-assessment is to know as much about learners as possible. There are several reasons why pre-assessment is useful.

## Purpose

- Identify learners' individual needs in order to design adjustable assignments.
- Develop multiple strategies to meet learners' needs.
- Measure students' knowledge and skills to determine appropriate content and pacing.
- Compare pre-assessments with summative assessments to see growth.
- Determine what students already know and understand about a unit of content.
- Determine which areas of content will require review, reteaching, or enhancement.
- Gain knowledge of students' interests, readiness, and learning profiles to help determine flexible groups.

## Characteristics

- Precedes instruction.
- Used to check for prior knowledge and skill levels, identify misconceptions, and measure learners' readiness, interests, and learning preferences.
- Not graded.

## Examples

**Checklists.** Checklists can be set up in different formats, ranging from very simple yes or no questions to more complex surveys that rate skills on a scale. For example, you might create a writing assessment checklist in which students check off whether they know writing mechanics and story elements and can identify or define them. Or you might create an assessment checklist for evaluating technology skills.

A checklist can be created in table format, with the assessment items in the first column, space for checkmarks in the second column, and space for comments in the third column (Fig. 9.4).

 **Add Tech!**   Checklists can be easily set up in Word or Excel by creating a table with several columns and rows. You can also customize a checklist by using the online PBL Checklist Generator at http://pblchecklist.4teachers.org.

| Technology Skill: Multimedia<br><br>*Students will plan, design, and communicate a simple multimedia project for an audience.* | Level<br>N= Novice<br>D = Developing<br>H = High | | | Comments |
|---|---|---|---|---|
| | N | D | H | |
| Can choose an appropriate design layout. | | | | |
| Can choose an appropriate background. | | | | |
| Can present the multimedia project in electronic and printed format. | | | | |
| Can insert text. | | | | |

FIGURE **9.4** ■ Sample tech assessment checklist

**Entrance Cards.** Prior to a lesson, students respond in writing to a question or set of questions posed by the teacher or physically move to a part of the classroom that defines their knowledge about a certain topic.

**Add Tech!**

**Create questions in Word or Publisher** and print them or make the documents available for students to use. Another way technology can help you is in the making of classroom signs. You could create your signs in Word or Publisher or use the online tool Project Poster at http://poster.4teachers.org. Make four signs such as Hardly Ever, Sometimes, Often, and All the Time, or words of your choice. Print the signs and post them in four corners of your room. Ask students to respond to your prompt by moving to the corner of the room with the sign that most closely matches their learner knowledge of the topic.

**KWL Charts.** KWL charts are used to assess what students already know (K), what students want to know (W), and what students have already learned (L). KWL charts are an effective pre-assessment tool as well as a tool for evaluating students' level of understanding.

**Add Tech!**

**A KWL chart can be created in Word** by inserting a table with three columns. You can also use one of the KWL charts found in the Resources section.

**Observations and Anecdotal Records.** Students complete a task or activity as the teacher observes, takes notes, and records progress using a checklist or form. Observation is a fine assessment tool that can be used at any time.

| | |
|---|---|
| **Add Tech!** | **You can create your own custom form in Word** and print several copies to use on a clipboard in the classroom. If you have a handheld computer, you could create a form for that device and use it to record your observational notes on your handheld for upload later to your laptop or desktop computer. More information about handheld assessment as well as two forms from Saskatchewan Learning are listed in the chapter resources. |

**Pretests.** Pretests are designed to point out where students are in particular content areas and skills and can be used for guiding differentiated instruction. Pretests are often used in conjunction with curriculum compacting. We described strategies for compacting curriculum in chapter 5.

| | |
|---|---|
| **Add Tech!** | **Teachers can use technology for pretesting and scoring.** Many teachers use posttests, or a derivation of them, as pretests. Newer software also empowers you to create your own. Take a look at Electronic Assessment Creation Tools in the Resources section, which provides several sites for you to explore. In addition, you might want to look at some of the Microsoft tutorials for creating your own tests. |

**Response Cards and Devices.** Students use paper cards to respond to questions posed by the teacher. The students hold up their answers for the teacher to check responses. (Example: Yes/No cards are cards students make, with Yes on one side and No on the other. Teachers ask a review or introductory question. Students who know the answer hold up the Yes card; students who don't know the answer hold up the No card. This tool is especially useful when introducing new vocabulary words that students need for a new unit of study.)

| | |
|---|---|
| **Add Tech!** | **Response cards can be made** with word processing software and laminated for long-term use. Better yet, have your students design them in Kid Pix or similar software. New handheld response devices made by eInstruction, CPS, and other companies make responses really exiting. These tools are about the size of a TV remote control device. Students press buttons on the tools to respond to questions and other content posed by the teacher. Each response is recorded, and the sum of responses can be shown statistically. The teacher can also see who has and hasn't answered questions because each remote device has its own tracking number. |

**Surveys and Inventories.** Surveys and inventories are forms that contain a set of questions for gathering information.

| | |
|---|---|
| **Add Tech!** | **Surveys and inventories can be designed using Word.** You can create a form and protect it so that it can't be altered. You can also create a form for posting on the Web. However, exciting new Web-based software does a lot of the work for you in terms of design. Both Zoomerang and SurveyMonkey offer free (limited) accounts. Check out the Resources section to explore these tools. |

## Formative Assessment

Just as pre-assessment is an important strategy, so is ongoing assessment. The purpose of ongoing assessment is to take a "temperature check" of the classroom climate. Teachers will also want to offer corrective feedback in a timely manner so that students have opportunities to improve and you can document student performance to guide instructional decisions.

In *Classroom Instruction that Works* (Marzano, Pickering, & Pollock, 2001), the authors quote researcher John Hattie, who states, "[T]he most powerful single modification that enhances achievement is feedback. The simplest prescription for improving education must be 'dollops' of feedback" (p. 96).

The authors discuss four generalizations about the use of feedback:

1. Feedback should be corrective in nature.
2. Feedback should be timely.
3. Feedback should be specific to a criterion.
4. Students can effectively provide some of their own feedback.

### Purpose

- Provides students with information about what they currently understand and have learned up to a particular point in time.
- Provides students with information about how they might improve their understanding and skills.
- Provides feedback as soon after assessment as possible.
- Identifies gaps in learning or where students have exceeded expectations.

### Characteristics

- It occurs in the context of an activity or process.
- Feedback is from a variety of perspectives: peer, self, and teacher.
- Criteria for assessment are relevant to the content and context at hand.
- Feedback can be in the form of praise, constructive criticism, and guidance.

### Examples

**Anecdotal Records.** Short accounts or descriptive notes that describe students' behavior.

**Add Tech!**   **Since anecdotal records are really teacher notes,** teachers can use technology to set up forms for recording or they can use handheld devices to record the information as they walk around the classroom. The resources section offers sample forms and information about using handhelds for assessment.

**Checklists.** Formatted lists of behaviors that teachers check off as specific actions are carried out or skills have been mastered. Checklists should be specific, easily observable behaviors that are age appropriate. Checklists can be set up in different formats ranging from very simple, checking yes or no, to more complex, rating skills on a scale.

**Add Tech!**   **Previously discussed under pre-assessment,** checklists are also valuable tools for ongoing assessment.

**Discussion Questions.** Open-ended questions that help teachers gather information on students' readiness.

**Add Tech!**   **The contemporary format of classroom discussion questions** is the blog or electronic discussion group. As long as a blog can be contained on a secure server (nonpublic), it can be safe for students to use. Commercial products such as Gaggle (www.gaggle.net) and KidzBlog (www.haranbanjo.com/kidzblog/) offer safe and secure settings; however, any blog must be monitored. Blogs can be used for almost any topic, including novel discussion, sharing ideas, and ongoing assessment.

**Peer Review.** A process that allows learners to give written or verbal feedback to other learners. Peers can use checklists or rubrics, or give a written or verbal response to peers' work.

**Add Tech!** **Peer review documents can be created in Word** and used electronically or in print. The Resources section offers several examples of peer review forms.

**Learning Logs.** Short, ungraded, unedited writing that reflects on learning activities. The writings serve as a sort of journal for children to promote thinking in their writing.

**Add Tech!** **Learning logs can be created in Word** and used electronically or in print format. The Resources section offers an example of a learning log form.

**Observations.** A method for circulating among flexible groups to learn how students are processing ideas and understanding concepts.

**Add Tech!** **Use the anecdotal forms** described earlier in this section or create a checklist using technology.

**Reflective Journals.** A process that can be used for students to reflect on their own learning. They can be open-ended, or the teacher can provide guiding, reflective questions for students to respond to. Journals provide insight on how students are synthesizing their learning, but they also help students make connections and better understand how they learn.

**Add Tech!** **Journal page samples are provided** in the Resources section; however, it's easy for you to make your own template in Word or Publisher or a similar program. A newer software program, Stationery Studio, encourages young writers to record their thoughts and reactions to writing prompts. Printed pages from this software could be bound into a journal at the end of the year.

**Response Cards.** A strategy used with the whole class for responding on cue, as a group, to teacher questions. Response cards are similar to exit cards except they're used during instruction and before the end of a unit.

> **Add Tech!** **Previously described** in the pre-assessment section of this chapter, response cards are also useful for ongoing assessment.

**Running Records.** A tool used to record the errors or miscues students make while reading. Running records help determine the difficulty level of texts so that teachers select appropriately leveled books and materials.

> **Add Tech!** **Forms for running records** used in reading assessment can be created in Word. Samples and printable forms are listed in the Resources section.

## Summative Assessment

The paper and pencil tests referred to earlier in this chapter were usually post-learning assessments teachers gave to assign grades. Today's after-learning assessment strategies take on different shapes and forms.

### *Purpose*

- Assess students' success in attaining knowledge, concepts, and skills that were the goals of instruction.

### *Characteristics*

- May allow for a demonstration of learning using a preferred mode of learning.
- Allows for demonstration of what students have learned.
- Represents a culmination of learning experiences.

## *Examples*

**Checklists.** Checklists use an easy-to-score format, with a key or space for tallying results. They can be used to identify steps completed or understood, as well as skills that have been mastered.

| Add Tech! | **Checklists are easy to create** using a word processor. Check the Resources section for examples and tips. |
| --- | --- |

**Exit Cards.** Exit cards are an easy 5-minute activity to check student knowledge before, during, and after a lesson or complete unit of study. Students respond to two to three questions posed by the teacher. Teachers can quickly read the responses and plan necessary instruction.

| Add Tech! | **Exit cards can be created using PowerPoint** to show to the entire class, or using Publisher or Word for individual cards. Check the Resources section for examples. |
| --- | --- |

**Portfolios of Work Samples.** Portfolios contain artifacts of students' work. Traditional portfolios are paper and pencil, while electronic portfolios may be entirely digital. That is, students' 100% digital portfolios contain products made only with technology tools. Older students may create a portfolio in PowerPoint, for example, and hyperlink to digital art and artifacts created in MS Paint, MS Office, and other software. An example of a student-led conference and portfolio template is available as a download at www.rst2.edu/ctee/files/elecPort.ppt/.

Cathleen Chamberlain's site (www.electricteacher.com/onlineportfolio/) includes examples, tips, pre-steps, and more about digital portfolios. Dr. Helen C. Barrett's page (http://electronicportfolios.com/ALI/) offers guides to creating portfolios in several software applications. Check our Web site (www.everythingdi.net) for directions on making a portfolio in PowerPoint.

| Add Tech! | **Electronic portfolios can be created** with PowerPoint, Word, FrontPage, or similar software, or with commercial portfolio software. These digital portfolios contain artifacts created with technology software. |
| --- | --- |

**Product Assessment Tools.** You can assess student products constructed according to guidelines and rubrics that are presented prior to product development. Students can use project-scoring guides and self-assessment exercises to self-grade their products.

**Add Tech!** **Product assessments can be created** in Word or Publisher in the form of rubric tables or Likert scales for self-grading of products. Open-ended student-reflective exercises can also be created to assess self and team.

**Rubrics.** Rubrics are scoring tools that list the criteria for a product or performance. They show gradations of quality for each criterion in a range from poor to excellent. Rubrics should be both qualitative and quantitative. Use specific language to help students understand goals. Figure 9.5 is an example (from a writing rubric) of the way many teachers write rubrics. These details are too vague for students.

FIGURE **9.5** ■ Rubric that is too vague for proper assessment

| | Expert | Almost There | On the Way | Starting |
|---|---|---|---|---|
| Mechanics | **No** grammatical, spelling, or punctuation errors. | **Almost no** grammatical, spelling, or punctuation errors. | **A few** grammatical spelling, or punctuation errors. | **Many** grammatical, spelling, or punctuation errors. |

The revisions shown in Figure 9.6 make the rubric more specific. Now there's clear, concise, qualitative, and quantitative language.

FIGURE **9.6** ■ Rubric improved with more specific language

| | Outstanding 4 points | Good 3 points | Satisfactory 2 points | Beginning 1 point |
|---|---|---|---|---|
| Mechanics | **0%–5%** of the writing has grammatical, spelling, or punctuation errors. | **6%–10 %** of the writing has grammatical, spelling, or punctuation errors | **11%–19 %** of the writing has grammatical, spelling, or punctuation errors. | **20% or more** of the writing has grammatical, spelling, or punctuation errors. |

**Add Tech!** **Construct your own rubrics** by looking at those created by other teachers. Examples abound at RubiStar, the Chicago Public Schools, and Kathy Schrock's Guide. One caution about rubrics: although RubiStar and other sites foster the creation of rubrics, we've seen many rubrics that are not high quality.

**Self-assessments.** Students use self-assessments to reflect on their own learning and to evaluate specific criteria in order to assess that learning. Teachers may use checklists, rubrics, or open-ended questions to prompt students in their self-assessments.

> **Add Tech!** Teachers can use Word to set up checklists or surveys, or use self-assessment examples from the resources section.

**Teacher-made tests.** These assessments are constructed by teachers to determine what students have learned after teachers have taught a skill or a unit of instruction. Teacher-made tests may include open-ended and essay questions, multiple choice and true or false questions, fill in the blank and matching questions, and blank-page assessments in which students write what they know about the topic.

> **Add Tech!** Tests can be easily made in Word or any word processing program. However, newer online test creation software (see Electronic Assessment Creation Tools in the Resources section) is fun to use as well as productive. If you use Discovery Education *unitedstreaming*, Quiz Center is a unique way to combine assessment with video streaming content.

Another engaging way to assess a group of students is through an electronic game format such as Jeopardy or Millionaire. Free PowerPoint game templates are available on the Web. However, we like the commercial products from FTC Publishing (www.ftcpublishing.com). Links and sample games are available in the resources section at the end of the chapter.

The sample screenshots below illustrate matching and Jeopardy-like games that can be purchased from FTC Publishing.

In the Deliberation game, you place a picture of your choice on a background layer behind the game board. The picture is slowly revealed as players match pairs of text, images, or text with image.

For this fourth-grade example, we used Michigan state symbols and asked students to match a picture of each symbol to its corresponding words. The team or student calls out two numbers, such as 4 and 12. The teacher "shows" what is behind the numbers 4 and 12. If there's a match, part of the picture is revealed. If there isn't a match, the teacher "hides" the mismatch, and the numbers for the next pair are called. Students eventually remember matching pairs and the picture behind the board is revealed.

The Communication game features a Jeopardy-like board in a colorful format. Using this game, we created a Women's History Month game for fifth-grade students. As in the real Jeopardy game, three individual players or three student teams select a category and answer in the amount of $100–$500. The answer is revealed and the correct question must be asked to gain credit. Score can be added as the game continues. A Final Challenge and wager complete the game.

Chalkboard Challenge, another Jeopardy-like game, offers a more traditional look for two classroom teams or group assessment. Using this game template, we created a Revolutionary War game with five categories (People 1, People 2, Battles, Places, and Things) for fifth-graders. It's played in the same way as the Communication game.

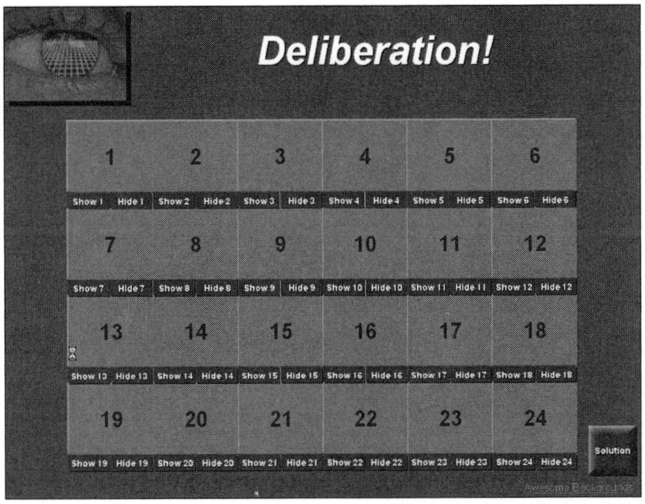

FIGURE **9.7** ▣
FTC Publishing's
Deliberation!
matching game

© FTC Publishing. Reprinted with permission.

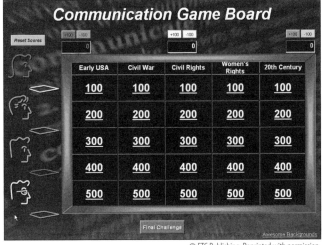

FIGURE **9.8** ▣
FTC Publishing's
Communication
question and
answer game

© FTC Publishing. Reprinted with permission.

# Wrapping Up Assessment + Technology

We hope you see numerous new ways to use technology to assess the various stages of student learning. For additional help, please check out the resources section to investigate strategies to use in your classroom. Also check out www.everythingdi.net.

## Resources for Chapter 9

| | | |
|---|---|---|
| **Assessment and Rubric Links** | A Checklist for Effective Questioning | www.pgcps.org/~elc/isquestion7.html |
| | Scholastic Assessments | www.teacher.scholastic.com/professional/assessment/indexbk.htm |
| | Discovery School/Kathy Schrock's Assessments | http://school.discovery.com/schrockguide/assess.html |
| | Authentic Assessment Toolbox | http://jonathan.mueller.faculty.noctrl.edu/toolbox/ |
| **Blogs** | Class Blogmeister | http://classblogmeister.com |
| | Education World | www.education-world.com/a_tech/tech/tech217.shtml |
| | Gaggle Blogs | http://gaggle.net/gen?_template=/templates/gaggle/html/blog/ |
| | KidzBlog | http://haranbanjo.com/kidzblog/ |
| **Books** | *Resources for Student Assessment* (Kelly & Haber, 2006) | |
| **Checklists** | Computer Skills | www.kgcs.k12.va.us/tech/ss/elementary_middle_school_curriculum.htm |
| | Computer Skills | www.mcsdk12.org/dept/computer/comp_elem_skills.htm |
| | Make a Checklist in Word | http://office.microsoft.com/en-us/assistance/HA011624511033.aspx |
| | Math Skills | www.pvsd.k12.pa.us/salisbury/Math Skills Lists/MathSkills.htm |
| | Number, Data, and Space | http://investigations.scottforesman.com/assessment.html |
| | PBL Checklist Generator | http://pblchecklist.4teachers.org |
| | Reading Skills | www.pvsd.k12.pa.us/salisbury/Reading Skills Lists/ReadingSkills.htm |
| **Curriculum, Assessment, and Instruction Models** | FLAG (Field-tested Learning Assessment Guide) | www.flaguide.org/start/assess_in_context.php |
| | Manatee School District | www.manatee.k12.fl.us/curriculum/assessment/assessment.htm |
| | USD 204 Bonner Springs/ Edwardsville, KS | www.usd204.k12.ks.us/cia/ |

*continued*

## Resources for Chapter 9 *(continued)*

| | | |
|---|---|---|
| **Electronic Assessment** | Online Assessment Resources for K–12 Teachers | www.uwstout.edu/soe/profdev/assess.shtml |
| | Using Electronic Assessment to Measure Student Performance | www.nga.org/Files/pdf/ELECTRONICASSESSMENT.pdf |
| **Electronic Assessment Hardware** | CPS Response Pads | www.pearsonncs.com/cps/index.htm |
| | eInstruction | www.einstruction.com/index.cfm?fuseaction=K12.Display&Header=K12 |
| | Handheld Assessment | http://thejournal.com/the/learningcenters/center/?msid=14 www.tribeam.com/educator.html |
| **Examples and Forms** | Anecdotal Record Form | www.sasked.gov.sk.ca/docs/wellness/pdfs/pdf10.pdf www.sasked.gov.sk.ca/docs/kindergarten/anecdot.pdf |
| | Create Class Surveys with Excel | www.educationworld.com/a_tech/techtorial/techtorial082.shtml |
| | Create Survey Forms from a Word Table | www.bbk.ac.uk/ccs/docs/word/5–110.pdf |
| | Design a Survey Using Microsoft Word, Then Evaluate the Data Using Microsoft Access | www.microsoft.com/education/designsurvey.mspx |
| | Journal Pages | http://penmanship.donnayoung.org/journal.htm www.abcteach.com/MonthtoMonth/June/journal1.htm |
| | How Did I Do At? | www.saskschools.ca/~ischool/physedpd/MAY11-FINALLY/assessment/pages/p228.htm |
| | How Did I Help My Team | www.readwritethink.org/lesson_images/lesson218/help.pdf |
| | KWL Chart | www.eduplace.com/graphicorganizer/pdf/kwl.pdf www.nwrel.org/learns/resources/organizers/kwl.pdf |
| | KWL Form | http://teacher.scholastic.com/lessonplans/graphicorg/kwl.htm |
| | Learning Log | www.accessola.com/osla/toolkit/Resources.html |
| | Peer Assessment | www.saskschools.ca/~ischool/physedpd/MAY11-FINALLY/assessment/pages/p225.htm |
| | PowerPoint Flash Cards | www.thinkbright.org/teachers/viewResource.asp?contentid=4401 |
| | Reading Log (download Reading Log 4–5 and Reading Log K–3) | http://aumedal.net/dnn/ohes/Download/tabid/267/ |
| | Self-Assessment Rubric | www.readwritethink.org/lesson_images/lesson277/rubric.pdf |
| | Student Assessment Form | www.saskschools.ca/~ischool/physedpd/MAY11-FINALLY/assessment/pages/p220.htm |
| | Student Grid Assessment | www.readwritethink.org/lesson_images/lesson851/grid.pdf |
| | Technology Self-Assessment | www.bham.wednet.edu/technology/techself.htm |

*continued*

## Resources for Chapter 9  *(continued)*

| | | |
|---|---|---|
| **Electronic Assessment Creation Tools** | APlus Math Flashcard Creator | www.aplusmath.com/Flashcards/Flashcard_Creator.html |
| | Creating Tests with Microsoft Word | www.educationworld.com/a_tech/techtorial/techtorial020.shtml |
| | Discovery School Quiz Center | http://school.discovery.com/quizcenter/quizcenter.html |
| | Easy Test Maker | www.easytestmaker.com |
| | E.L. Easton | http://eleaston.com/quizzes.html |
| | Game-O-Matic | http://clear.msu.edu/dennie/matic/ |
| | Hot Potatoes | http://hotpot.uvic.ca |
| | MS Templates for multiple-choice and true/false tests | http://office.microsoft.com/en-us/templates/ TC100357581033.aspx?pid=CT101435311033 http://office.microsoft.com/en-us/FX012319191033.aspx |
| | Personal Educational Press | www.educationalpress.org |
| | QuizStar | http://quizstar.4teachers.org |
| | SurveyMonkey | www.surveymonkey.com/Pricing.asp |
| | RubiStar | http://rubistar.4teachers.org |
| | Chicago Public Schools— Ideas and Rubrics | http://intranet.cps.k12.il.us/Assessments/Ideas_and_Rubrics/ ideas_and_rubrics.html |
| | Kathy Schrock's Guide | http://school.discovery.com/schrockguide/assess.html |
| | Test Pilot | www.clearlearning.com |
| | The Kid-Friendly 4-Point Rubric for Students | www.cde.state.co.us/cdeassess/documents/csap/rubrics/Kid-Friendly 4-PtRubricStudents_Eng.pdf |
| | Zoomerang | http://info.zoomerang.com/products.htm |
| **Exit Cards** | Exit cards | www.mcps.k12.md.us/curriculum/enriched/giftedprograms/ instructionalstrategy.shtm |
| | Exit slips | www.saskschools.ca/curr_content/bestpractice/exit/ |
| | Sample card | www.animalrangeextension.montana.edu/amazgraze/images/ exitcard3-large.gif |
| **Portfolios** | Create Student Portfolios with Hyperlinks | www.educationworld.com/a_tech/techtorial/techtorial044.shtml |
| | Electronic Portfolios in the K–12 Classroom | www.educationworld.com/a_tech/tech/tech111.shtml |
| | Electronic Portfolios: Students, Teachers, and Lifelong Learners | http://eduscapes.com/tap/topic82.htm |
| | E-portfolio Fever | www.educationworld.com/a_tech/techtorial/techtorial038.shtml |

*continued*

## Resources for Chapter 9   *(continued)*

| | | |
|---|---|---|
| **PowerPoint Games** | FTC Publishing | http://ftcpublishing.com |
| | Jefferson County Schools' PowerPoint Collection | http://jc-schools.net/ppt.html |
| | Parade of Games in PowerPoint | http://facstaff.uww.edu/jonesd/games/ |
| | PowerPoint Games | http://jc-schools.net/tutorials/PPT-games/ |
| | Write On: PowerPoint Games | http://jc-schools.net/write/games/ |
| **Pre-Assessments** | Counter Squares | www.amblesideprimary.com/ambleWeb/mentalmaths/countersquare.html |
| | Dolch Site Words | www.mrsperkins.com/dolch.htm |
| | Group Response Cards | www.interventioncentral.org/htmdocs/interventions/classroom/ groupresp.php |
| | Multiplication Table | http://office.microsoft.com/en-us/templates/TC060900071033.aspx? CategoryID=CT063739921033 |
| | PowerPoint Collection | http://jc-schools.net/ppt.html |
| | Project Poster | http://poster.4teachers.org |
| | Scribble Square | www.amblesideprimary.com/ambleWeb/mentalmaths/scribblesquare.html |
| | Student Peer Assessment | http://office.microsoft.com/en-us/templates/TC012120231033.aspx? pid= CT101442071033 |
| | Multiplication Tables through 12x12 (PowerPoint template) | http://office.microsoft.com/en-us/templates/TC060900071033. aspx?pid=CT101446261033 |
| | Multiplication Tables 9/pg (Excel template) | http://office.microsoft.com/en-us/templates/TC010184091033. aspx?pid=CT101446261033 |
| | The Table Trees | www.amblesideprimary.com/ambleWeb/mentalmaths/tabletrees.html |
| **Running Records** | Reading a-z.com | www.readinga-z.com/newfiles/levels/runrecord/runrec.html |
| | Running record forms | www.readinga-z.com/guided/runrecord.html |
| | Forms, tips, and codes | www.hubbardscupboard.org/guided_reading.html#RunningRecords |
| **Software** | Destination Math | http://rivapprod2.riverdeep.net/portal/page?_pageid=353,110730&_ dad=portal&_schema=PORTAL |
| | Destination Reading | www.riverdeep.net/portal/page?_pageid=353,138397,353_138398&_ dad=portal&_schema=PORTAL |
| | Fastt Math | www.tomsnyder.com/Products/product.asp?SKU=FASFAS |
| | FTC Publishing | http://ftcpublishing.com |
| | Stationery Studio | www.fablevision.com/stationerystudio/product.htm |
| | StudyDog (Free version which can track up to 20 users) | www.famlit.org/studydog/ |
| | StudyDog (Commercial version) | www.studydog.com |

## CHAPTER 10

# Using Technology *to* Manage Your Differentiated Classroom

In a previous chapter we referred to the many hats teachers wear during their teaching careers. In addition to all the roles we play in the classroom, other substantial responsibilities consume our time and energy. In fact, the administrative tasks we must perform tap some of the time and energy reserves needed to maintain teaching at high levels for the benefit of our students.

Beyond the physical demands of teaching our students, we must adhere to local, state, and national standards that require formal assessment. Teachers of the 21st century also have to cope with the emotional challenges and baggage that students carry with them, which can impact the learning environment, the students' ability to perform, and the safety of all students, staff, and administrative personnel. Sometimes it seems as if we're acrobats on a tightrope, striving to keep our balance as we're pulled in different directions!

These challenges are sizable. As we turn to the day-to-day operation of our own classrooms, we may wonder if managing a differentiated classroom will seem overwhelming, too. Students are always on the move as a result of learner choice and flexible grouping. Honoring all of our students' diverse learning profiles, levels of readiness, and interests may seem next to impossible. Establishing an emotionally encouraging learning community and an inviting physical environment is no easy task. However, you might already have met those challenges head on, without the support of two powerful allies: technology, and instructional and management strategies. This chapter covers this important area of differentiation.

In this chapter, we discuss administrative concerns and effective tactics that will help you create an organized, successful classroom, such as the creation of a positive learning environment and classroom setup. Tactics include scaffolding, a support mechanism that's a form of guided practice, enabling students to make the leap to a more advanced academic level. They also include anchor activities (sometimes called anchoring, or extending), a management strategy that can cultivate student autonomy and enhance comprehension of key concepts. When students have completed their current task, they can move to tech-related anchor activities that supply meaningful options. Students can choose from a menu of activities based on their interest and readiness.

As promised in chapter 5, "Using Technology to Differentiate by Content," we'll investigate learning contracts because they marry nicely with anchoring and make room for many choices and higher levels of student responsibility. Technology and instructional and management strategies will surely add to your poise and grace as you perform your daily tightrope act in the classroom.

## The Learning Environment: A Critical Component for Success

There is a particular practice that provides the framework for our current educational system, although its success truly defies human comprehension. What are we describing? A classroom of 25 or more elementary students of the same age! Think for a moment how remarkable it is that your classroom functions effectively on a daily basis and pat yourself on the back! Now consider the interruptions and the challenges you and your pupils confront each day. We're certain you can come up with a fairly lengthy list.

Whether you've taught for 9 months or 9 years, you recognize the obstacles that present themselves as you attempt to establish a positive learning atmosphere: unruly behavior, numerous assessments, movement to encore classes, human self-centeredness, dysfunctional family situations that affect individual students (and in turn, those around them), and various interruptions from phone calls to P.A. announcements (and, sadly, bomb threats and other safety-related concerns).

Carol Tomlinson (2001) recently acknowledged the weighty significance of the learning environment in DI classrooms by identifying it as a classroom element. In *How to Differentiate Instruction in Mixed-Ability Classrooms*, she lists seven characteristics of an "effective learning community" (pp. 21–24). We'd like to take a moment to name the characteristics for you and briefly describe their importance. You'll observe that the majority if these traits address emotional concerns.

1. **"Feeling welcomed."** An effective learning community is one in which students and teachers realize that success comes in all sizes, and they take pride in their accomplishments. Their value for one another translates into mutual encouragement and genuine compassion.

2. **"Mutual respect is non-negotiable."** Our respect for and acceptance of our differences is key to the building of a team atmosphere.

3. **"Students feel safe in the classroom."** Security extends beyond the boundaries of academic work. Educators and pupils feel free to tackle risky educational ventures, knowing that neither failure nor requests for help will be criticized.

4. **"There is a pervasive expectation of growth."** Teachers involve students in goal-setting activities, and some form of growth is expected (and celebrated) in individualized and group tasks.

5. **"The teacher teaches for success."** In an effective learning community, teachers gently push their students beyond their learning comfort zones in an effort to guide them step-by-step down the educational path toward independence. This path accommodates multiple and varied types of assessments and fosters a sense of self-sufficiency in the learning journey.

6. **"A new sort of fairness is evident."** Increased diversity within the classroom walls requires more flexibility. We must be willing to allow for alternative methods and options for our very diverse students if our wish is that all students experience some sense of success.

7. **"Teachers and students collaborate for mutual growth and success."** As we  impart more responsibility to our students via promotion of peer support, involvement in problem solving, and increase in accountability for classroom tasks and academic work, we usually witness some positive results. Students become more concerned with "shepherding" others while simultaneously developing autonomy.

Attending to the emotional aspects of our learning communities is usually much more complicated than arranging a welcoming physical space. Nevertheless, we can't overlook the impact of the physical environment on our students' ability to learn and perform. Obviously, we're somewhat limited in terms of the kinds of modifications we're able to make to the physical layout and condition of the classroom, but we can make minor improvements.

Following are some ways we can make over our classrooms to ready them for differentiated instruction. These tactics are based on the principle that pleasing physical surroundings translate into an increased comfort level for our students. When our students feel at ease, they experience a heightened sense of security, and safety is one of the characteristics of an effective learning community.

1. Organize and place your materials in such a way that they're accessible to students (at their eye-level and within their grasp).

2. Appeal to your students' five senses in other ways, such as the use of music or slideshows as they enter the classroom to focus their attention on the topic of the lesson at hand.

3. To meet the demands of flexible grouping, do the following:

   ▪ Allow for adequate space between tables or desks.

   ▪ Vary seating arrangements.

   ▪ Allocate a specific area of the classroom for group meetings, independent work, and free time.

   ▪ If possible, position technology hardware in a spot that easily accommodates frequent use. (If you have only one computer or must move to another area, such as a lab, to use technology, don't worry. Many resources are available to help you successfully work within these parameters.)

Isn't it amazing to consider all the factors we must take into account before we even begin communicating content to our students? The good news is that the establishment of an upbeat learning atmosphere is well worth the effort. Students who feel at home in their classrooms typically work with more confidence and success. Now let's examine some of those helpful instructional and management strategies that we mentioned in the introduction. We'll begin with scaffolding.

## Support Mechanism: Scaffolding

What foreman would willingly put his employees at risk by refusing to allow scaffolds at a job site during the construction process? When construction workers renovate old buildings or erect new ones, scaffolds are necessary to support the structure. The failure to use scaffolding is a risky venture, particularly when the building project reaches high into the sky!

The same is true in the classroom. Our students are not unlike the old edifices that undergo remodeling or the new ones that are raised. No matter how independent or advanced they may seem, we still need to make sure we provide necessary support as they progress to higher levels of skill or knowledge. As a teacher who practices differentiated instruction, you're probably familiar with the support mechanism called scaffolding, which truly does resemble the type of framework used by construction workers. Moreover, you might have used some types of scaffolding already, such as manipulatives, organizers, reading buddies, or study guides.

Why is it so imperative to supply scaffolding for our students? Scaffolding (sometimes referred to as "guided practice") helps students build on the knowledge they've already mastered and the skills they've already developed. As students take a step up to the next level of knowledge or skill, they might be tentative because they're uncertain. They're unsure about what lies ahead, and the step up seems more like a huge leap. You might envision scaffolding as a booster chair or stepladder that helps students attain a higher level of skill and emotionally encourages them along the pathway to continued achievement and autonomy.

You might find that your students also need scaffolding to assist them with some of the technology you incorporate into a particular activity because they haven't learned how to operate it or can't use it efficiently. It may be necessary to provide small-group instruction to those who aren't as proficient with a particular technology, or to allow students to work through one of the numerous tutorials online to become more familiar with specific software or hardware. In the section that follows, we'll describe a wonderful support mechanism called peer coaching that you might employ to assist those who aren't as skilled with technology.

Perhaps the most effective way to provide scaffolding for students who are more technologically challenged is to use various technological devices to frame the learning activities you develop, or to embed them so that they seem to be a natural part of student tasks. For example, in the documents you create, you might include WordArt, hyperlinks, highlighting, comment boxes, or embedded objects. These devices appeal to your technology enthusiasts, too, and can work to save time. If you embed several files (even of different types) within one document, this prevents you and your students from having to open each file within each individual software program. If you supply a number of hyperlinks within one document, you and your students won't have to type or copy and paste each link into an Internet browser. You might be surprised to find that even your less adept students will warm up quickly to these user-friendly devices.

The Kent School District in Washington has a very valuable Web site called Scaffolding for Learning (www.kent.k12.wa.us/KSD/IT/TSC/scaffolding/). On this Web site you'll find numerous resources that describe types of scaffolds and their purposes, articles about scaffolds, sample lessons involving scaffolds, and a link to scaffolded templates and activities designed by Kent staff, all at (www.kent.k12.wa.us/curriculum/tech/scaffolds/scaffolds.xls).

In addition, here are some basic steps you can use to offer scaffolding throughout a lesson with new or difficult material. The technology-enhanced project we'll use as a model below is the image of an explorer that students design (using Microsoft Paint) for their bookmarks, as described in the I-Search lesson plan in chapter 2.

1. **Present the task or skill to your students.**
   First, select an explorer ahead of time that you'll not allow any of your students to choose. If possible, print or project a large, clear photo of the explorer in color (perhaps from clip art, an online encyclopedia, or other resource so that students can see what he looks like). Explain that you'll use Paint to produce your own portrait of this explorer, which will later become a part of the final artifact: a bookmark with images and brief text about his life. Make sure you're able to project your computer screen so that students can observe the creation process.

2. **As you model the task, think out loud.**
   You might say something like, "Look at the tool pictures on the left-hand side of the screen. If you can't remember what a tool is used for, you can drag the mouse over the tool's picture.

   "Think about the shapes and colors that we could use to build a computer image of this explorer. Does he have any distinct features?

   "Let's create a portrait from the shoulders up. A good place to start would be our explorer's head."

3. **Work together to practice the task as a whole class.**
   Show students how to position and draw the head in a central location on the screen. After outlining the head, ask them for input. For which features should you use a brush, airbrush, or pencil? Which colors should you choose for his face, hair, and clothing?

   As they answer your questions, you can complete the computer image, reminding them of the names of the tools as you use them. Offer them any tips, hints, or expertise. When your picture is complete, select Save As, type the name of the picture, and then click on Save.

4. **Divide students into flexible groups so that they can learn the skill cooperatively.**
   You might decide to have students generate an image of the same explorer, or you could select a different one for all the students to try. If possible, allow them to work in pairs so that they each have more hands-on practice with Paint.

5. **Invite individual students to model the learned task as independent learners.**
   Students are now ready to begin work on the pictures of the explorers for their bookmarks.

While you, as the teacher, are responsible for designing and supplying scaffolding for your students, there's another outstanding support mechanism that requires little work from your end: peer coaching.

# Support Mechanism: Peer Coaching

Whether you're aware of it or not, you might have some superstars in your classroom who can assist their peers *and* their teacher! Although we teachers may not always recognize it as such, technology is a friend to most of our 21st-century students. When we integrate technology into our coursework, our students respond with eagerness and an increased level of motivation.

Have you ever found yourself in the middle of a technology problem only to be bailed out by one of your tech-savvy students? After overcoming any initial embarrassment, maybe you've come to the realization that you have some budding peer coaches on hand. What a great resource to have at your fingertips—make sure you put it to good use! Even though some of your students struggle with core material, they may be technological whiz kids who can come to the aid of others. Allowing students to assume the role of technology peer coaches usually inspires them, particularly those who are below-level students in core curricular areas. Peer coaching affords them a chance to shine for a moment and excel in an area that is "cool" to students of the digital age. In most cases, students who aren't as skilled with technology are not ashamed to receive help from others because they want to succeed with it.

We invite you to experiment with this useful support mechanism. You can put it to use in various ways, and it doesn't seem to matter whether students share one computer or have their own. For the sake of example, we've arranged students into mini-groups in lab situations, with computers for each individual. When students encounter difficulties, they go directly to the students who've been appointed as their group leaders. If the group leaders can't resolve the problem, they take it a step further by asking their leader peers next. If the leader peers can't answer the question, one of them asks the teacher for help. Sometimes the teachers won't have an adequate response. When this happens, one way to handle it is to put forth the problem to the whole group to see if someone else might be able to solve it. Here's yet another instance of decision and consensus making in a community of learners!

We've addressed the importance of cultivating a healthy physical and emotional learning environment for our students and supporting them with techniques such as peer coaching and scaffolding. Let's see what anchor activities can offer to teachers and students as they work together in the differentiated classroom.

# Anchoring or Extending

Sometimes teachers and students confuse anchoring (aka "anchor activities" or "extending") with a more unpleasant activity: "busy work." Actually, anchor activities serve a higher purpose. Not only do anchor activities benefit students because they promote responsibility and independence (which in turn reduces classroom disorder), but they also free us up to monitor struggling students and whole-class or group tasks, or to test out a new activity.

Anchor activities are a part of the unit students are currently studying and are tied to the assignment students have just completed. They present additional opportunities to extend students' comprehension of essential concepts, and they allow for choices based on levels of readiness and interest. Most important, they offer purposeful options that reinforce and deepen the connection between the overarching unit theme and the distinct assignments that make up that unit. Most teachers give some type of credit or grade for anchor activities because they're included in the assessment plan.

If you haven't tried anchoring activities in your classroom, we think you'll find they don't involve heavy grading on your part. Nonetheless, they carry weight with students because they realize you'll be assessing their work.

Don't mistakenly categorize anchoring as an inflexible strategy, because you can adapt it to your needs. You might use it

- after students have finished an assignment,
- as a component of learning contracts,
- as a warm-up or opening activity,
- independently,
- while students await your assistance on a task,
- with learning and interest centers,
- as a booklet or other expression of culminating activities.

If you have a low-tech classroom, you'll be happy to discover that we can offer either non-tech or tech-driven anchor activities. As you can see in the table that follows, technology can function as both a creative and research tool.

TABLE **10.1** ■ Non-tech and tech-related anchor activities

| Non-tech Anchor Activities | Tech-related Anchor Activities | |
|---|---|---|
| Creative activities using books, crayons, glue, paper, puppets, stories, and so forth | Creative activities using computer software, such as: | |
| | **Microsoft Paint or TuxPaint** | www.tuxpaint.org |
| Culminating booklet students work through as a part of the creation of a final product | Teacher and students create booklets made from downloads or software, such as Microsoft Word or Publisher (or via a teacher-created Web site that allows students to complete sections of the work online and submit) | |
| Games, riddles, and puzzles | Games—online and teacher-created using technology: | |
| | **VA Kids, K–5th—Games & Activities** | www.va.gov/kids/k-5/games_activities.asp |
| | **Kid's Page at Valley Forge** | www.ushistory.org/valleyforge/kids/ |
| | **ABCya! Elementary Computer Games** | www.abcya.com |
| | **Mrs. Dell Interactive Learning Activities** | http://mrsdell.org/quiaactivities.html |
| | **Parade of Games in PowerPoint** | http://facstaff.uww.edu/jonesd/games/ |
| | **Jefferson County Schools Science Presentations and PowerPoint Games** | http://jc-schools.net/PPTs-science.html#GradesK-5 |
| Graphic organizers, outlines, and thinking maps created by hand | Graphic organizers, outlines, and thinking maps made with computer software, such as: | |
| | **Learning Resources: Graphic Organizers** | www.eduscapes.com/tap/topic73.htm |
| Illustrations, images, and maps from print resources or made with art supplies such as crayons, markers, colored pencils | Illustrations, images, and maps from digital resources or made with computer drawing software, such as: | |
| | **Microsoft Paint, TuxPaint, Comic Creator** | www.readwritethink.org/student_mat/student_material.asp?id=21 |
| | **Xpeditions** | www.nationalgeographic.com/xpeditions/ |
| Journal writing, learning logs, and newspapers | Journal writing, learning log, and newspapers—created with computer software such as: | |
| | **Publisher, Word, or Printing Press** | www.readwritethink.org/student_mat/student_material.asp?id=36 |
| Math (or other subject) "problem of the day" | Web site resources that offer online problems of the day or week, such as: | |
| | **Aunty Math** | www.dupagechildrensmuseum.org/aunty/ |

*continued*

TABLE **10.1** ■ Non-tech and tech-related anchor activities   *(continued)*

| Non-tech Anchor Activities | Tech-related Anchor Activities | |
|---|---|---|
| Research investigations (inquiry learning, problem-based learning, project-based learning) using library or classroom resource materials | Research investigations (inquiry learning, problem-based learning, project-based learning) using the Web and software such as WebQuests and online encyclopedias: | |
| | **Bernie Dodge's WebQuest Collections** | http://edWeb.sdsu.edu/Webquest/Webquest_collections.htm |
| | **The WebQuest Place** | www.thematzats.com/Webquests/intro.html |
| | **WebQuests Created by eMints Teachers** | www.emints.org/Webquest/ |
| | **Saskatoon (East) School Division WebQuests** | http://sesd.sk.ca/teacherresource/Webquest/Webquest.htm |
| | **Fact Monster** | www.factmonster.com |
| | **World Almanac for Kids** | www.worldalmanacforkids.com |
| Scrapbook or portfolio (paper based) | Electronic scrapbook or portfolio using computer software such as Microsoft PowerPoint, Microsoft Publisher, Microsoft Word, Adobe Photoshop, Art Explosion Scrapbook Factory Deluxe, and Creating Keepsakes Scrapbook Designer Deluxe | |
| Silent reading | Silent reading online or via printable materials from computer software or Internet, such as: | |
| | **Starfall** | www.starfall.com |
| | **World Wide School** | www.worldwideschool.org/library/catalogs/bysubject-top.html |
| | **KidSpace at the Internet Public Library** | www.ipl.org/kidspace/browse/rzn0000 |
| | **International Children's Digital Library** | www.icdlbooks.org |
| | **Interactive Stories** | http://Web.bsu.edu/00smtancock/EDRDG430/430stories.html |
| Teacher-made ancillary packets of materials | Teacher- and student-made packets from downloads or software, such as: | |
| | **Enchanted Learning** | www.enchantedlearning.com |
| | **abcteach** | www.abcteach.com |
| Worksheets from workbooks (spelling, vocabulary, math) | Worksheets from downloads or computer software: | |
| | **teAchnology** | www.teach-nology.com/worksheets/ |
| | **edHelper** | www.edhelper.com |

The key to successfully implementing anchor activities is to model how they operate and to communicate behavioral and academic expectations to our students in advance. Here are a few tips and techniques some teachers use that might help you effectively incorporate anchor activities into your classroom repertoire:

1. Settle in advance on grouping and seating arrangements (and meeting place) for the unit. Classify by color, name, or number and post in an appropriate location.

2. Tell students what they specifically need to accomplish, using assignment sheets or role cards.

3. To reduce movement in the classroom, set ground rules for the number of students who may physically come to you for help or wait for your assistance.

4. Appoint two classroom assistants to the following roles to decrease movement in the classroom and allow you to focus on struggling students and behavioral issues, monitor students' progress, and so forth:

   - a materials manager, whose job is to compile and gather materials for the assignment.

   - a peer mentor or expert of the day, who might proofread, collect papers, answer some classmates' questions about your instructions, and so forth. (Restrict the number of students who approach this student for help, too.)

5. Devise a signal that communicates to students that the noise level in the classroom is too elevated.

The following diagram might help you to better envision how you can progressively acclimate your class to working in an environment where multiple tasks (involving anchor activities) are occurring concurrently.

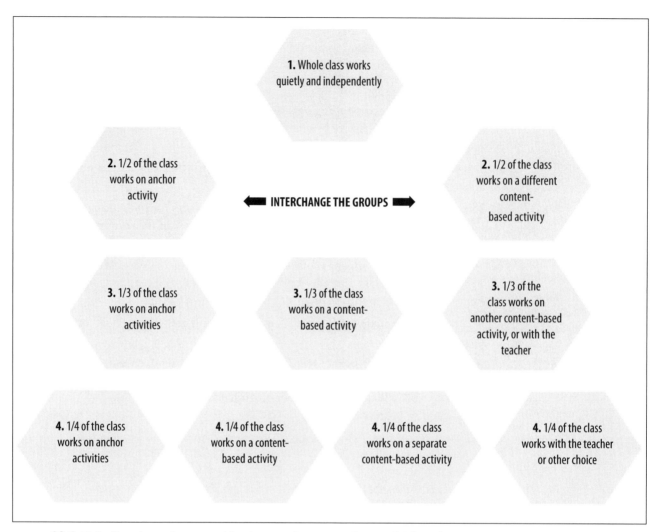

FIGURE **10.1** ■ Acclimating a class to working in an environment where multiple tasks are occurring concurrently

We mentioned early on in this section that anchor activities can serve as a key component of a learning contract, which is our next instructional and management strategy. If you haven't attempted to use this strategy in your classroom, we think you'll be pleasantly surprised with the results. They actually function as both a teaching strategy and an assessment tool, and they're a vehicle for self-directed learning.

## Learning Contracts

Throughout this book, we've stressed that differentiated instruction is grounded in student choice and accountability. Sometimes, however, it's difficult for teachers to relinquish control to students. But by transferring some of the responsibility to them, both parties—students and teachers alike—reap many benefits. Some of them are:

- Students experience heightened self-worth and self-sufficiency.
- Students and teachers build trust in their relationships with one another.
- Students improve decision-making skills.
- Students feel more motivated because they have a say in directing their educational path.
- Teachers' stress and workload actually decrease slightly.

Learning contracts are a signed agreement between you and an individual student. The first time you try a learning contract with students, expect to encounter some opposition. Not only are you changing the rules by holding students accountable for their own learning, but also they have to promise (with a signature, no less!) to fulfill the outlined objectives.

As you might assume, the mere use of a learning contract doesn't guarantee that students will cooperate with enthusiasm. At first, they might seem intimidated by the thorough listing of learning goals, working conditions, rubrics, guidelines, timelines, tasks, and deadlines that the contract specifies. These components clarify expectations and standards by which students will be assessed. However, by spelling out your criteria, you halt any attempts to claim that deadlines haven't been announced or that expectations weren't made clear.

Although learning contracts contain some required elements, they also give students options that will personalize their own learning experiences. The good news is that while contracts may be differentiated to accommodate students' diverse interests, learning profiles, and levels of readiness, it doesn't mean you have to create 20 or 30 separate contracts!

Here are some practical recommendations that will help you formulate and implement learning contracts:

1. As a general rule, develop three broad templates that relate to three typical levels of students:

    a) self-directed students who have a good command of core content,

    b) students who need to work through core materials from start to finish to comprehend them, and

    c) struggling students who don't understand core concepts.

2. Introduce anchoring at the beginning of the unit and help students elect their preferred anchor activities from a list of options.

3. Include tasks that involve choices from an assortment of interests or learning styles.

4. Build in assessment and progress checks at different points in the contract.

   a) Pre-contract activity:
      - Use KWL charts to find out what your students know and what they'd like to investigate.

   b) In-progress activities:
      - Meet and consult with your students as they work on their individual assignments.
      - Record group participation and homework grades to make sure they're on target.
      - Fill out self-evaluations to help them improve time management and organizational skills (optional).

   c) Post-contract activities:
      - Assess student work.
      - Have students complete self-evaluations.

While students might at first be a little distressed by this new approach, most will come to appreciate learning contracts. They should respond positively to the freedom they have to work at their own pace, the absence of busy work and review of material that they've already mastered, and the opportunity to engage in tasks that appeal to their interests.

### A Sample Differentiated Learning Contract Using Technology

It's possible you've never seen a learning contract before, so we're going to show you one designed for fifth-graders. We recently visited a fifth-grade teacher to talk with her about how she teaches English and language arts. We interviewed some students and the teacher about a unit they'd just completed on the Newberry Award-winning novel *From the Mixed-Up Files of Mrs. Basil E. Frankweiler,* by E. L. Konigsburg. These are some of their comments and thoughts on typical classroom activities.

**Students' Perspective:**

In our study of the novel, Mrs. Wright usually leads a discussion with lots of questions to make sure we understand what certain words mean and what has happened in the chapter or chapters we had to read for class. Sometimes she reads a chapter or part of a chapter out loud, and other times, she asks us to read out loud.

More often than not, Mrs. Wright gives us a study guide for each chapter that has 5 to 10 questions. Most of the time, we have to write out the answers to the questions and turn them in so she can check them over. She frequently uses those questions to guide our discussion, so it doesn't really matter if we've written out the answers ahead of time. We can just listen to the answers in class and fill them in on our papers before she collects them. It gets kind of boring because we do the same thing all the time.

At the end of our unit, we have to write a book report and take a test on the novel. We take quizzes every other chapter.

**Mrs. Wright's Perspective:**

In most cases, I use whole group instruction with English/language arts to make sure everyone understands what's happened in the text we're reading. Next school year, though, I'd like to challenge my students and myself by providing differentiated options for students in our unit on *From the Mixed-Up Files of Mrs. Basil E. Frankweiler.*

I think offering differentiated student choices would increase students' enthusiasm for reading and discussing the text. Furthermore, whole group instruction is becoming increasingly difficult, as I have lots of interruptions with students leaving the classroom at various times. I'd like to integrate some technology and anchor activities and try out a learning contract to give students more input.

### *Grace and Stephanie's Perspective*

Suppose, for this learning contract, that you're in Mrs. Wright's class and studying *From the Mixed-Up Files of Mrs. Basil E. Frankweiler,* which is usually read in the fourth, fifth, or sixth grade.

We fast forward to the next school year and discover that Mrs. Wright has introduced the unit with a PowerPoint slideshow full of images associated with the text, images such as Michelangelo, the Metropolitan Museum of Art, the fountain there, and artifacts in various galleries. She invites students to predict the kind of mystery that Jamie and Claudia (the protagonists) might solve.

Students are comfortable working individually or in flexible groups, and they're adept at using the software applications mentioned in the Learning Activities section of the contract. Mrs. Wright has described how the learning contract works and what students will complete independently and in pairs.

## Sample Learning Contract

On the following pages is a sample learning contract that Mrs. Wright might present to you.

*From the Mixed-Up Files of Mrs. Basil E. Frankweiler*

Your Name: _____

**Learning Contract**

This learning contract covers your investigation of the book *From the Mixed-Up Files of Mrs. Basil E. Frankweiler* as well as three products you will create. You will be able to do some of your work independently and some with a partner. Check off each box once you have completed an activity.

**Required Activities**

**1.** Review some of the important places, people, and things in the novel.

☐ You may play Concentration, a matching game; do a word search; or review with flashcards at www.quia.com/custom/3227main.html.

☐ Print a copy of the completed activity (or activities) and attach the printed page(s) to this contract.

**2.** With a partner, read biographical and autobiographical information about the author, E. L. Konigsburg.

☐ Share a computer to investigate the following Web sites. Take notes individually (on paper) regarding some of the connections between E. L. Konigsburg's writings and her real life, such as childhood experiences she had that might have appeared in her writing, people in her life she modeled her characters on, and so forth.

☐ Discuss the facts with your partner to make sure you understand them.

| ✓ **when complete** | **Title and Web Page Address (URL)** |
|---|---|
| | E. L. Konigsburg's Biographical and Autobiographical Information<br>http://cms.westport.k12.ct.us/cmslmc/resources/authorstudy/authors/konigauto.htm |
| | Meet E. L. Konigsburg<br>www.eduplace.com/kids/tnc/mtai/konigsburg.html |
| | *Museumkids "Mixed-Up Files"* Issue<br>www.metmuseum.org/explore/publications/pdfs/MusKids_MixedUp/MKids_MixedUp_EntireGuide.pdf |

**3.** Opinion Paragraph

☐ Work independently and use your notes to write an opinion paragraph on your interpretation of how experiences and people in E. L. Konigsburg's real life have come to life in her books, particularly in *From the Mixed-Up Files of Mrs. Basil E. Frankweiler.*

☐ Support your opinion with the facts you recorded from the Web sites. Facts can be checked for accuracy. An opinion is based on a personal belief or view.

☐ Attach your opinion paragraph after you write it.

| OPINION PARAGRAPH RUBRIC | | | |
|---|---|---|---|
| **Categories** | **Criteria** | | **My Score** |
| | 1 point | 0 points | Score |
| **Capitalization** | I have zero to two errors in capitalization. | I have three or more errors in capitalization. | |
| **Conclusion** | My paragraph has a conclusion. | My paragraph does not have a conclusion. | |
| **Descriptive Adjectives** | My writing has pizzazz. My adjectives are descriptive. I may have used a thesaurus. | My writing isn't very colorful; it's somewhat dull. | |
| **Format** | My writing has a title, a body, and the author's name. It's neatly written. | My writing may be missing the title or author's name. It is not neatly written. | |
| **Organization** | My paragraph is well organized and in logical order. | My paragraph is poorly organized and hard to understand. | |
| **Position Statement** | My opinion position is clearly stated. | My opinion position is not clear. | |
| **Punctuation** | I have zero to two errors in punctuation. | I have three or more errors in punctuation. | |
| **Sentence Structure** | More than two-thirds of my sentences are mostly correct. | More than one-third of my sentences are incorrectly written. | |
| **Source of Evidence** | My sources for evidence are included. | My sources for evidence are not included. | |
| **Supporting Evidence** | My evidence supports my position. | My evidence is unrelated to or does not support my position. | |
| TOTAL POINTS | | | |

**4.** Choice of Learning Activities

Choose one option from each column of the following table and discuss with your teacher what you would like to do to learn more about the book.

| Be a Writer! | Be an Artist! | Be a Historian! |
|---|---|---|
| ☐ Write an essay that persuades the reader whether or not Jamie and Claudia could pull off the same feat today. (Use Word.) | ☐ Make a floor plan of the Metropolitan Museum of Art in New York. (Use MS Publisher or the drawing tools in PowerPoint or Word.) | ☐ Like the Met, the Art Institute of Chicago was founded in the late 1800s. Craft a brochure that provides visitors with general information about the museum, such as location, hours, admission fees, dining options, history, and possible hiding places for Jamie and Claudia. (Use Publisher.) |
| ☐ Write a news article describing the mystery that Jamie and Claudia solved as though it just happened yesterday. (Use Publisher.) | ☐ Draw your version of the "Angel" statue in the book. (Use Paint.) | ☐ Create a slide show about Michelangelo's life and works. Find digital pictures to insert into the slides. (Use PowerPoint.) |
| ☐ Posing as Jamie or Claudia, write several diary entries about your escapade in the Metropolitan Museum of Art. (Use Word.) | ☐ Design a poster that identifies Jamie and Claudia as missing children. Include a written description of them, their ages, where they were last seen, whom to contact with information, and so forth. (Use Publisher.) | ☐ Jamie and Claudia were intrigued by the historical artifacts they saw in some of the art galleries in the museum. Research one of the following topics: Knights (arms and armor), Greek & Roman Art (sarcophagus), or Egyptian Art (mummies). Create a Webbe or booklet to publish your historical findings. (Use Word for a Webbe and Publisher for a booklet.) |

**Citizenship and Work Habits**

I agree to the following learning conditions:

☐   I agree to follow our class ground rules.

☐   I agree to complete my work on time.

☐   I agree to do my personal best.

Student's Signature: _____ Date: _____

Teacher's Signature: _____ Date: _____

Learning contracts are extremely effective because they clearly outline the tasks that need to be completed and the requirements students must fulfill. You might also want to supply additional supports, such as pacing guides and checklists, to increase students' chances for success. Self-evaluation and peer evaluation, a collaboration rubric, and display and sharing of final products are other important activities.

The sample learning contract we developed is simply a model to give you an idea as to what one might look like and how you can use it with your students. You can spice up your contracts with color or clip art and make yours even more detailed. There are no absolutes in terms of length, so don't feel pressured to include numerous tasks within the contract. In fact, it would be wise to start off short and sweet and then move forward to more elaborate contracts. Our intent here is to provide a middle-of-the-road idea. Regardless of the physical design, we think you'll encounter positive results in your classroom when you offer your students more learning choices. On top of all the benefits, you'll be pleased to discover that learning contracts modify your teaching responsibilities and engage you in many favorable ways as you witness the development of students' final products!

Supervising one's classroom and managing all the additional administrative duties have become awesome responsibilities for teachers. With all the demands on our time and the workload we shoulder, it seems exceedingly obvious to say that instructional and management strategies are essential tools for day-to-day survival! In this chapter, we shared some beneficial strategies that support a differentiated classroom, such as scaffolding, anchoring, peer coaching, and learning contracts. Through our investigation of those strategies, we've learned that technology is also an invaluable tool to help manage our classrooms. We also reviewed the characteristics of an effective learning community and how it's critical to our students' overall comfort level and, in turn, their success. Although it sometimes seems like a great deal of work to get ourselves organized to try out new strategies, we think that you'll find they're a valuable addition to your classroom.

## Resources for Chapter 10

| | | |
|---|---|---|
| **Anchor Activities** *(and other digital resources that might be used for assessment)* | AAA Math | www.aaamath.com |
| | abcteach | www.abcteach.com |
| | Best Practices: Instructional Strategies and Techniques | http://wblrd.sk.ca/~bestpractice/anchor/ |
| | Especially for Elementary | http://rozauer.tripod.com/elem.htm |
| | Montgomery Public Schools Anchor Activity Worksheet | www.mcps.k12.md.us/curriculum/enriched/giftedprograms/docs/ Anchor Worksheet.doc |
| | Reading a-to-z.com | www.readinga-z.com |
| | teAchnology | www.teach-nology.com/Web_tools/ |
| **Computer Lab Resources** | Kings Park Elementary Third Grade Lessons, Units, Web Activities and Resources | www.fcps.edu/KingsParkES/staff/third-resources.htm |
| | The Computer Lab | www.sabine.k12.la.us/vrschool/complab.htm |
| | Strategies for Setting Up Computer Labs | www.wtvi.com/teks/labstrategies/ |
| | Elementary Computer Labs | www.fi.edu/fellows/fellow4/may99/ |
| **Copyright-Related Issues** | United States Patent and Trademark Office Kids' Pages | www.uspto.gov/go/kids/kidantipiracy.htm |
| | Copyright Kids | www.copyrightkids.org |
| **Creating Your Own Teacher and Class Web Sites** | TeacherWeb | www.teacherWeb.com |
| **Differentiated Instruction Links** | Polk Schools | www.polk-schools.com/Differentiated.htm |

*continued*

## Resources for Chapter 10 (continued)

| | | |
|---|---|---|
| *From the Mixed-Up Files of Mrs. Basil E. Frankweiler* | E. L. Konigsburg | www.Webenglishteacher.com/konigsburg.html |
| | E. L. Konigsburg Biographical and Autobiographical Information | http://cms.westport.k12.ct.us/cmslmc/resources/authorstudy/authors/konigauto.htm |
| | Meet E. L. Konigsburg | www.eduplace.com/kids/tnc/mtai/konigsburg.html |
| | *Museumkids* "Mixed-Up Files" Issue | www.metmuseum.org/explore/publications/pdfs/MusKids_MixedUp/MKids_MixedUp_EntireGuide.pdf |
| | Online Activities Using the Metropolitan Museum of Art's Siteto Help Enrich/Extend E. L. Konigsburg's *From the Mixed-Up Files of Mrs. Basil E. Frankweiler* | www.k111.k12.il.us/King/mixed_up.htm |
| | Quia: *From the Mixed-Up Files of Mrs. Basil E. Frankweiler* | www.quia.com/custom/3227main.html |
| | Teacher Cyber Guide: *From the Mixed-Up Files of Mrs. Basil E. Frankweiler* | www.sdcoe.k12.ca.us/score/fris/fristg.htm |
| | Webquesting: *From the Mixed-Up Files of Mrs. Basil E. Frankweiler: 30 Years Later* | www.hobart.k12.in.us/Webquests/jonesquest/filequest.html |
| Learning Contracts | Alaska Department of Education and Early Development's Collection of Assessment Strategies (including learning contracts, graphic organizers, self- and peer evaluation, journals/learning logs, and others) | www.eed.state.ak.us/tls/Frameworks/mathsci/ms5_2as1.htm |
| | Best Practices Sample Learning Contract | http://wblrd.sk.ca/~bestpractice/contract/assets/pdf/sheet321.pdf |
| Microsoft Office | Management Contracts | http://office.microsoft.com/en-us/templates/CT101527321033.aspx |
| Rubrics and Rubric Generators | Rubistar | http://rubistar.4teachers.org |
| | Teach-nology | www.teach-nology.com/Web_tools/rubrics/ |
| | Tech for Learning | http://myt4l.com/index.php?v=pl&page_ac=view&type=tools&tool=rubricmaker |
| Scaffolding | San Diego City Schools Technology Grant Triton and Patterns Projects | http://projects.edtech.sandi.net/staffdev/patterns2000/reception.html |
| | | http://projects.edtech.sandi.net/staffdev/patterns2000/transformation.html |
| Technology in Education | Resource Center | www.rtec.org/rtec.cfm?rtec_id=2 |

# BIBLIOGRAPHY

Armstrong, T. (1994). *Multiple intelligences in the classroom.* Alexandria, VA: Association for Supervision and Curriculum Development.

Armstrong, T. (2000). *Multiple intelligences in the classroom (2nd ed.).* Alexandria, VA: Association for Supervision and Curriculum Development.

Axelrod, A. (1997). *Pigs will be pigs: Fun with math and money.* New York: Aladdin.

Benjamin, A. (2003). *Differentiated instruction: A guide for elementary school teachers.* Larchmont, NY: Eye on Education.

Bloom, B. S. (1956). Taxonomy of educational objectives, handbook I: Cognitive domain. New York: David McKay Co., Inc.

Duncan, D., & Lockhart, L. (2000). *I-search, you search, we all learn to research.* New York: Neal-Schuman.

Campbell, L., & Campbell, B. (1999). *Multiple intelligences and student achievement.* Alexandria, VA: Association for Supervision and Curriculum Development.

Chapman, C., & King, R. (2005). *Differentiated assessment strategies: One tool doesn't fit all.* Thousand Oaks, CA: Corwin Press.

Gardner, H. (1993). *Multiple intelligences: The theory in practice.* New York: Basic Books.

International Society for Technology in Education. (2000). *Connecting curriculum and technology.* Eugene, OR: Author.

International Society for Technology in Education. (2002). *Multidisciplinary units for grades 3–5.* Eugene, OR: Author.

Jacobs, H. H. (1997). *Mapping the big picture: Integrating curriculum and assessment K–12.* Alexandria, VA: Association for Supervision and Curriculum Development.

Kelly, M. G., & Haber, J. (2006). *Resources for student assessment.* Eugene, OR: International Society for Technology in Education.

Leedy, L. (1999). *Celebrate the 50 states!* New York: Holiday House.

Lerman, J. (2005). *101 best web sites for elementary teachers.* Eugene, OR: International Society for Technology in Education.

Macrorie, K. (1988). *The I-search paper: Revised edition of searching writing.* Portsmouth, NH: Boynton/Cook.

Marzano, R. J., Pickering, D. J., & Pollock, J. E. (2001). *Classroom instruction that works: Research-based strategies for increasing student achievement.* Alexandria, VA: Association for Supervision and Curriculum Development.

McKenzie, W. (2002). *Multiple intelligences and instructional technology: A manual for every mind.* Eugene, OR: International Society for Technology in Education.

Montgomery County Public Schools. (2005). Math stations. Retrieved May 27, 2005 from www.mcps.k12.md.us/curriculum/enriched/giftedprograms/mathstations.shtm

Reis, S. M., Burns, D. E., & Renzulli, J. S. (1992). *Curriculum compacting: The complete guide to modifying the regular curriculum for high ability students.* Mansfield Center, CT: Creative Learning Press.

Scholastic Professional Books. (1998). *The kid's book of the 50 great states: A state-by-state scrapbook filled with facts, maps, puzzles, poems, photos, and more.* New York: Author.

Shumway, M. (1993, Summer). To be a bridge. *Focus on Faculty,* (BYU Faculty Center Newsletter) *1*(3), 4. Available: http://fc.byu.edu/opages/reference/newslet/v1n3.pdf

Sternberg, R. (1999). Thinking styles. New York: Cambridge University Press.

Tomlinson, C. A. (2001). *How to differentiate instruction in mixed-ability classrooms (2nd ed.).* Alexandria, VA: Association for Supervision and Curriculum Development.

Tomlinson, C. A. (2003). *Fulfilling the promise of the differentiated classroom: Strategies and tools for responsive teaching.* Alexandria, VA: Association for Supervision and Curriculum Development.

Tomlinson, C. A., & Eidson, C. C. (2003). *Differentiation in practice: A resource guide for differentiating curriculum grades K–5.* Alexandria, VA: Association for Supervision and Curriculum Development.

# National Educational Technology Standards

## National Educational Technology Standards for Students (NETS•S)

The National Educational Technology Standards for students are divided into six broad categories. Standards within each category are to be introduced, reinforced, and mastered by students. Teachers can use these standards as guidelines for planning technology-based activities in which students achieve success in learning, communication, and life skills.

**1. Creativity and Innovation**

Students demonstrate creative thinking, construct knowledge, and develop innovative products and processes using technology. Students:

**a.** apply existing knowledge to generate new ideas, products, or processes.

**b.** create original works as a means of personal or group expression.

**c.** use models and simulations to explore complex systems and issues.

**d.** identify trends and forecast possibilities.

**2. Communication and Collaboration**

Students use digital media and environments to communicate and work collaboratively, including at a distance, to support individual learning and contribute to the learning of others. Students:

**a.** interact, collaborate, and publish with peers, experts, or others employing a variety of digital environments and media.

**b.** communicate information and ideas effectively to multiple audiences using a variety of media and formats.

**c.** develop cultural understanding and global awareness by engaging with learners of other cultures.

**d.** contribute to project teams to produce original works or solve problems.

3. **Research and Information Fluency**

Students apply digital tools to gather, evaluate, and use information. Students:

**a.** plan strategies to guide inquiry.

**b.** locate, organize, analyze, evaluate, synthesize, and ethically use information from a variety of sources and media.

**c.** evaluate and select information sources and digital tools based on the appropriateness to specific tasks.

**d.** process data and report results.

4. **Critical Thinking, Problem Solving, and Decision Making**

Students use critical-thinking skills to plan and conduct research, manage projects, solve problems, and make informed decisions using appropriate digital tools and resources. Students:

**a.** identify and define authentic problems and significant questions for investigation.

**b.** plan and manage activities to develop a solution or complete a project.

**c.** collect and analyze data to identify solutions and make informed decisions.

**d.** use multiple processes and diverse perspectives to explore alternative solutions.

5. **Digital Citizenship**

Students understand human, cultural, and societal issues related to technology and practice legal and ethical behavior. Students:

**a.** advocate and practice the safe, legal, and responsible use of information and technology.

**b.** exhibit a positive attitude toward using technology that supports collaboration, learning, and productivity.

**c.** demonstrate personal responsibility for lifelong learning.

**d.** exhibit leadership for digital citizenship.

6. **Technology Operations and Concepts**

Students demonstrate a sound understanding of technology concepts, systems, and operations. Students:

**a.** understand and use technology systems.

**b.** select and use applications effectively and productively.

**c.** troubleshoot systems and applications.

**d.** transfer current knowledge to the learning of new technologies.

# National Educational Technology Standards for Teachers (NETS•T)

All classroom teachers should be prepared to meet the following standards and performance indicators.

### I. Technology Operations and Concepts

Teachers demonstrate a sound understanding of technology operations and concepts. Teachers:

**A.** demonstrate introductory knowledge, skills, and understanding of concepts related to technology (as described in the ISTE National Educational Technology Standards for Students).

**B.** demonstrate continual growth in technology knowledge and skills to stay abreast of current and emerging technologies.

### II. Planning and Designing Learning Environments and Experiences

Teachers plan and design effective learning environments and experiences supported by technology. Teachers:

**A.** design developmentally appropriate learning opportunities that apply technology-enhanced instructional strategies to support the diverse needs of learners.

**B.** apply current research on teaching and learning with technology when planning learning environments and experiences.

**C.** identify and locate technology resources and evaluate them for accuracy and suitability.

**D.** plan for the management of technology resources within the context of learning activities.

**E.** plan strategies to manage student learning in a technology-enhanced environment.

### III. Teaching, Learning, and the Curriculum

Teachers implement curriculum plans that include methods and strategies for applying technology to maximize student learning. Teachers:

**A.** facilitate technology-enhanced experiences that address content standards and student technology standards.

**B.** use technology to support learner-centered strategies that address the diverse needs of students.

**C.** apply technology to develop students' higher-order skills and creativity.

**D.** manage student learning activities in a technology-enhanced environment.

## IV. Assessment and Evaluation

Teachers apply technology to facilitate a variety of effective assessment and evaluation strategies. Teachers:

**A.** apply technology in assessing student learning of subject matter using a variety of assessment techniques.

**B.** use technology resources to collect and analyze data, interpret results, and communicate findings to improve instructional practice and maximize student learning.

**C.** apply multiple methods of evaluation to determine students' appropriate use of technology resources for learning, communication, and productivity.

## V. Productivity and Professional Practice

Teachers use technology to enhance their productivity and professional practice. Teachers:

**A.** use technology resources to engage in ongoing professional development and lifelong learning.

**B.** continually evaluate and reflect on professional practice to make informed decisions regarding the use of technology in support of student learning.

**C.** apply technology to increase productivity.

**D.** use technology to communicate and collaborate with peers, parents, and the larger community in order to nurture student learning.

## VI. Social, Ethical, Legal, and Human Issues

Teachers understand the social, ethical, legal, and human issues surrounding the use of technology in PK–12 schools and apply that understanding in practice. Teachers:

**A.** model and teach legal and ethical practice related to technology use.

**B.** apply technology resources to enable and empower learners with diverse backgrounds, characteristics, and abilities.

**C.** identify and use technology resources that affirm diversity.

**D.** promote safe and healthy use of technology resources.

**E.** facilitate equitable access to technology resources for all students.

# INDEX